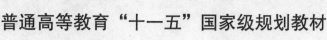

普通高等教育"十一五"国家级规划教材

U0127584

畅通英语

高级教程教师参考书 （第二版）

Changtong Yingyu Gaoji Jiaocheng Jiaoshi Cankaoshu

Upper-Intermediate

Teacher's book (2nd Edition)

Channel your English

H.Q.Mitchell-J.Scott

《畅通英语》改编组

mm publications

高等教育出版社·北京

HIGHER EDUCATION PRESS　BEIJING

图书在版编目（CIP）数据

畅通英语高级教程教师参考书/《畅通英语》改编组改编. —2 版.
—北京：高等教育出版社，2011.6
ISBN 978 – 7 – 04 – 031425 – 0

Ⅰ．①畅… Ⅱ．①畅… Ⅲ．①英语–高等职业教育–教学参考资
料 Ⅳ．①H31

中国版本图书馆 CIP 数据核字（2011）第 062614 号

策划编辑 闵 阅　　责任编辑 张慧勇　　封面设计 张 志　　版式设计 孙 伟
责任校对 张慧勇　　责任印制 刘思涵

出版发行	高等教育出版社	网　　址	http://www.hep.edu.cn
社　　址	北京市西城区德外大街 4 号		http://www.hep.com.cn
邮政编码	100120	网上订购	http://www.landraco.com
印　　刷	北京中科印刷有限公司		http://www.landraco.com.cn
开　　本	889 ×1194　1/16		
印　　张	16.25	版　　次	2005 年 7 月第 1 版
字　　数	498 000		2011 年 6 月第 2 版
购书热线	010 – 58581118	印　　次	2011 年 6 月第 1 次印刷
咨询电话	400 – 810 – 0598	定　　价	37.50 元

本书如有缺页、倒页、脱页等质量问题，请到所购图书销售部门联系调换
版权所有　侵权必究
物 料 号　31425 – 00

第二版前言

《畅通英语》（第二版）系列教材是普通高等教育"十一五"国家级规划教材开发编写计划中的一种，是在引进改编英国MM出版公司2003年出版的Channel your English形成的第一版的基础上进一步修编而成的。本系列教材既保留了原版教材新颖的教学设计模式和先进的教学理念，又结合国内高职高专英语教学的实际，增编了适量的辅教辅学和助考的内容和练习。本系列教材可供三年制和五年制高职高专学生使用。

《畅通英语》（第二版）以真实的交际型语言活动为基础，按照语言表达的难易程度分级编写，注重语言应用能力培养。从初级到中高级的英语学习全过程都有效地整合了听、说、读、写、译5种语言技能训练。该书布局系统全面、科学合理，将功能、语法、词汇、语音和跨文化交际技能尽收其中，利于教师按照语言学习和应用的规律有效地安排教学内容与进度，既提高学习者兴趣，又锻炼学习者能力，使所学内容与涉外交流、人际交往的真实话题和场景紧密结合，反复强化，达到学、练、用合一的理想效果。

本系列教材的特点主要体现在如下几个方面：

教材内容贴近日常生活，真实生动，丰富有趣。学习者在生动的多元文化环境中学习语言，掌握技能。教材中阅读文章题材广泛，如不同国家的节日介绍、世界体坛名人和户外极限运动介绍、性格测试、书信写法等；题材大多是学习者感兴趣的话题，如学习工作、休闲娱乐、求职指导、服饰打扮、饮食喜好、旅游探险、真诚友谊等。教材话题内容全面，覆盖诸多领域，如科技、网络、文化、社会、经济等，使学习者在不同场合能够充分感知语言环境，通过语言操练掌握语言技能。

体现语言的人际、意念、语篇三大功能，实用性强。各单元的对话体现了许多常用的表达和意念功能，如介绍与陈述、赞同与反对、问题与解决方案、给予与获取、需求与允诺、推理与预测等。阅读与写作文体多样实用，主要介绍应用文体，如广告、个人简历、景点介绍、论文、信件等。另外，以话题情景为中心归纳、联想、即学即用的词汇积累建档法，也十分有效，很值得推荐。

注重综合能力的培养。教材采用基于话题任务的交际教学法，突出强调涉外交流活动中必需的英语交际会话能力培养。使学生能以话题和情景为基础，灵活运用英语完成交际任务；强调学以致用，真正将语言学习与使用结合起来，能听会说，读写并重，达到"学好，用好，考好"的目的。

图文并茂，新颖活泼。教材配有大量与各种功能相关的富于启发性的图片，为语言学习者提供了形象的训练情景，有效地培养学习者对语言的领悟能力。

教学体系完备，教学资源丰富。本系列教材由学生用书、教师参考书、学生拓展练习册、MP3听力光盘、DVD视频光盘和电子教案等组成，形成完备、集成、立体化的英语教学资源体系。

本系列教材包括初、中、高各级的学生用书、学生拓展练习册和教师参考书各5册，含《基础教程》1、2册，《中级教程》1、2册和《高级教程》1册。《基础教程1》适合初学者水平，《基础教程2》适合初中起点水平，《中级教程1》适合高中水平，《中级教程2》和《高级教程》适合高中以上水平。学习者可以根据自己的实际水平，从不同的分册开始学习。每册包括12个单元，每单元包括3课内容。第1课以会话引入为主，包括情景对话、词语表达、语法结构和口语实践，并配有语音语调训练；第2课重在以听、读为主的接受型技能训练，包括阅读、词语表达、语法、听力实践等部分；第3课重在以说、写为主的产出型技能训练，包括听、说、读、写4种技能综合训练。学生用书每3个单元之后，还编有阶段复习测试题，配有单元主题扩展阅读短文及同步练习，供复习巩固所学语法结构、词语表达及阅读技能之用。学生用书后还附有词汇表和词组表等，供学生查阅参考。

本系列教材各级均配有学生拓展练习册，内含学生用书中各单元主题扩展阅读短文、各课的配套同步练习和针对"高等学校英语应用能力考试"大纲中所规定的项目和要求设计的模拟试题，供师生结合实际教学情况选用操练。学完本系列教材的前4册可以参加"高等学校英语应用能力考试"的B级考试，学完全系列教材可参加"高等学校英语应用能力考试"A级考试和大学英语四级考试。

本系列教材的对话、陈述、课文都配有MP3光盘，并配有电子教案。《畅通英语》（第二版）的教师参考书提供了详细的"教法和教材说明"，还增编了各单元的"文化背景知识介绍"、"课文语言点注释"、"课文参考译文"、"听力文字材料"和"补充练习答案"。

《畅通英语》（第二版）是一套汇集中外英语教育工作者长期教学研究最新成果的引进改编系列教材，其新颖的教学理念、实用的教学模式和贯穿始终的培养学生语言应用能力的教学活动定会给中国英语学习者、教育者新的启迪。

《畅通英语》（第二版）系列教材由四川大学石坚教授和电子科技大学冯斗教授担任总主编。本书为《畅通英语高级教程教师参考书》，主编为曾路教授（西南民族大学外国语学院），副主编为何颖副教授（电子科技大学成都学院）、陈玉堂（西南民族大学外国语学院），编者为胡杰辉（电子科技大学外国语学院）、彭琳（西南民族大学外国语学院）、廖莉（西华师范大学外国语学院）。

编　者

2011年2月

第一版前言

为了深入贯彻《中共中央国务院关于深化教育改革全面推进素质教育的决定》，进一步落实教育部等7部门《关于进一步加强职业教育工作的若干意见》，全面实施《2003~2007年教育振兴行动计划》，推动职教教材多样化发展，教育部制定了《2004~2007年职业教育教材开发编写计划》。计划内的教材出版后将向全国职业学校推荐选用。

《畅通英语》系列教材是上述教材开发编写计划中的一种，是在英国MM出版公司2003年出版的*Channel your English*的基础上改编而成的。本套教材既保留了原版教材新颖的教学设计模式和先进的教学理念，又结合国内高职高专英语教学的实际，增编了适量的辅教辅学内容和练习。本套教材可供五年制和三年制高职高专学生使用。

《畅通英语》以真实的交际型语言活动为基础，按照语言表达的难易程度分级编写，注重语言应用能力培养。从初级到中高级的英语学习全过程都有效地整合了听、说、读、写、译5种语言技能训练。该书布局系统全面、科学合理，将功能、语法、词汇、语音和跨文化交际技能尽收其中，利于教师按照语言学习和应用的规律有效地安排教学内容与进度，既提高学习者兴趣，又锻炼学习者能力，使所学内容与涉外交流、人际交往的真实话题和场景紧密结合，反复强化，达到学、练、用合一的理想效果。

本套教材的特点主要体现在如下几个方面：

教材内容贴近日常生活，真实生动，丰富有趣。学习者在生动的多元文化环境中学习语言，掌握技能。教材中阅读文章题材广泛，如不同国家的节日介绍、中国属相介绍、心理测试、神秘的UFO等；题材大多是学习者感兴趣的话题，如学习工作、休闲娱乐、求职指导、服饰打扮、饮食喜好、旅游探险、真诚友谊等。教材话题内容全面，覆盖诸多领域，如科技、网络、文化、社会、人物、经济、文摘、广告、说明等，使学习者在不同场合能够充分感知语言环境，掌握语言技能，加以强化操练，便可表达自如。

体现语言的人际、意念、语篇三大功能，实用性强。各单元的对话体现了许多常用的人际交往表达和意念功能，如介绍与陈述、赞同与反对、问题与解决方案、给予与获取、需求与允诺、推理与预测等。阅读与写作文体多样实用，主要介绍应用文体，如广告、人物、景点、论文、信件等。另外，以话题为中心归纳、学习、使用和积累词汇，也是本书的一大特色。

注重综合能力的培养。教材采用基于话题任务的交际教学法，突出强调涉外交流活动中必需的英语交际会话能力培养。使学生能以话题和情景为基础，灵活运用英语完成交际任务；强调学以致用，真正将语言学习与使用结合起来，能听会说，读写并重，达到"学好，用好，自然会考好"的目的。

教学体系完备，教学资源十分丰富。本套教材由学生用书、教师用书、学生练习册、录音带、多媒体光盘等组成，形成完备、集成、个性化、立体化的英语教学资源体系。

图文并茂，新颖实用。教材配有大量与各种功能相关的富于启发性的图片，为语言学习者提供了形象的训练情景，有效地培养学习者对语言的领悟能力。

本套教材结构科学合理，布局系统全面。主要包括以下内容：

《畅通英语》学生用书共5册，含《基础教程》2册、《中级教程》2册和《高级教程》1册。《基础教程1》适合于初学者水平，《基础教程2》适合于初中水平，《中级教程1》适合于高中水平，《中级教程2》和《高级教程》适合于高中以上水平。学习者可以根据自己的实际水平，从不同的分册开始学习。每册包括15~16个单元，每单元包括3课内容：第1课以会话引入为主，包括情景对话、词语表达、语法结构和口语实践，并结合语音语调训练；第2课重在以听读为主的接受型技能训练，包括阅读、词语表达、语法、听力和口语实践等部分；第3课重在以说写为主的产出型技能训练，包括听、说、读、写4种技能综合训练。学生用书每3~4个单元之后，还编有阶段复习题，供复习巩固所学语法结构和词语表达使用。学生用书后还附有交际活动卡片、词汇表和词组表等，供学生查阅参考。

该书各级均配有学生练习册，内含学生用书中各单元主题扩展阅读短文、各课的配套同步练习及课内外各种活动设计安排，供师生结合实际教学情况选用操练。《中级教程2》和《高级教程》的学生练习册中各单元还配有反映《高等学校英语应用能力考试大纲和样题》中所规定的项目和要求的模拟试题。学完本套教材的前4册可以参加"高等学校英语应用能力考试"的B级考试，学完全套教材可参加A级考试。

全套教材的对话、陈述、课文都配有录音带，并配有对话部分的多媒体光盘。

《畅通英语》的教师参考书提供了详细的"教法和教材说明"，还增编了"文化背景知识介绍"、"课文语言点注释"、"课文参考译文"、"听力文字材料"和"补充练习答案"等。

《畅通英语》是一套集中外英语教育工作者长期教学研究最新成果的引进改编系列教材，其新颖的教学理念、实用的教学模式和贯穿始终的培养学生语言应用能力的教学活动定会给中国英语学习者、教育者新的启迪与裨益。

本套教材由北京联合大学杨亚军教授和电子科技大学冯斗教授担任总主编。《畅通英语高级教程教师参考书》主编为湖南邵阳学院曾建湘，副主编为彭俊广、谢王艳、杨志豪和肖尊岚，编者为刘文红、刘涛、刘让强、马若飞、肖红梅、袁红平和陈晚姑。

编　者

2005年6月

Introduction

Outline of the course

Channel your English Upper-Intermediate is an innovative course, which smoothly takes teenage learners of English from intermediate to a higher level of fluency. It has been meticulously designed to boost students' existing knowledge and build their ability to communicate their ideas accurately and confidently. The main concern of the writers of this book has been to explicitly demonstrate how English is used in real-life situations, thus enabling students to use it in meaningful contexts, as well as to prepare students wishing to sit the official First Certificate in English (FCE) examination. Other important factors such as the learners' age and interests have been taken into consideration in the planning and design of this book. The topics have been carefully selected to attract students' interest and motivate learning.

Channel your English Upper-Intermediate uses an integrated approach to all four language skills (reading, listening, speaking, writing) in a well-organised, user-friendly syllabus combining functions, structures, vocabulary and communication skills. The book is divided into 12 well-developed and carefully structured units, each of which is based on a general topic and divided into three lessons. Vocabulary and grammar are systematically categorised and presented in each lesson helping teachers to manage and organise their time efficiently. Communicative language teaching is viewed as a practical activity rather than a theoretical notion.

Channel your English Upper-Intermediate is suitable for upper-intermediate level students. By the end of the book, students will have mastered the functions and structures out-lined in the contents. Additionally, they will have developed all four skills, having been given adequate practice throughout the book. The material included can be covered in approximately eighty hours. The precise time needed will vary according to factors such as school organisation, class size, learner ability and motivation.

There are certain key features in the book that add to the challenging and motivating material of the course, such as the authentic reading material and the special emphasis given to vocabulary building, including phrasal verbs, collocations, lexical sets, idioms, words easily confused and derivatives.

Course components

•Student's Book

The Student's Book contains:
● Table of contents presenting the topics as well as vocabulary, structures and functions presented and practised in each unit.
● Twelve eight-page units, each divided into three lessons, arranged in four modules.
● Four four-page revision units appearing at the end of each module.
● A Grammar reference section with useful tables, examples and explanations of the grammatical structures dealt with in each unit.
● Glossary
● Useful expression

•Workbook

The Workbook is divided into units and lessons in accordance with the Student's Book and contains exercises for further practice of the items dealt with in the Student's Book. The exercises may be done in class or assigned for homework. The reading texts appearing in each unit are thematically linked to the topic of each unit and offer further reading comprehension practice. There are exam-oriented tasks to give students further practice and consolidation of the structures and vocabulary practised in every unit. Each unit is rounded up with a writing section consisting of a model writing for students to elaborate on followed by a writing task.

•Teacher's Book

The Teacher's Book contains:
- An introduction.
- Teacher's Reference includes: tables with the functions, structures and active vocabulary introduced in each lesson, useful tips and notes for lesson planning, answers to all exercises and ideas for optional activities.
- The transcripts for the listening exercises.
- Additional reference consists of 3 components: culture notes, language points and translation of texts in each unit.
- Workbook (Teacher's Edition) mainly provides teachers with keys to exercises included in the Workbook.
- The last part of Teacher's Book is Key to supplementary exercises, which gives appropriate explanation to supplementary exercises in the Workbook.

•Student's Audio CDs

The CDs include all the recorded material from the sections in the Student's Book where the symbol appears.
 : Transcripts for the listening sections.

The structure of the units (units 1-12)

Each of the twelve units is divided into three lessons, which are discussed in detail below.

•Lesson One

Lesson One is divided into three basic sections: presentation, words and phrases and grammar.

Presentation

The aims of this section are to present vocabulary, structures and functions in the context of a reading or listening text and to familiarise students with the topic of the unit.

The presentation can be either a reading or a listening text. It is accompanied by a variety of tasks. Initially, students have to answer questions of personal response. Thus a short discussion is generated through visual and verbal information with the aim of introducing the topic of the unit as well as that of the short text they will hear or read. Students are encouraged to get involved personally in an activity that creates expectations and motivates them to move on to the next stage. As this is usually a warm-up activity, it is advisable that students should not spend more than a few minutes doing it. Once this stage is complete, students are asked to read or listen to a text in order to carry out a variety of task types. These cover ordering or spotting the mistakes on pictures, T/F sentences, open ended questions, matching paragraphs with pictures or headings with paragraphs, etc. Finally, students are asked questions in order to expand on the topic of the reading or listening text. These questions might appear either in the Student's or the Teacher's Book.

Words and phrases
Elaborating on the presentation stage, the purpose of these activities is to familiarise Ss with a variety of lexical items (i.e. phrasal verbs, colloquial expressions, derivatives, idioms, collocations, words easily confused, prepositional phrases) introduced in the text.

Grammar
The grammar section in this lesson deals with grammatical structures appearing in the presentation stage and are clearly presented, while usage is illustrated through notes and/or examples. However, Students are always actively involved in the understanding of grammar through various language awareness activities. Students are asked to refer to the text of the presentation stage in order to make inferences about the functions and usage of grammatical structures. The accompanying tasks vary, and require students to complete tables or match structures with functions or rules. The grammar section always ends with a short exercise giving students the opportunity to practise the grammatical structures in context. If time is scarce, we suggest that it be assigned for homework. In some units, there is a separate section entitled *English in Use*, which gives students further practice in structural accuracy through an open cloze or multi-

ple choice cloze activity. Students should rely on previous knowledge as well.

Lesson Two

Lesson Two focuses on receptive skills (reading and listening) and deals with the target language (grammar and lexis) appearing in the reading text. Lesson Two is divided into four sections: reading, vocabulary, grammar and listening.

Reading
In this section, students are exposed to a wide variety of reading material, such as magazine and newspaper articles, literary texts and encyclopaedic extracts.The texts are authentic, specially adapted to suit teenage and young adult learners' needs and interests. They cover a broad range of motivating and contemporary topics and provide students with interesting, multi-cultural information about the real world. The main aim is to provide intensive reading practice although they also lend themselves to presenting target vocabulary and grammar in context. Each module focuses on specific micro skills. The tasks simulate exam-type tasks (such as FCE) and are graded in terms of difficulty reaching the FCE level.

To begin with, students are asked to carry out a pre-reading task which smoothly introduces them to the topic of the reading text by relating it to their personal experience and/or preferences. This task appears in the Teacher's Book in the form of questions that generate a short discussion or visual/verbal stimuli for students to predict the content of the reading text. Following this initial stage, students skim read the text for the first time in order to understand the gist and/or check their predictions at the same time. It is advisable that students be given sufficient time to carry out the task and that teachers point out to them that unknown words should not worry them at this stage.

Students then read the text again with a view to developing certain reading micro skills, such as skimming for the main ideas, scanning for specific information and understanding text organisation. The task types vary and include matching headings/summary sentences with paragraphs, gapped texts with missing sentences/paragraphs and multiple choice questions. These tasks also aim at familiarising students with FCE-type tasks. When classroom time is scarce, they can be assigned for homework.

A post-reading stage mainly appears in the Teacher's Book as an optional activity but it is recommended that it be done systematically to round up the reading section. Its aim is to help students expand on the topic of the reading text relating it to their personal preferences and experience. Students should be encouraged to use as much of the topic-related vocabulary in the text as possible.

Words and phrases
As with the activity under the same heading in Lesson One, this activity gives students further practice with various lexical items, such as phrasal verbs, expressions, collocations and derivatives appearing in the reading text. The tasks vary and expand on the vocabulary introduced in the text.

Grammar
In this section, the grammatical items introduced in the reading text are dealt with, similarly to what has been described in the corresponding section in Lesson One.

Listening
The process of listening is very similar to that of reading. There is always a direct or indirect thematic link between the listening and the reading text. A variety of spoken text types and task formats have been employed, through which important listening micro skills are developed.

To start with, a pre-listening activity appearing in the Teacher's Book smoothly introduces the topic of the listening activity, activating Ss' background knowledge and preparing them for the task at hand. Then, students listen once to understand the gist. The next stage is listening for detail or specific information. Students listen to the text again and carry out the task. Task types vary and include T/F exercises, multiple choice, multiple matching, note taking, and matching speakers to what they said. All activities in this stage also familiarise Ss with exam-type tasks such as those of the FCE examination.

It is advisable that the teacher ask students to read the instructions carefully before they do each activity, making sure they fully understand what they are expected to do. After making sure that students have understood the instructions and the language included in the tasks, the teacher can play the CD. When answers are elicited from students, we suggest that students should be asked to justify their answers. Then, if necessary, the CD may be played again and any points that have not been understood can be clarified.

•Lesson Three

Lesson Three focuses on the productive skills (speaking and writing).

Speaking

The aim of the speaking section in Lesson Three is to enable students to use some of the vocabulary, grammar and functions introduced in the unit in a meaningful context. The activities are interesting, they closely approximate real-life tasks and there is always a goal to be achieved through the activity. Students always work in pairs and perform a variety of tasks. They discuss or exchange information, make suggestions, make decisions or express personal opinion in order to achieve their goal. Other tasks include speculating, prioritising, comparing and contrasting pictures. The speaking tasks are based on visual and/or verbal stimuli. For most speaking activities, support is provided through tables including vocabulary and/or expressions related to the topic of the speaking in order to facilitate students so as to carry out the task successfully.

To achieve optimum results, it is advisable to set a time limit for the activity. During the activity, the teacher should go round the classroom and listen to the discussions taking place and make sure that students speak only in English. Whenever necessary, help and support should be provided. As the aim of the activity is to enhance students' fluency, it is not recommended to interrupt them in order to correct their errors. It is preferable that the teacher keep a record of common or basic mistakes and comment on them at the end of the activity. There is ample opportunity to focus on accuracy and correct errors while doing other types of exercises.

Writing

Like speaking, writing is a productive skill and one that students often have difficulty with. Students are introduced to different exam-type writing tasks: story writing, informal letters, formal letters, articles, reports and discursive compositions. This section is also divided into stages. There are two or three pre-writing stages depending on the unit. In the first pre-writing stage, students are asked questions related to the topic of the writing task. In the second stage, students are introduced to a model text and elaborate on it in a variety of ways. The tasks at this stage focus on understanding gist and identifying style, register, purpose and target reader as well as elaborating on format/layout. In the next stages, labelled either *Plan* or *Improve your style,* various activities focusing on a number of sub-skills (planning and organising ideas, editing to improve writing style, etc.) prepare students for the actual *Writing task,* the final stage, which should be assigned for homework. It is very important to make sure that students have fully understood what they are expected to do. Moreover, they should be familiarised with a correction code, like the one suggested below, which will help them identify and correct their own mistakes.

WW:	wrong word
S:	spelling
P:	punctuation
T:	tense
A:	article
WO:	word order
^ :	something missing

Revision Units

The four Revision Units with exam-type tasks could be done either at home or in class, depending on the time available. The exercises thoroughly revise the functions, grammar and vocabulary that have been taught in the preceding units. Since the Revision Units are not tests, we suggest that you allow Ss to refer to the relevant units when doing the exercises if they need to.

Each revision unit consists of reading comprehension texts, also deriving from authentic sources. The aim is to consolidate the sub-skills already practised in the module. There is also a *Use of English* section, which familiarises Ss with FCE-type tasks. Finally, there is a listening task, which helps Ss further practise their listening skills and consolidate the sub-skills already practised in the module.

Optional activities

In the Teacher's Book there are various optional activities which help Ss get a better understanding of the presentation texts and the reading or listening texts and give them further practice with various grammatical structures or forms.

Abbreviations used in Teacher's Book

adj → adjective
adv → adverb
e.g. → for example
etc → et cetera
n → noun
p → page
pp → pages
prep → preposition
sb → somebody
sth → something
Ss → students
v → verb
TB → Teacher's Book

Contents

01 Been around the world?

Lesson One

Functions

Talking about lifestyles and habits
Expressing habits in the present

Structures

Present Simple
Present Progressive

Vocabulary

Words

anniversary	gathering (n)	notice (v)
approve (of)	guarantee (n)	overturned
chat (v)	habit	pile
compliment (n)	handshake (n)	punctual
custom	helping	disrespectful
elsewhere	host (n)	volume

Phrasal verbs

look down on	pull up	take off	throw in

Expressions

at the stroke of midnight
bear in mind
be in for
do the trick
have a ball

have a go
it's the effort that counts
it's worth a try
Off we go ...

Conversational English

Got to go.   I suppose so.

presentation

Aim: to present vocabulary and structures in the context of an article about different habits and customs around the world

Background Notes:
• Spain is a country in southwestern Europe, Thailand is in southeast Asia, Bolivia is in South America and Zambia in south-central Africa.
• *'Auld Lang Syne'*, meaning 'Old Long Ago', is the title of a popular song traditionally sung at midnight on New Year's Eve. It was written by the Scottish poet Robert Burns (1759-1796) and is about friendship and times gone by.

1 Aims: • to interpret the title of the article in order to predict its content
• to relate the topic of the article to Ss' personal experiences
• Ask Ss to look at the title of the article and discuss the questions.

> **optional**
> You may also ask Ss a few more questions:
> e.g. *Have you heard of any customs and habits in other countries that are different from those in your country?*
> *Have you ever visited a foreign country and thought that some of the local habits and customs were strange or unusual?*

2 Aim: to give Ss practice in reading for specific information
• Have Ss read the first paragraph and ask them question a.
• Elicit and check answers.
• Ask Ss to read the rest of the text paragraph by paragraph without worrying about the unknown words. After each paragraph, ask Ss the corresponding questions. (Questions b and c are about Thailand, question d is about Bolivia, question e is about Zambia.)
• Elicit and check answers.

Key

a. Spaniards eat twelve grapes at the stroke of midnight because they hope that it will bring them good luck in the coming year.
b. Thais consider it rude when a visitor doesn't take off his / her shoes before entering the house. They also consider it rude if someone touches them on the head.
c. Young people in Thailand try to keep their heads lower than those of older people at social gatherings because they don't want to give them the impression that they are looking down on them.
d. Guests at dinner parties in Bolivia should finish everything on their plates and throw in a compliment about the food during dinner.
e. No, they aren't. It is not always certain whether they will keep the appointment they have made or not.

• When this activity is over, ask Ss some more questions.
  e.g. *If you wanted to shake hands with a Bolivian whose hand is dirty, what would he most probably do?*
  What do Zambians consider rude at dinner parties?
• Encourage Ss to guess the meaning of new vocabulary such as *huge, disrespectful* and *helping*. Provide explanations through definitions or example sentences.

words and phrases

1 Phrasal verbs and expressions

Aim: to give Ss practice in inferring the meaning of the phrasal verbs and expressions in the article through a matching activity

- Refer Ss to the article.
- Ask Ss to do the activity.
- Check answers.

Key

1. h	6. a
2. e	7. b
3. g	8. d
4. i	9. f
5. c	

optional

If there is time, ask Ss to make their own sentences using the phrasal verbs and expressions and check them.

2 Words easily confused

Aim: to give Ss practice in distinguishing between words that can easily be confused

- Refer Ss to the verbs **watch** and **notice** in the article. (*If you **watch** Thais at social gatherings, you will **notice** that young people try ...*).
- Encourage Ss to work out the difference in meaning.

watch = look at sb / sth for a long time, paying attention to what is happening
notice = become aware of sb / sth
look = turn your eyes in a particular direction

- Ask Ss to do the rest of the exercise, one set at a time. For each set, explain the difference through definitions and / or examples. You can also refer Ss to the article whenever necessary.

consider = think of sb / sth in a particular way (*They **consider** it extremely rude.*)
judge = form an opinion about sb / sth, based on certain information or evidence
think (about sth) = examine carefully all the possibilities before making a decision

allow + full infinitive / *let* + base form = give permission to sb to do sth
approve (of) = think that sb / sth is good
(*... Zambians don't **approve** of that, either!*)

escape from sth = get away from an unpleasant or dangerous situation
prevent (sb from doing sth) = stop sb from doing sth
avoid + -ing form = not let sth unpleasant or embarrassing happen (*... to **avoid** giving an impression of looking down on them.*)

- Check answers.

Key

a. noticed	b. watched	c. looked
a. judge	b. is / was thinking	c. considers
a. let	b. allow	c. approve
a. escape	b. prevent	c. avoid

optional

If there is time, ask Ss to make their own sentences using the words presented above and check them.

Teacher's Notes

grammar

1 **Aim: to revise some uses of the Present Simple and present some new ones through a matching activity**

- Ask Ss to read through the rules. Ensure that Ss understand the terms used. If necessary, provide explanations.
- Ask Ss to read through the examples.
- Have Ss do the activity.
- Elicit and check answers.

Key

a. 4	b. 5	c. 3	d. 2	e. 1

2 **Aim: to revise some uses of the Present Progressive and present some new ones through a matching activity**

- Ask Ss to read through the rules. Ensure that Ss understand the terms used. If necessary, provide explanations.
- Ask Ss to read through the examples.
- Have Ss do the activity.
- Elicit and check answers.

Key

a. 3	b. 4	c. 2	d. 1

3 **Aim: to give Ss practice in using the Present Simple and the Present Progressive in context**

- Ask Ss to read through the conversation taking place in an *Internet chat room* (= an area on the Internet where people from all over the world can communicate with each other) and complete the blanks.
- Check answers and ask Ss to provide justification.
- If time is scarce, assign the exercise for homework.

Key

(1) have
(2) 's / is
(3) 'm turning / am turning
(4) 's / is
(5) listen
(6) 're organising / are organising
(7) 'm going / am going
(8) 'm taking / am taking
(9) needs

Teacher's Notes

Lesson Two

Structures

Be used to + -ing form
Stative verbs

Vocabulary

Words

boom (v)	gasp (v)	option	tip (v)
ceremony	highway	(fast food) outlet	vast
chapel	loosen	powder	vehicle
endless	mild	proper	version
fairly	minimart	status	weird

Phrasal verbs and expressions

at a low cost	date back to
at peak times	grab a bite (to eat) / a cup (to drink)
be short of	it's no wonder
be the case	life-on-the-go
catch a movie	out of the ordinary
catch on	

reading

Background Notes:

- *Drive-ins* were places where you could eat or watch films while sitting in your car. Nowadays, they have been replaced by *drive-throughs*. These are restaurants, cinemas, minimarts or even banks where you can be served quickly and efficiently without having to get out of your car.
- The letters *ATM* stand for *Automated Teller Machine* (a machine outside a bank from which you withdraw money from your bank account using a special plastic card).
- A *movie theatre* is the American equivalent of *cinema*.

optional pre-reading activity

- Ask Ss to read the title of the reading text and look at the picture accompanying it.
- Ask Ss to predict the topic of the reading text. You can ask Ss the following questions.
  e.g. *What kind of place is shown in the photograph?*
  What do you think "Living in the Fast Lane" means?
- Discuss and elicit answers.

1 **Aim: to help Ss understand the organisation of a gapped text**

- Ask Ss to read through the text for gist, without worrying about the gaps.
- Ask Ss to try to guess what each of the missing sentences is about.
- Ask Ss to look at the sentences A-F which have been removed from the text and ensure that they understand them.
- Point out to Ss that they should always look for clues in the sentences which precede or follow the gaps. To this end, Ss may be helped by determiners (*this*, *that*) and subject / object personal pronouns (*we / us*, *they / them*) which refer to things or people mentioned in previous or later sentences. When there are no such cohesive devices, Ss should rely strongly on context.
- Ask Ss to read the first paragraph of the text and decide which sentence best fits the first gap.

- Check answers and ask Ss to underline the key words / phrases which helped them decide.
- Ask Ss to read the text paragraph by paragraph and do the rest of the activity.
- Point out to Ss that if they cannot decide what fits in a gap, they should move on and get back to it later.
- Check answers and ask Ss to provide justification.

Key

1. C **Text**
Then, you drive ...
... do your shopping
in no time.

Missing sentence
... when you can't ... to park ... in the back seat. *This,* at the beginning of the sentence, refers to the idea of doing your shopping in the manner described in the paragraph.

2. D **Text**
... fast food outlets and burger bars ...
... grab a bite to eat ...
... the business is still booming ...

Missing sentence
... endless lines of cars ... these places ... between 12:30 and 2:30 pm. (=lunchtime)

3. A **Text**
... designed for families ...
... get dressed up or find ...

Missing sentence
... were particularly popular ... the age of discos ... hang out there a lot. These places, at the beginning of the sentence, refers to the places mentioned previously in the text.

4. F **Text**
... drive-through wedding chapels ...
This practice refers to getting married in the manner described in the missing sentence.

Missing sentence
... drive up, park and the ceremony ... the window. They refers to the couple mentioned previously in the text. *Ceremony* refers to wedding ceremonies which are related to the wedding chapels mentioned previously in the text.

5. B **Text**
... cars were more than just a means of transport.

Missing sentence
They were status symbols ... works of art. They, at the beginning of the sentence, refers to the word cars mentioned previously in the text.

Extra sentence: E

- When the activity is over, explain unknown words through definitions or example sentences.

2 **Aim: to expand on the topic of the reading text**
- Ask Ss the questions and generate discussion.

words and phrases

1 Phrasal verbs and expressions

Aim: to give Ss practice in inferring the meaning of the phrasal verbs and expressions in the article through a matching activity

- Refer Ss to the article.
- Ask Ss to do the activity.
- Check answers.

Key

a. out of the ordinary
b. catch a movie
c. are short of
d. grab a bite to eat
e. it's no wonder
f. catching on
g. at a low cost

2 Word building

A **Aims:** · **to introduce positive and negative suffixes of adjectives and adverbs**
· **to give Ss practice in adjective and adverb formation**

- Read and explain the introductory comment as well as the examples in the table.
- Ensure that Ss understand the procedure.
- Have Ss do the activity and check answers.

Key

noun	adjective (noun + ful)	adjective (noun + less)	adverb (noun + fully)	adverb (noun + lessly)
use	useful	useless	usefully	uselessly
end	-	endless	-	**endlessly**
beauty	beautiful	-	**beautifully**	-
care	**careful**	**careless**	**carefully**	**carelessly**
doubt	**doubtful**	**doubtless**	**doubtfully**	doubtlessly
need	-	needless	-	**needlessly**
harm	**harmful**	**harmless**	harmfully	**harmlessly**

B **Aim: to give Ss practice in using nouns, adjectives and adverbs in context**

- Have Ss do the activity and check answers.

Key

a. beautifully
b. carelessly
c. doubt
d. harmless
e. endlessly
f. need

---

optional

If there is time, ask Ss to make their own examples with the rest of the words from exercise A and check them.

Teacher's Notes

grammar

1 **Aim: to demonstrate how present habits are expressed through elicitation**

- Ask Ss to read through the table and provide them with any explanations if necessary.
- Refer Ss to the text on pages 4-5 and ask them to complete the table with examples from the text.
- Elicit and check answers.

Key

- *People often go there to catch a movie and eat in their cars.*
- *... but most Americans are used to eating in their cars nowadays.*
- Read out and explain the note. If necessary, provide Ss with further examples.

2 **Aim: to elicit the different uses of stative verbs in present forms**

- Ask Ss to read the first set of sentences.
- Elicit answers.
- Do the same for the second set of sentences.

Key

1. a. believe / be under the impression (state)
   b. search for sth using your hands (action)
2. a. believe / have an opinion (state)
   b. consider (action)

- Read out and explain the note. If necessary, provide Ss with further examples.

STATE	ACTION
• They *have* a house in the suburbs.	• She *is having* lunch at the moment.
• Oh no! I *see* Jane coming towards us!	• I *am seeing* my lawyer tomorrow morning at 9:00.
• Mmm! The soup *tastes* delicious!	• He *is tasting* the sauce to see if it needs more salt.
• These roses *smell* really nice!	• Why *are* you *smelling* the milk? Has it gone off?
• I don't like Bruce at all! He *is* so rude and selfish!	• *Are* you *being* sarcastic or is it my imagination?

English in use

Aim: to check structural accuracy through an error correction exercise

- Ask Ss to read through the text for gist, without trying to correct anything.
- Ask Ss to read the text again, one sentence at a time and try to identify which of the lines are correct and which contain a word which should not be there.
- Check answers and ask Ss to provide justification.

Key

1. are	4. he	7. own	10. ✔
2. ✔	5. on	8. any	11. ✔
3. so	6. it	9. being	

listening

Aim: to give Ss practice in listening for gist through a matching activity

- Ask Ss to read through the statements A-F. Make sure that they understand what they mean.
- Point out to Ss that they can note possible choices during the first listening, but should finalise their answers only after the second listening since there is one extra answer which could confuse them.
- Play the CD twice.
- Check answers.

Key

Speaker 1: F
Speaker 2: C
Speaker 3: E
Speaker 4: D
Speaker 5: B

Extra letter: A

optional post-listening activity

You may ask Ss further questions of personal response to the listening text.

e.g. *Has anything embarrassing happened to you during a visit to a foreign country?*

Teacher's Notes

Lesson Three

Vocabulary

affectionate	hectic	schedule
caring	isolation	space
cosy	major	vet
domestic	motivated	

Expressions
drop sb a line
feel like a fish out of water
get the hang of things
hold sth against sb
look on the bright side

speaking

1 Aim: to generate discussion based on Ss' personal experiences and preferences
- Ask Ss to look at the questions and generate discussion.

2 Aim: to give Ss practice in relating words / phrases to context
- Tell Ss to look at photographs a and b.
- Then ask Ss to look at the box and decide which words / phrases can be used to describe each photograph. Ensure that Ss don't have any unknown words. If necessary, provide them with explanations and / or examples.
- Elicit answers.

Key

Photograph a: pollution, isolation (= *the state of being alone or feeling lonely /* figurative use), different forms of entertainment, traffic jams, more facilities.
Photograph b: isolation (= *the state of being far away from places where other people live /* literal use), healthy food, fresh air, few job opportunities, open spaces.

3 Aim: to give Ss practice in comparing and contrasting two photographs
- Divide Ss into pairs.
- In each pair, tell one student to talk about what life is like in each of the situations shown in the photographs. Encourage him / her to use some of the words / phrases from exercise 2.
- Now ask the second student the question: *Which of the two lifestyles best suits you / do you prefer?*
- Elicit answers.

Key

Suggested ideas:
- Photograph *a* was taken on the tube / in the city. / Photograph *b* was taken in the country.
- There's a lot of pollution in big towns / cities. / The

air in the country is cleaner.
- Traffic jams are quite common in cities. / No traffic problems in the country / more open spaces.
- Cities offer different forms of entertainment and more facilities. / Life in the country is more difficult as there are few job opportunities.
- Cities are crowded places but people do not frequent contact with one another. / In the country, people might feel isolated / people living there eat healthier food because they grow it themselves.

4 Aim: to elaborate and expand on the topic of the speaking activity
- Ask Ss to read the questions and generate discussion.

5 Aim: to give Ss practice in relating adjectives to context
- Tell Ss to look at photographs c and d.
- Then ask Ss to look at the box and decide which words / phrases can be used to describe each photograph. Ensure that Ss don't have any unknown words. If necessary provide them with explanations and / or examples.
- Point out to Ss that some words might be used for both photographs.
- Elicit answers.

Key

Photograph c: caring, domestic, relaxed, monotonous, responsible, affectionate, demanding
Photograph d: professional, hectic, stressed / stressful, monotonous, demanding, responsible, determined, motivated, exhausted

6 Aim: to give Ss practice in comparing and contrasting two photographs
- Divide Ss into pairs.
- In each pair, tell one student to talk about how the women in the photograph feel. Encourage him / her to use some of the adjectives from exercise 5.
- Now ask the second student the question: *Can women successfully combine motherhood with a career today? / Which of the two situations is more familiar to you?*
- Elicit answers.

Key

Suggested ideas:
- Photograph *c* shows a woman at home. Photograph *d* shows a woman at work.
- Being a full-time mother is quite demanding / can be stressful at times / exhausted by the end of the day / monotonous. / Having a career can also be demanding and quite stressful as well as hectic on busy days.
- Being a mother involves a lot of responsibility. / Career women are quite determined and motivated to succeed.

writing

1 **Aims:** · to activate Ss' background knowledge
· to prepare Ss for the writing task
· Ask Ss the questions and generate discussion.

2 **Aim:** to help Ss identify the purpose, audience and stylistic features of a letter
· Ask Ss to read through the letter and answer the questions a-c.
· Elicit and check answers.

Key

a. To give Tim his / her news about his / her life in New Zealand.
b. The writer uses informal language. You can tell from:
· the layout – greeting (*Dear Tim*), indented paragraphs
· the language – informal expressions (*How's it going?, I thought I'd drop you a line, trust me, I'm finally getting the hang of things*).
· the punctuation - exclamation marks (*... there is plenty of water around!, ... pretty unfamiliar!, ... the hang of things!, ... really windy sometimes!*), contracted forms (*How's, haven't, I'd, I'm*).
c. They are probably friends or cousins.

3 **Aim:** to familiarise Ss with the stylistic features of different types of letters
· Tell Ss to read through the three closing paragraphs.
· Ask Ss to decide which closing paragraph is most suitable for the letter in exercise 2.
· Elicit answers.
· Ask Ss the questions.
· Elicit answers.

Key

· Closing paragraph *b* best concludes the letter in exercise 2.
· Because closing paragraph *a* best concludes a letter of apology while closing paragraph *c* best concludes a letter of invitation.

4 **Plan**

Aim: to help Ss plan their writing and encourage them to include relevant information in it
· Ask Ss to do the exercise.
· Check answers.

Key

· Greeting ⇨ d
· Opening paragraph ⇨ e
· Main part ⇨ a
· Closing paragraph ⇨ c
· Signing off ⇨ b

5 **Writing task**

Aim: to give Ss practice in writing a letter giving news
· Assign the writing task for homework.

Teacher's Notes

02 Eureka!

Lesson One

Functions

Expressing opinions

Structures

Present Perfect Simple
Present Perfect Progressive

Vocabulary

Words and expressions

accompany	entirely	put an end to
alert (n)	fake	receiver
appliance	fraud	refund
attached (to)	furious	sculpted
beloved	instalment	sentence (v)
beware	instantly	squeaky clean
breakthrough	javelin	squeeze in(to)
calendar	leading (adj)	stay in touch
commercialised	long jump	strap (n)
credit	momentarily	thick
debt	nifty	undoubtedly
discus	not lift a finger	uninterruptedly
dumb-bell	patch (n)	

Phrasal verbs

let down	take in	work out
miss out on	throw in	
put sth off	wander (away)	

presentation

Aim: to present vocabulary and structures in the context of four classified advertisements about unusual inventions

1 **Aims:** · **to activate Ss' background knowledge**
· **to help them predict the content of the classified advertisements**

· Ask Ss the questions and generate discussion.
· Elicit answers.

optional

You may also ask Ss a few more questions:
e.g. *If you were an inventor, what sort of gadget would you come up with?*

2 **Aim: to give Ss practice in reading for specific information through a T / F activity**

· Have Ss read the first advertisement and ask them to decide whether the first statement is True or False.
· Elicit and check answers. Ask Ss to provide justification.
· Ask Ss to read the other three advertisements, without worrying about the missing words. After each advertisement, ask Ss the questions.
· Elicit and check answers. Ask Ss to provide justification.

Key

1. F   2. T   3. F   4. F

· When this activity is over, ask Ss some more questions.
  e.g. *Where can you buy Marvellous Magnetic Slippers?*
  How does a Telephone Dumb-bell work?
  Is it difficult to use the Automatic Dog-Washer?
  What does the Anywhere Desk consist of?
· Encourage Ss to guess the meaning of new vocabulary such as *leading*, *refund*, *alert*. Provide explanations through definitions or example sentences.

Teacher's Notes

words and phrases

1 Phrasal verbs

**Aim:to give Ss practice in inferring the meaning of
the phrasal verbs in the advertisements
through a matching activity**

- Refer Ss to the advertisements.
- Ask Ss to do the activity.
- Check answers.

Key

1. e
2. f
3. d

4. a
5. b
6. c

> **optional**
> If there is time, ask Ss to make their own sentences
> using the phrasal verbs and expressions and check
> them.

2 Words easily confused

**Aim:to give Ss practice in distinguishing between
words that can easily be confused**

- Refer Ss to the words **cash** and **credit** in the third
  advertisement (*Pay cash or by credit card ...*).
- Encourage Ss to work out the difference in meaning.

cash = money in the form of coins and banknotes
credit = an arrangement you make with a shop to
pay later for something you buy
cheque = a printed form that you can write a sum of
money on and then sign it to be used as a way of
paying for something instead of cash

- Ask Ss to do the rest of the exercise, one set at a
  time. For each set, explain the difference through
  definitions and / or examples. You can also refer Ss
  to the advertisements whenever necessary.

imitation = a copy of something, especially of
something expensive (*... don't be taken in by
imitations!*)
fake = an object (e.g. a work of art, a coin or a piece
of jewellery) that is not genuine but has been made
to look as if it is
fraud = the crime of deceiving somebody in order to
get money or goods illegally

invention = the production of something that has not
existed before (*It is the most amazing invention I've
ever seen!*)
discovery = the act of finding something that was not
known about before
experiment = a scientific test that is carried out in

order to gain new knowledge

refund = a sum of money that is paid back to you
when you return goods to a shop (*... we'll give you
a full refund!*)
debt = a sum of money that somebody owes
instalment = one of a series of payments that are
made regularly over a period of time until something
has been paid off

device = a piece of equipment that has been
designed for a particular purpose (*This nifty device
consists of ...*)
appliance = a machine that is designed to do a
particular thing in the home (e.g. preparing food,
heating or cleaning)
tool = an instrument used for making or repairing
things

- Check answers.

Key

a. credit	b. cash	c. cheque
a. imitation	b. fraud	c. fake
a. experiment	b. invention	c. discovery
a. debt	b. refund	c. instalment
a. appliances	b. tools	c. device

> **optional**
> If there is time, ask Ss to make their own sentences
> using the words presented above and check them.

Teacher's Notes

10   Channel your English

grammar

1 **Aim: to revise some uses of the Present Perfect Simple and the Present Perfect Progressive through a matching activity**

- Ask Ss to read through the sentences a-d from the presentation. Then ask Ss to read through the questions 1-4. Ensure that Ss understand the terms used. If necessary, provide explanations.
- Have Ss do the activity.
- Elicit and check answers.

Key

1. b
2. a
3. d
4. c

2 **Aims:** • **to elaborate on exercise 1**
　　　• **to revise Present Perfect Simple vs Past Simple**

- Ask Ss to read through the sentences a-c. Then ask Ss to read through the rules that follow. Ensure that Ss understand the terms used. If necessary, provide explanations.
- Have Ss do the activity.
- Elicit and check answers.

Key

- **be** + _adjective_ (in the superlative degree) + **Present Perfect Simple**.
- the _Present Perfect Progressive_ is used to show annoyance resulting from a recent action.
- the **Past Simple** is used for actions that happened in the past and the exact _time_ is mentioned.

3 **Aim: to give Ss practice in using the Present Perfect Simple, the Present Perfect Progressive and the Past Simple in context**

- Ask Ss to read through the text for gist.
- Have Ss do the activity.
- Check answers and ask Ss to provide justification.
- If time is scarce, assign the exercise for homework.

Key

(1) have undoubtedly become	(7) have changed
(2) were	(8) have been successfully competing
(3) went on	
(4) have been around	(9) have been complaining
(5) did not / didn't come	
(6) included	(10) have become

Lesson Two

Structures

Past Perfect Simple
Past Perfect Progressive

Vocabulary

Words and expressions related to money

currency	pay up front	transaction
hard cash	receipt	

Other words and expressions

acceptable	financial	perception
authenticity	fixed (adj)	pros and cons
banknote	gossip (n)	region
be bound to	identifying (adj)	spade (n)
capacity	indispensable	spread (v)
circulate	issue (n)	suspicious
consequence	lace	thud
craze	obligation	trade (v)
dare (v)	obtain	tribal (adj)
debate	official	undesirable
developing (adj)	originate	valuable
dimension	outrageous	value (n)
exchange	peer (v)	

Idioms with money
be rolling in money
get one's money's worth
money doesn't grow on trees
put some money into
throw one's money around

reading

optional pre-reading activity
- Ask Ss to read the title of the reading text and look at the picture accompanying it.
- Ask Ss to predict the topic of the reading text. You can also ask Ss the following questions:
  e.g. *What forms of payment are you familiar with? How do you usually pay for the things you buy?*
- Discuss and elicit answers.

1 **Aim: to help Ss identify the main idea of each paragraph through a matching exercise**
- Ask Ss to read through the text for gist, without worrying about the gaps.
- Ask Ss to read through the summary sentences A-G and ensure that they understand them.
- Before the second reading, point out to Ss that they should always look for key words or phrases in the text which are related to those in the summary sentences. When there are no such cohesive devices, Ss should rely strongly on context.

- Now ask Ss to read the first paragraph of the text and decide on the sentence which best summarises it. Ask Ss to underline the key words / phrases which helped them decide. Check answers.
- Ask Ss to read the text paragraph by paragraph and do the rest of the activity.
- Point out to Ss that if they cannot decide on the summary sentence of a specific paragraph, they should move on and get back to it later.
- Check answers and ask Ss to provide justification.

Key

1 G Text
... how people traded ...
Summary sentence
... to carry out their transactions.

2 C Text
... shells, knives and even spades ...
Summary sentence
... various objects ...

3 F Text
The Chinese developed the earliest forms of coins ... in the kingdom of Lydia that the first real coins were made ...
Summary sentence
The idea of using coins in financial transactions originated in Asia.

4 D Text
... banknotes ... having money in paper form was warmly received ...
Summary sentence
... the advantages of having money in the form of printed paper.

5 A Text
... credit cards ... to pay up front ...
Summary sentence
.... buying now and paying later.

6 E Text
... revolutionise ... Smart cards will contain ...
Summary sentence
... open the door to a new dimension.

Extra summary sentence: B

- When the activity is over, explain unknown words through definitions or example sentences.

optional post-reading activity
Ask Ss questions of personal response to the topic of the reading text.
e.g. *How helpful do you think credit cards are? What do you think of smart cards? Can you think of any drawbacks they might have?*

words and phrases

2 Word building

A Aim: to introduce noun and verb formation and give Ss practice in it
- Read out and explain the introductory comment.
- Discuss the examples given.
- Have Ss do the exercise and check answers.

Key

noun	verb = noun + -ise
revolution	*revolutionise*
symbol	**symbolise**
memory	memorise
apology	apologise
economy	economise
victim	**victimise**

B Aim: to introduce noun and adjective formation and give Ss practice in it
- Read out and explain the introductory comment.
- Discuss the examples given. Point out to Ss the difference between *historic* (= important in history and likely to be remembered, e.g. *A number of festivities were held to mark the President's historic visit to our country*) and *historical* (= belonging to history; related to sth that happened in the past or to the study of history, e.g. *Alexander the Great is a major historical figure*).
- Have Ss do the exercise. Point out the difference between *economic* (= related to economy or the field of economics, e.g. *The country's economic situation has finally stabilised*) and *economical* (= inexpensive, saving money, e.g. *My car is more economical than yours*).
- Check answers.

Key

noun	adjective = noun with -ic or -ical
history	*historic / historical*
economy	**economic / economical**
hero	**heroic**
medicine	**medical**
science	scientific
chemistry	chemical

2 Idioms

Aim: to introduce the meaning of idioms related to money by giving Ss practice in using them in context
- Ask Ss to read through the meanings 1-5 and the sentences a-e. Explain any words Ss might not know.
- Have Ss do the exercise and check answers.

Key

a. 5   b. 1   c. 3   d. 4   e. 2

Teacher's Notes

grammar

1 **Aim:** **to present the Past Perfect Simple and the Past Perfect Progressive**
- Refer Ss to the reading text on pages 12-13.
- Ask Ss to underline any examples of the Past Perfect Simple and the Past Perfect Progressive.
- Have Ss do the activity.
- Elicit answers.

Key

- By that time, money **had become** so important that the developing societies started circulating their own coins....
- In actual fact, people **had been using** coins for about 1 600 years until banknotes made their historic appearance.
- ... but by the early 11th century these receipts **had been given** fixed values and became official. (Passive Voice)

2 **Aim:** **to elicit the uses of the Past Perfect Simple and the Past Perfect Progressive**
- Ask Ss to read through the rules and ensure that they understand the terms used. If necessary, provide explanations.
- Ask Ss to refer to the sentences in exercise 1 and do the activity.
- Check answers.

Key

a. We use the _Past Perfect Simple_ to describe an action that was completed _before_ another action in the past. The second action is expressed with the _Past Simple_.
b. We use the _Past Perfect Progressive_ to emphasise the duration of an action that _happened / took place_ before another action in the past.

3 **Aims:** • **to give Ss practice in using the Past Perfect Simple and the Past Perfect Progressive vs the Simple Past in context**
• **to help Ss comprehend which time expressions are used to express different time relations**
- Ask Ss to read through the text for gist. Explain any words Ss might not know.
- Have Ss do the exercise.
- Check answers.

Key

(1) had been doing	(6) before
(2) after	(7) got
(3) heard	(8) put
(4) by then	(9) imagined
(5) had stopped	(10) lifted

listening

1 **Aim:** **to give Ss practice in listening for specific information through a matching exercise**
- Ask Ss to read statements 1-6.
- Explain any words Ss might not know.
- Play the CD twice.
- Check answers.

Key

1 K	2 G	3 C	4 K	5 G	6 K

optional post-listening activity

You may ask Ss further questions of personal response to the listening text.
e.g. Do you think that credit cards can trick you into buying more than you want?
Do you think that smart cards can have undesirable consequences? If so, do you agree that we should prevent their circulation?

Teacher's Notes

Lesson Three

Vocabulary

Words

beneficial	insist (on)	radiation
concession	interrupt	rank (v)
confirm	misuse (v)	regularly
drastically	peeler	seemingly
(dys) function (n)	potential (adj)	similarly

Phrases and expressions

a must-have accessory	the other way around
give priority	worth mentioning
more often than not	

speaking

1 **Aim: to give Ss practice in prioritising**

- Divide Ss into pairs.
- Tell Ss to look at the pictures and ensure that Ss know the name of each invention. If necessary, provide them with explanations (*a computer, a hairdryer, a video cassette recorder / DVD player, a dishwasher, a satellite dish, an electric toothbrush, a pair of batteries, an air-conditioner*).
- Tell Ss to look at the suggested expressions and involve them in meaningful collaborative tasks.
- Generate disussion.

Key

Suggested ideas:

- I think that computers are the most important invention in recent years. They can store huge amounts of data and have made our lives a lot easier.
- I agree and I'd like to add that with the introduction of the Internet, communication has become simpler and quicker.
- I can't imagine my life without my VCR because I like watching films at home.
- I believe that the least important invention in recent years is the electric toothbrush. It hasn't really changed our lives because we can use conventional toothbrushes and get the same results.
- As far as I'm concerned, one of the most helpful inventions in recent years is the air conditioner because it creates a pleasant atmosphere at home or at work both in summer and in winter.
- Having a dishwasher is necessary because it saves lots of time and energy.

2 **Aim: to elaborate and expand on the topic of the speaking activity**

- Ask Ss the questions and generate discussion.

Teacher's Notes

writing

1 **Aim: to help Ss identify the purpose and the organisation of a one-sided essay**
- Tell Ss to read through the essay. Explain any words Ss might not know.
- Ask Ss to read through the introductions a-c and then choose the one which best fits the essay. Explain any words Ss might not know.
- Elicit answers. Ask Ss to provide justification for their choice.

Key

Introduction *b* best fits the essay. It introduces the topic of the essay and prepares the reader for what is to follow, that is the negative effects of mobile phones on people and human interaction. (Introduction *a* would best fit a one-sided essay on the advantages of mobile phones while introduction *c* would best fit an essay on technology).

2 Plan

Aim: to help Ss plan their writing and encourage them to include relevant information in it
- Refer Ss to the essay.
- Ask Ss to do the exercise.
- Check answers.

Key

a. Y
b. N
c. Y
d. Y
e. Y

3 Linking ideas

Aim: to present linking words through a listing activity
- Ask Ss to read through the list of linking words and the headings that follow. Explain any words Ss might not know.
- Have Ss do the activity.
- Check answers.

Key

- **LISTING POINTS**
  furthermore, in addition
- **GIVING AN EXAMPLE**
  such as, take for instance
- **EXPRESSING RESULT AND CONSEQUENCE**
  therefore, as a result
- **EXPRESSING CONCESSION / CONTRAST**
  contrary to the above ideas, on the other hand, even though
- **SUMMING UP**
  to sum up, on the whole

4 Writing task

Aim: to give Ss practice in writing a one-sided essay
- Assign the writing task for homework.

Teacher's Notes

03 Fast forward

Lesson One

Functions

Talking about the future
Making predictions

Structures

Future *Will*
Future *Going to*
Future Progressive
Future Perfect

Vocabulary

Words and phrases

at a brisk / steady pace   restricted (area)
carer   scan (v)
holographic   significant
know-how (n)   temporarily
match sth against sth else   transmit
orbit   transplant (n)
proposal   wire (n)

Prepositional phrases (*in / out of*)

in agreement   in / out of sight
in charge   in the long run
in favour   out of breath
in / out of control   out of the question
in / out of hand

Collocations with *set* and *put*

put a strain on / effort into / the blame on
set a task / eyes on / foot in / the standard

presentation

**Aim: to present vocabulary, structures and functions in
the context of a radio talk show about the future**

Background Note:
A conventional TV set has a two-dimensional (2-D)
screen, while a *holographic* TV set projects
three-dimensional (3-D) images.

1 **Aim: to generate discussion and introduce the
topic of the presentation**
· Ask Ss to read through the extracts 1-6. Explain any
words Ss might not know.
· Ask Ss to match the extracts with the pictures a-f.
· Generate discussion and elicit answers.

Key

1. untrue (Graham Bell invented the telephone
in1875)
2. untrue
3. true (Dr Christian Barnard performed the first heart
transplant before the end of 1967)
4. true
5. untrue
6. untrue

a 4   b 2   c 5   d 6   e 3   f 1

2 **Aim: to predict the content of the dialogue
based on Ss' background knowledge**
· Ask Ss to read through the statements a-e.
· Ask Ss whether they think the ideas expressed in
these statements will be possible in the future or not.
· Elicit answers. However, don't check Ss' answers at
this stage.

3 **Aim: to give Ss practice in listening for the
main ideas expressed in the dialogue in
order to check their predictions**
· Ask Ss to listen to the dialogue carefully. Play the
CD once. If necessary, play the CD again.
· Check answers.

Key

a, c

Teacher's Notes

words and phrases

1 Prepositional phrases

A **Aim: to present prepositional phrases with *in* and *out of***

- Ask Ss to read through the words in the box. Explain any words Ss might not know.
- Discuss the examples given.
- Have Ss do the exercise.
- Check answers.

Key

in	out of
the long run	—
hand	*hand*
control	control
sight	sight
favour	—
charge	—
—	breath
order	order
agreement	—
—	the question

B **Aim: to give Ss practice in using the prepositional phrases in context**

- Have Ss do the exercise. Explain any unknown words if necessary.
- Check answers.

Key

a. in favour   c. out of sight   e. out of breath
b. in agreement d. out of order

> **optional**
> If there is time, ask Ss to make their own sentences using the rest of the prepositional phrases from exercise 1A and check them.

2 Collocations

A **Aim: to present collocations with *set* and *put***

- Ask Ss to read through the words in the box. Explain any words Ss might not know.
- Read out and discuss the examples given.
- Have Ss do the exercise.
- Check answers.

Key

set	put
the standard	*an end to*
foot in	the blame on
a task	effort into
eyes on	a strain on

B **Aim: to give Ss practice in using some of the collocations in context**

- Have Ss do the exercise. Explain any unknown words if necessary.
- Check answers.

Key

a. set foot in   c. will put the blame on
b. set eyes on   d. have put a strain on

> **optional**
> If there is time, ask Ss to make their own sentences using the rest of the collocations from exercise 2A and check them.

Teacher's Notes

grammar

1 Aim: to revise the basic uses of the Future Will, the Future Going to, the Future Progressive and the Future Perfect
- Ask Ss to read through the sentences a-d.
- Discuss which future form is used in each sentence.
- Elicit answers.
- Ask Ss to read through the rules. Ensure that Ss understand all the terms used.
- Have Ss complete the rules.
- Elicit answers.

Key

a. *will create* - Future *Will*
b. *will be working* - Future Progressive
c. *is going to put* - Future *Going to*
d. *travel will have improved* - Future Perfect
The Future Will is used to make predictions about the future.
The Future Going to is used to make predictions based on evidence.
The Future Progressive is used for actions that will be in progress at a specific time in the future.
The Future Perfect is used for actions that will be completed before a specific time or another action in the future.

2 Aim: to revise some further uses of the Future Will and the Future Going to
- Ask Ss to read through the sentences.
- Ask Ss to read through the set of rules.
- Discuss and elicit answers.

Key

The **Future Will** is also used for *on-the-spot decisions*, *threats*, *promises*, and *offers*.
The **Future Going to** is also used for future *plans*.

3 Aim: to give Ss practice in using the future tenses in context
- Have Ss do the activity.
- Check answers and ask Ss to provide justification.

Key

1. b   2. a   3. b   4. b   5. a

English in use

Aim: to give Ss practice in structural accuracy through an open cloze exercise
- Ask Ss to read through the text for gist, without worrying about the missing words.
- Ask Ss to fill in the gaps with one word only.
- Check answers and ask Ss to provide justification.

Key

(1) has
(2) than
(3) no
(4) will
(5) that / which
(6) soon
(7) How
(8) your
(9) if
(10) have

── Teacher's Notes ──

Lesson Two

Structures

Conditional sentences (Zero Type & Type 1)
Time clauses (present / future)

Vocabulary

Words

activate	kink
badge	miserable
concept	overpriced
correspondence	priceless
currently	release (v)
decoder	stimulate
experimental	tiny
fingerprint	transform (into)
gizmos	ultimate
glow	valueless
instruction manual	

Phrasal verbs and expressions

battle it out	iron out
be a hit	take action
go on	take off
in the first place	

reading

optional pre-reading activity

- Ask Ss to read the title and the sub-headings of the reading text and look at the pictures accompanying them.
- Ask Ss to predict the topic of the reading text. You can also ask Ss the following questions.
  - e.g. *What do you think is so special about these gadgets?*
    Do you think they can really help improve the quality of our lives in the future?
- Discuss and elicit answers.

1 Aim: to give Ss practice in scanning a text to find specific information

- Ask Ss to read through the text for gist, without worrying about the unknown words.
- Ask Ss to read through questions 1-8. Explain any unknown words.
- Before the second reading, point out to Ss they should look for key words / phrases in the text.
- Ask Ss the first question and allow them some time to answer it.
- Check answers and ask Ss to underline the key words / phrases which helped them decide.
- Do the same for the rest of the questions.

- Point out to Ss that the answer to question 9 relies heavily on their global understanding of the text.
- Check answers and ask Ss to provide justification.

Key

1 **A** (*... holographic TV is bound to revolutionise our concept of TV in the future.*)
2 **C** (*... are developing a method of transmitting messages through TV sets.*)
The answers to questions 1 and 2 may appear in any order.
3 **B** (*... if your washing machine is about to break down ... it sends a warning message to the computer link and informs you in time to take action.*)
4 **A** (*... you'll be able to enjoy the delicious aromas of roast chicken and potatoes, apple pie, chocolate soufflé ...*).
5 **C** (*... transmitting messages through TV sets ...*),
6 **D** (*... your boring old wristwatch will be transformed into a handy little videophone ... / ... will be activated by the wearer's voice.*)
7 **E** (*Simply put on your badge in public ...*)
The answers to questions 6 and 7 may appear in any order.
8 **E** (*If your profile matches someone else's, both badges will glow.*)
9 **B** (Ss' overall impression of the text)

- When the activity is over, explain unknown words through definitions or example sentences.

2 Aim: to expand on the topic of the reading text

- Ask Ss the questions and generate discussion.

Teacher's Notes

words and phrases

1 Phrasal verbs and expressions

Aim: to give Ss practice in inferring the meaning of the phrasal verbs and expressions in the reading text through a matching activity

- Refer Ss to the reading text.
- Ask Ss to do the activity.
- Check answers.

Key

1. d   2. c   3. e   4. a   5. f   6. b

optional

If there is time, ask Ss to make their own sentences using the phrasal verbs and expressions and check them.

2 Adjectives

A Aims: • to familiarise Ss with the concept of strong adjectives
- to help Ss deduce the meaning of the adjectives from the context

- Ask Ss to read through the extracts from the text.
- Ask Ss to explain the meaning of the adjectives in bold.
- Generate discussion and elicit answers.

Key

overpriced = very expensive, highly priced
delighted = very pleased

B Aim: to help Ss identify the degree of strength of various adjectives describing price and emotions

- Ask Ss to read through the adjectives in the box. Explain any unknown words if necessary.
- Have Ss do the activity. Ensure that Ss understand the procedure.
- Check answers. Provide Ss with explanations when necessary (e.g. demonstrate the difference between *valueless* = having no value and *priceless* = invaluable, beyond price).

Key

adjectives describing price		adjectives describing emotions	
least	valueless	least	miserable
	cheap		unhappy
	overpriced		satisfied
	valuable		pleased
most	priceless	most	*delighted*

C Aim: to give Ss practice in using strong adjectives in context

- Have Ss do the activity and check answers.

Key

a. priceless   b. satisfied   c. miserable   d. overpriced

optional

If there is time, ask Ss to make their own sentences using the rest of the adjectives from exercise B and check them.

— Teacher's Notes —

grammar

1 **Aims:** · **to elicit the uses and the structures of Zero type and Type 1 Conditional Sentences**
· **to expand on Conditional Sentences**
· **to introduce Time Clauses**

· Ask Ss to read through the two extracts from the text.
· Ask Ss to read through the rules. Ensure that Ss understand the terms used. If necessary, provide explanations.
· Have Ss do the activity.
· Elicit and check answers.

Key

If clause	Main Clause
If + Present Simple →	*Future Will* / modal verbs / imperative

Conditional sentences Type 1 express something that is likely to happen in the *present* or *future*.

If clause	Main Clause
If + Present Simple →	*Present Simple*

The **Zero Conditional** is used for *general truths*.

· Ask Ss to read through the extracts from the text and the rules that follow. Ensure that Ss understand the terms used. If necessary, provide explanations.
· Have Ss do the activity.
· Elicit and check answers.

Key

Conditional sentences can also be introduced with *provided*, providing and *as long as*.

Time clauses are introduced with *as soon as*, *when*, *after*, *before* and *while*.

We never use *Future Will* in time clauses.

· Now read out and explain the note. If necessary, provide Ss with examples.

2 **Aim: to give Ss practice in using Conditional Sentences and Time Clauses in context**
· Have Ss do the exercise and check answers.
· If time is scarce, assign the exercise for homework.

Key

a. Unless <u>you pay for your ticket, you can't come with us.</u>
b. You'll be late <u>if you don't take a taxi / unless you take a taxi.</u>
c. As long as <u>you are back by midnight, I'll let you go to the concert.</u>
d. You must work hard if <u>you want to get the promotion you want.</u>
e. If you press the red button, <u>the light goes off.</u>
f. As soon as <u>I go home, I'll give you a ring.</u>

listening

Aim: to give Ss practice in listening for gist through a multiple choice exercise

· Ask Ss to read through the six situations. Explain any unknown words if necessary.
· Play the CD twice.
· Check answers.

Key

1 B   2 C   3 C   4 B   5 A   6 C

---

optional post-listening activity
You may ask Ss questions of personal response to the topic of the listening activity.
e.g. *Does the idea of travelling in space appeal to you?*
Do you enjoy watching science fiction films?
What do you think of smart robots?

Teacher's Notes

Lesson Three

Vocabulary

Words

advanced	intelligence
aspect	literally
chore	magnetic levitation
command (n)	medieval
conventional	on-board (adj)
gesture	streamlined design
humanoid	surgery
hypersonic	time-consuming
infrared (adj)	workforce

speaking

Background Note:
- *Hypersonic travel* occurs when you travel faster than the speed of sound.
- *Infrared* involves the use of electromagnetic waves which are longer than those of red light in the spectrum and cannot be seen.
- *Magnetic levitation* involves the use of powerful electric magnets which raise the train just above the track. The massive reduction in friction results in a faster, more efficient train.

1 **Aims:** • to generate discussion based on Ss' personal experiences and preferences
  • to introduce the topic of the first set of photographs
- Ask Ss to look at the questions and generate discussion.

2 **Aim: to give Ss practice in relating words / phrases to context**
- Tell Ss to look at photographs a and b.
- Then ask Ss to look at the box and decide which words can be used to describe each picture. Ensure that Ss don't have any unknown words. If necessary, provide them with explanations and / or examples.
- Elicit answers.

Key

Photograph a: fuel consumption, conventional, inefficient
Photograph b: on-board computer, environmentally friendly, streamlined design, hypersonic travel, magnetic levitation

3 **Aim: to compare and contrast two photographs**
- Divide Ss into pairs.
- In each pair, tell one student to talk about the different types of trains shown in the two photographs. Encourage him / her to use some of the words above.
- Now ask the second student the question: *Which of the two trains would you like to travel in? Why?*
- Elicit answers.

Key

Suggested ideas:
Photograph *a* shows a conventional train which is slow and inefficient while the streamlined design of the train in photograph *b* indicates that it is faster and environmentally friendly.

4 **Aim: to elaborate and expand on the topic of the speaking activity**
- Ask Ss to read the questions and generate discussion.

5 **Aim: to give Ss practice in forming collocations related to technology**
- Ask Ss to read through the words in the boxes. Ensure that Ss don't have any unknown words.
- Have Ss do the exercise.
- Check answers.

Key

artificial intelligence, infrared signal, humanoid robots, built-in sensors

6 **Aim: to compare and contrast two photographs**
- Divide Ss into pairs.
- In each pair, tell one S to talk about how different the two forms of labour shown in the two pictures are. Encourage him / her to use some of the collocations in the exercise above.
- Now ask the second S the question: *Have robots taken over people's jobs in your country? If so, how do you feel about it?*
- Elicit answers.

Key

Suggested ideas:
- Photograph *c* shows women working in a factory / Photograph *d* shows a robot assembling a car.
- Working without the help of technology can be time-consuming / Humanoid robots work without making mistakes with the help of artificial intelligence.

7 **Aim: to elaborate and expand on the topic of the speaking activity**
- Ask Ss to look at the questions and generate discussion.

Key

Suggested ideas:
- A robotic workforce would be more efficient and reliable than a human workforce but many people would be made redundant as a result.
- They probably will, because they will have a lot of free time on their hands since robots will be doing everything for them.
- I would feel uneasy because I wouldn't trust a machine to perfom an operation / I would feel confident that nothing could go wrong.

writing

1 Aim: to activate Ss' background knowledge

• Ask Ss the questions and generate discussion.

2 Aim: to help Ss identify the purpose and stylistic features of an essay expressing an opinion

• Ask Ss to read through the essay. Explain any unknown words if necessary.
• Have Ss do the exercise.
• Check answers.

Key

Virtual reality will be invaluable in the future

Virtual reality is already widely used for entertainment purposes as well as in medicine to train future doctors and assist in operations. Sometimes it is hard to say where reality stops and virtual reality begins. As computers become more advanced, the virtual experience will become even more realistic. In the future, virtual reality will be used more and more.

To begin with, virtual reality will make learning much easier and more fun. For instance, people will be able to experience things they could only read about before, like living in a medieval castle, meeting an Egyptian pharaoh or exploring the inside of a volcano.

Virtual reality is also the future of computer games. People will not just play games on their computers; they will, quite literally, be inside the games escaping into a fantastic 3-D world. Actually, it will not be long before we can all enjoy the virtual reality experience in the comfort of our homes.

On the whole, virtual reality is the future and, in my opinion, it will undoubtedly change every aspect of our lives.

3 Plan

Aim: to help Ss plan their writing and encourage them to include relevant information in it

• Ask Ss to do the exercise.
• Check answers.

Key

• linking words
• introduction of the subject of the essay
• relevant points to support your opinion
• formal language

4 Improving your style

Aim: to familiarise Ss with the register and style of an essay expressing an opinion

• Ask Ss to read through the extract first.
• Have Ss do the exercise.
• Check answers.

Key

Suggested answer:

Scientists around the world are trying to build smart robots. To begin with, they will help us with household chores, perform time-consuming tasks and teach us how to do certain things. In addition, robots will replace pets in the future. However, these electronic pets will be our companions rather than our servants. What is more, they will be able to interact with us instead of simply reacting to voice commands, touches and gestures, just like ordinary pets. For this purpose, they will have sensors in order to become familiar with their surroundings and avoid bumping into walls and furniture.

5 Writing task

Aim: to give Ss practice in writing an essay expressing an opinion

• Assign the writing task for homework.

Teacher's Notes

Revision 01-03

reading

1 **Aim: to give Ss further practice in reading for specific information through a multiple choice exercise**

- Draw Ss' attention to the picture and to the title of the article and ask them to predict what it is about.
- Ask Ss to read the text for gist to see if their predictions are accurate.
- Discuss answers.
- Ask Ss to read through the statements. Explain any unknown words if necessary.
- Ask Ss to read the stem of each question (not the options).
- Ask Ss to read the text again paragraph by paragraph and try to find the part of the text each question refers to.
- Point out to Ss that they have to pay close attention to specific details in the text in order to answer the questions since some of the options may be distracting.
- Ask Ss to read the options of each question and choose the answer that fits according to the meaning of the text.
- Check answers and ask Ss to provide justification.

Teacher's Notes

reading (continued)

Key

1 C (*… the Thousand Islands is the name given to the stretch of the St Lawrence river from Kingston to Brockville, on the Canadian side and the length of Alexandria Bay, on the US side.*)

2 C (*… he had saved up enough money to go to Texas to work for himself …*)

3 D (*… he was offered the job of steward …*)

4 B (*… and raised the quality of service to levels never before experienced. As a result, he was offered the job of managing the Waldorf Astoria …*)

5 A (*Ss have to rely on their knowledge of vocabulary to answer this question.*)

6 A (*He purchased an estate from Congressman E.K. Hartin in 1895, a part of which was an island called Hart and changed the name of Hart to Heart.*)

7 B (*…when a telegram arrived … which read Stop the work, Mrs Boldts is dead. Until his death in 1916 Bolts never visited the castle again.*)

- When the activity is over, explain unknown words through definitions or example sentences.

Use of English

1 **Aim: to revise various language forms through a multiple choice cloze exercise**

- Ask Ss to read through the text for gist, without paying attention to the gaps.
- Ask Ss to read the text again, one sentence at a time.
- Ask Ss to read the four options carefully, before deciding which one best fits each space.
- Have Ss do the activity.
- Check answers.

Key

(1) B
(2) D
(3) A
(4) B
(5) A
(6) C
(7) A
(8) A
(9) B

Use of English

Key (continued)

(10) C
(11) B
(12) D
(13) C
(14) C
(15) B

2 Aim: to check structural accuracy through an open cloze exercise
- Ask Ss to read through the text for gist, without paying attention to the gaps.
- Ask Ss to fill in the gaps with one word only.
- Have Ss do the activity.
- Check answers.

Key

(16) F
(17) D
(18) N
(19) B
(20) H
(21) C
(22) J
(23) O
(24) L
(25) E

3 Aim: to check structural accuracy through an error correction exercise
- Ask Ss to read the text for gist, without trying to correct anything.
- Ask Ss to read the text again one sentence at a time and try to identify which of the lines are correct and which contain a word which should not be there.
- Have Ss do the activity.
- Check answers.

Key

26 lots
27 ✓
28 being
29 it
30 the
31 ✓
32 from
33 most
34 ✓
35 to
36 ✓
37 of
38 ✓
39 the
40 too

Aim: to translate into English the Chinese given in brackets through a translating exercise

- Ask Ss to read the text for gist.
- Point out to Ss that before completing the gaps, they should decide on which phrases are needed for each blank.
- Have Ss do the activity.
- Check answers.

Key

41	our budget was tight
42	we were very keen to see the Alps
43	After giving a helpful recommendation
44	thanked the couple warmly
45	the most memorable days of our lives

listening

Aim: to give Ss further practice in listening for specific information through a note taking exercise

- Ask Ss to read through sentences 1-8 and predict what kind of information is required.
- Explain any unknown words in the sentences.
- Point out to Ss that they should complete each of the sentences with a word or a short phrase from the listening text.
- Play the CD twice.
- Check answers.

Key

1. The US(A) / The States	5. million-dollar
2. hero	6. 1984
3. shorter skirts	7. 16 / sixteen hours
4. heavy metal	8. overnight

Teacher's Notes

Lesson One

Functions

Expressing obligation, necessity, possibility, permission
Criticising
Giving advice

Structures

Must, have to, need, may, could

Vocabulary

Words

admiration	imply	slip (of paper)
blotting paper	intently	snatch (v)
bout	keenly	utter (v)
coarse	lean (v)	well-lit
eagerness	murmur (v)	whereabouts
enclosure	observe	
frankly	perceive	

Words with prepositions

concentrate (on)	inquire (about)	stamp (with)
gaze (at)	reason (for)	suffer (from)
glance (at)	receive (from)	worry (about)

Phrasal verbs and expressions

draw over	in your heart of hearts
give sb a lift	not be sb's cup of tea
hold on	spring out

Key

- Sherlock Holmes was embarrassed by Mrs St Clair's question because he didn't want to let her know that her husband was dead.
- Sherlock Holmes was shocked when Mrs St Clair showed him Neville's letter because he thought Neville was dead.
- Sherlock Holmes was led to believe that the envelope wasn't addressed by Neville because the handwriting on the envelope wasn't Neville's.

Note: *From the different shades of the ink used on the envelope, Sherlock Holmes figured out that the sender's name and the address weren't written at the same time. Whoever addressed the envelope had to inquire about the address first. If it had been Neville, he would have known the address. Neville did write the letter and put the ring inside the envelope but it was someone else who addressed the envelope.*

- When the activity is over, ask Ss some more questions.
- e.g. *Why is Mrs St Clair asking Sherlock Holmes all these questions?*
  What was the date on the letter addressed to Mrs St Clair?
- Encourage Ss to guess the meaning of new vocabulary such as *bouts, coarse* and *enclosure.* Provide explanations through definitions or example sentences.

presentation

Aim: to present vocabulary, functions and structures in the context of an extract from *The Adventures of Sherlock Holmes* by Arthur Conan Doyle (1859-1930)

1 **Aim: to introduce the topic of the presentation by relating it to Ss' background knowledge**
- Ask Ss to look at the questions and generate discussion.
- Elicit answers.

2 **Aim: to give Ss practice in reading for specific information**
- Ask Ss to read through the story for gist, without worrying about the unknown words.
- Ask Ss to look at the questions.
- Ask Ss to read the story again.
- Have Ss answer the questions.
- Elicit and check answers.

Teacher's Notes

words and phrases

1 Words with prepositions

Aims: · **to present words followed by prepositions**
       · **to give Ss practice in using them in context**

· Ask Ss to read through the words with prepositions in the box. Explain any unknown words if necessary.
· Have Ss do the activity.
· Check answers.

Key

a. has suffered from / been suffering from
b. are inquiring / inquired / have been inquiring about
c. received ... from
d. worry about
e. reason for
f. unfamiliar with

> **optional**
> If there is time, ask Ss to make their own sentences using the words presented above and check them.

2 Words easily confused

Aim: to give Ss practice in distinguishing between words that can easily be confused

· Refer Ss to the verbs **hold** and **snatch** in the extract (*She stood smiling, **holding** up a little slip of paper. / He **snatched** it from her ...*).
· Encourage Ss to work out the difference in meaning.

snatch = take sth away from sb abruptly
hold = carry sth, have sth in one's hands or arms

· Ask Ss to do the rest of the exercise, one set at a time. For each set, explain the difference through definitions and / or examples. You may also need to refer Ss to the extract where appropriate.

glance (at) = look quickly at sth
observe = watch sb or sth carefully, especially to learn more about them
gaze (at) = look at sth for some time, either because you are very interested or surprised, or because you are thinking of sth else (*I had left my chair and was **gazing** at it over his shoulder.*)

murmur = say sth in a soft quiet voice that is difficult to hear or understand (*'Coarse writing,' I **murmured**.*)
whisper = speak very quietly to sb so that other people cannot hear what you are saying
utter = say sth

examine = look at sb or sth carefully in order to find out if there is anything wrong with them (*... and drew*

over the lamp to **examine** it intently.*)
investigate = carefully examine the facts of a situation, an event or a crime in order to find out the truth about it or how it happened
research = study a subject carefully and try to discover new facts about it

· Check answers.

Key

a. held / was holding	b. snatched / took	c. took
a. gazed	b. glanced	c. observe
a. murmured	b. utter	c. whispered / were whispering
a. examined	b. researching	c. are investigating

> **optional**
> If there is time, ask Ss to make their own sentences using the words presented above and check them.

Teacher's Notes

grammar

1 Aim: to present the functions of modal verbs through a matching exercise

- Ask Ss to read through the sentences 1-4.
- Ask Ss to read through the functions a-d. Ensure that Ss understand the terms used.
- Have Ss do the exercise.
- Check answers.

Key

1. b   2. d   3. a   4. c

- Now ask Ss the question that follows.
- Elicit and check answers.

Key

- Can and May can also be used to express possibility.

2 Aim: to present the use of the verb need both as a main and a modal verb through a matching activity

- Ask Ss to read through the sentences 1-2.
- Ask Ss to read through the patterns a-b. Ensure that Ss understand the terms used.
- Have Ss do the activity.
- Check answers.

Key

1. b   2. a

3 Aim: to expand on the functions of the modal verbs through a matching activity

- Ask Ss to read through the first set of sentences 1-2.
- Ask Ss to read through the two questions a-b. Ensure that Ss understand the terms used.
- Elicit and check answers.
- Do the same for each of the remaining sets of sentences and questions. Provide Ss with further explanations when necessary.
- Elicit and check answers.

Key

a. 2   b. 1   c. 4   d. 3   e. 6   f. 5

4 Aim: to give Ss practice in using the modal verbs in context

- Have Ss do the activity.
- Check answers.

Key

1 B   2 A   3 A   4 C   5 B   6 B

Teacher's Notes

Lesson Two

Structures

Should
Ought to
Had Better

Vocabulary

Words

abandon	horrified	reserve (n)
approach (v)	inexplicable	response
barely	inspire	tamed (adj)
bustling	lodge	tranquillity
constant	lush	tremendous
daring	nonetheless	vegetation
explore	overcome	venture
fascinating	perimeter	villain
fuss	perspective	visible
growling (adj)	pound (v)	wilderness
hesitant	rent (v)	

Phrasal verbs and expressions

at the crack of dawn	keep one going
bend down	make up for
be on guard	on the prowl
feel like home	put behind
feel under the weather	set up
get a good night's sleep	turn down

Collocations with *take*

take advantage	take offence
take for granted	take precautions
take into account	take the blame
take (no) notice (of)	

reading

optional pre-reading activity

- Ask Ss to read the title of the reading text and look at the picture accompanying it.
- Ask Ss to predict the topic of the reading text and try to interpret its title. You can also ask the following questions:
  e.g. *What do you know about jungles?*
  What kind of wildlife would you expect to find in a jungle?
- Discuss and elicit answers.

1 Aim: to give Ss practice in identifying the main ideas of the paragraphs in an article through a matching activity

- Ask Ss to read through the text for gist, without worrying about the gaps.
- Ask Ss to try to guess what each of the headings is about.

- Ask Ss to read through the headings A-H. Ensure that Ss understand them.
- Before the second reading, point out to Ss that they should look for key words / phrases in the text which are related to those in the headings.
- Now ask Ss to read the first paragraph of the text and decide on the most suitable heading. Ask Ss to underline the key words / phrases which helped them decide. Check answers.
- Ask Ss to read the text paragraph by paragraph and do the rest of the activity.
- Point out to Ss that if they cannot decide on the heading for a specific paragraph, they should move on and get back to it later.
- Check answers and ask Ss to provide justification.

Key

1 F (*Abandoning the bustling streets, the crowds and the constant running around for a while was something I needed to do.*)

2 E (*… using public transport … had a fifteen-kilometre walk on a dirt road … we were exhausted … a pickup van passed by and offered to give us a lift … This strange bird actually helped us put the difficulties of the day behind us.*)

3 A (*After surviving an uncomfortable drive, the unbearable heat and the blinding sun ... But as we ventured deeper into the jungle, things became more difficult.*)

4 D (*… that I would be on guard that night. / … I wasn't really sure what I was guarding the camp from …*)

5 G (*… a leaf with, believe it or not, a tiny brown frog on it!*)

6 H (*We didn't have much variety in our diet. Fish and rice for breakfast. Fish and rice for dinner, …*)

7 C (*… that made the trip so fascinating … an experience that inspired me …*)

Extra heading: B

- When the activity is over, explain unknown words through definitions or example sentences.

2 Aim: to expand on the topic of the reading text

- Ask Ss to look at the questions and generate discussion.

Key

Suggested ideas:
- be attacked by wild animals / run out of provisions / catch a disease / injure yourself / unbearable heat
- experience something new / escape from your daily routine / make you realise that we are part of a wider ecosystem that should be protected

words and phrases

1 Phrasal verbs and expressions

Aim: to give Ss practice in inferring the meaning of the phrasal verbs and expressions in the reading text through a matching activity

- Refer Ss to the reading text.
- Ask Ss to do the activity.
- Check answers.

Key

1. g
2. f
3. a
4. e
5. b
6. c
7. d

optional
If there is time, ask Ss to make their own sentences using the phrasal verbs and expressions and check them.

2 Collocations

Aims: • to introduce collocations with *take*
• to give Ss practice in using these collocations in context

- Ask Ss to read through the collocations in the box. Explain them if necessary.
- Have Ss do the exercise.
- Check answers.

Key

a. taking the blame
b. are taking ... precautions
c. take no notice / don't take any notice
d. take ... for granted
e. took advantage

optional
If there is time, ask Ss to make their own sentences using the collocations and check them.

grammar

1 **Aims:** • to give Ss practice in inferring the functions of *should*, *ought to* and *had better* through a matching activity
• to elaborate on the functions of *should* and *ought to* in the present / future and the past

• Ask Ss to read through the sentences 1-5.
• Ask Ss to read through the functions a-c.
• Have Ss do the activity.
• Elicit and check answers.

Key

1. a   2. c   3. a   4. a   5. b

• **Should / shouldn't**, *ought to* and *had better* + **base form** are used to give advice, express an opinion, make a suggestion or express mild obligation in the present or future.
• **Should / ought to + have + past participle** is used to express *criticism* or regret about something that didn't happen in the past.
• **Shouldn't / oughtn't to + have + past participle** is used to express *criticism* or regret about something that happened in the past and was wrong.

2 **Aim:** to give Ss practice in using *should / ought to* and *shouldn't / oughtn't to* in context

• Have Ss do the exercise. Ensure that they understand the procedure.
• Check answers.

Key

a. Suzanne shouldn't have bought that old car.
b. Tom shouldn't watch TV for so many hours.
c. Luke should / ought to have told his mother about the accident.
d. Polly should / ought to drive more carefully / Polly shouldn't / oughtn't to drive so carelessly.
e. You should / ought to go to the dentist's.

listening

Aim: to give Ss practice in listening for specific information through a T / F activity

• Ask Ss to read through the statements 1-7. Explain any unknown words if necessary.
• Point out to Ss that during the first listening they should listen carefully and only after the second listening should they finalise their answers.
• Play the CD twice.
• Check answers.

Key

1 F
2 F
3 F
4 F
5 T
6 F
7 T

optional post-listening activity

You may ask Ss further questions of personal response to the listening text.
e.g. *Would you ever take part in Gravity Formula 1 racing? Why / Why not?*
Have you heard of any other extreme sports?

Teacher's Notes

Lesson Three

Vocabulary

depart	possess
draft	purification
insect repellent	shelter (n)
location	strand (v)
optional	submit
out of order	

speaking

1 **Aim: to prepare Ss for the topic of the speaking activity by relating it to Ss' personal opinions and preferences**
- Ask Ss to look at the questions and generate discussion.

2 **Aim: to give Ss practice in reaching a consensus**
- Divide Ss into pairs.
- Tell Ss to look at the map of the island.
- Engage Ss in meaningful and realistic conversations.
- Point out to Ss that they should always give a reason for their choices and encourage them to use the expressions suggested in the box.
- Have Ss do the activity.
- Elicit answers.

Key

Suggested ideas:
- I think (that) location C is better than A because it is far away from the cannibals and the lake with dogfish and it is close to the ocean and the river.
- I wouldn't choose location A because it is rather dangerous since it is close to the cannibals and the jungle. I wouldn't choose location B either because it is close to the lake with dogfish and there are no trees to build a shelter under.

3 **Aim: to give Ss practice in prioritising**
- Divide Ss in pairs.
- Tell Ss to look at the items shown here. Ensure that Ss know what they are (*a first-aid kit, a mobile phone, binoculars, an axe, a compass, a tin opener, a pair of flippers, insect repellent, chocolate, special water purification tablets*). If necessary, provide explanations.
- Point out to Ss that they should always provide a reason for their choices.
- Have Ss do the activity.
- Elicit answers.

Key

Suggested ideas:
I would choose:
- the axe to cut down trees in order to build my shelter.
- the compass to orientate myself.
- the binoculars so that I'd be prepared for anything and so that I'd be able to spot ships in the distance.
- the special water purification tablets so that I'd have clean drinking water.

4 **Aim: to elaborate and expand on the topic of the speaking activity**
- Ask Ss the questions and generate discussion.

Key

Suggested ideas:
- determination, strong will, resourcefulness, adaptability, optimism
- Open answers

Teacher's Notes

writing

1 **Aims:** • **to activate Ss' background knowledge**
   • **to prepare Ss for the writing task**
- Ask Ss the question and generate discussion.
- Elicit answers.

2 **Aim: to familiarise Ss with the stylistic features**
   of different types of letters
- Tell Ss to read through the three extracts.
- Have Ss decide what types of letters the extracts are from.
- Elicit and check answers. Ask Ss to provide
  justification.

Key

a. a letter of complaint
b. a letter of application
c. a letter asking for information

3 **Improve your style**

Aim: to familiarise Ss with the conventions of a
   formal letter asking for information
- First tell Ss to read through the advertisement and
  the notes made on it. Explain any unknown words if
  necessary.
- Then ask Ss to read through the letter.
- Ask Ss to identify what is wrong with the letter, taking
  the features given here into consideration.
- Elicit and check answers.

Key

layout: The paragraphing is inappropriate. Formal
letters should be written in blocked paragraphs
(paragraphs should begin on the left-hand side of the
page leaving a blank line between them).

style: The letter is written in a rather informal style
because the writer has used a number of contractions
(*you're, I'm, I don't*) and abbreviations (*info* instead of
information). Furthermore, the writer has used too
many direct questions, while it would have been more
polite if she had used indirect ones.

linking words: The writer should have used more
linking words in order to introduce her requests in a
better way.

opening and closing paragraphs: The opening
paragraph used here sounds rather abrupt and
impolite. It would have been more appropriate if the
writer had begun her letter in a more polite and formal
way (e.g. *I am writing to ask if you could inform me
about …*). The closing sentence is also inappropriate
because it is too informal. The writer should have
written instead: *Thank you for your time and
assistance. I look forward to hearing from you at your
earliest convenience.* Furthermore, the writer should

have ended her letter by writing:
Yours sincerely,
(signature)
first name + surname

content: The writer hasn't included all the points
indicated in the notes.

4 **Writing task**

Aim: to give Ss practice in writing a formal letter
   asking for information
- Assign the writing task for homework.

Teacher's Notes

05 Mother Nature

Functions

Making suggestions / recommendations
Expressing agreement and disagreement

Structures

Infinitives and -ing forms I

Vocabulary

Words

blessed (adj)	function (v)	remarkable
bug	gemstone	resist
correspond	genteel	roam
crater	giant	sculpture
creepy-crawlies	long-haul	shooting star
curious	mammal	stroll (v)
earthquake	nightmarish	unravel
escalator	pioneer	video footage
evolution	raging	volcano
fierce	rare	wonder (n)

Expressions

a real feast for the eyes	jump at the chance
far reaches	on display
give sb the creeps	

presentation

Aim: to present vocabulary, functions and structures in the context of a brochure about the Natural History Museum in London

1 **Aim: to help Ss interpret the title of a text in order to predict its content**
- Ask Ss to look at the title of the text and discuss the question.
- Elicit answers.

Key

This type of text is more likely to be found in a brochure (b).

2 **Aim: to give Ss practice in scanning a text to extract specific information through a T / F activity**
- Have Ss read through the text for gist, without worrying about the unknown words.
- Have Ss re-read the text more carefully. Ask Ss the first question, which is based on their general understanding of the text.
- Elicit and check answers. Ask Ss to provide justification.
- Ask Ss the remaining three questions which correspond to each paragraph of the text respectively.
- Elicit and check answers. Ask Ss to provide justification.

Key

1. T (*... at the remarkable dinosaur exhibition. / ... all about mammals, the evolution of humans and the ways in which our minds and bodies function. / ...at the Ecology exhibition and discovering how plants turn the sun's energy into food?*)
2. F (*... and find out about the different creepy-crawlies that roam the planet!*)
3. F (*There are also 6 000 gemstones and crystals on display in the Earth Galleries ...*)
4. F (no mention of documents and findings belonging to pioneer voyagers)

- When this activity is over, ask Ss some more questions.
  e.g. *What is there in the Life Galleries that can give you an idea about how the universe works? How can visitors in the Earth Galleries actually 'feel' an earthquake? How can visitors to the Ecology exhibition travel through the centre of our planet?*
- Encourage Ss to guess the meaning of new vocabulary such as *unravel, evolution, fierce* and *sculpture*. Provide explanations through definitions or example sentences.

Teacher's Notes

words and phrases

1 Expressions

Aim: to give Ss practice in inferring the meaning of some expressions in the brochure through a matching activity

- Refer Ss to the brochure.
- Ask Ss to do the exercise.
- Check answers.

Key

a. give sb the creeps
b. jump at the chance
c. far reaches
d. a real feast for the eyes

> **optional**
>
> If there is time, ask Ss to make their own sentences using the expressions and check them.

2 Word building

Aim: to present and familiarise Ss with adjective and noun formation

- Read out and explain the introductory comment.
- Discuss the examples provided. Point out to Ss that adjectives are formed by adding either the suffix -ent or -ant to the verb root while nouns are formed by adding either the suffix -ence or -ance to the verb root.
- Have Ss do the activity.
- Check answers.

Key

Verb	Adjective	Noun
differ	*different*	difference
exist	*existent*	existence
ignore	ignorant	*ignorance*
confide	confident	*confidence*
assist	*assistant*	assistance
correspond	*correspondent*	*correspondence*
resist	*resistant*	resistance

B **Aim: to give Ss practice in using the adjectives and nouns presented above in context**

- Have Ss do the activity.
- Check answers.

Key

a. resistant
b. assistance
c. correspondent

d. ignorance
e. existence
f. different

grammar

1 **Aim: to help Ss identify the structural forms of the infinitive and the -ing form through a matching activity**

- Have Ss read through the sentences 1-10.
- Have Ss read through the patterns a-j.
- Have Ss do the matching.
- Check answers. If necessary, provide Ss with further explanations and / or examples.

Key

1. g	6. h
2. f	7. d
3. j	8. a
4. i	9. e
5. b	10. c

2 **Aim: to give Ss practice in using the infinitive and the -ing form in context**

- Have Ss read through the text for gist, without worrying about the gaps or the unknown words.
- Have Ss fill in the gaps.
- Check answers. Ask Ss to match the answers with the patterns presented in the previous exercise. If necessary, provide Ss with further explanations and / or examples.

Key

(1) taking	(6) to get
(2) visiting	(7) travelling
(3) make	(8) to go
(4) forget	(9) spending
(5) visiting	

Teacher's Notes

Lesson Two

Structures

Infinitives and -ing forms II

Vocabulary

Words

afterglow	hurl
blast	impending
coastal	insignificant
crop	livestock
cubic	matter (n)
death toll	sparsely
debris	turbulence
erupt	unreasonable
famine	vivid

Phrasal verbs and expressions

black out	in sight
blow off	the tip of the iceberg
bring about	to say the least
call out	wipe out

Expressions with *hot*

be hot on sb's trail	not feel too hot
hot air	piping hot
hot and bothered	

reading

optional pre-reading activity

- Ask Ss to read the title of the reading text and look at the pictures accompanying it.
- Ask Ss to predict the topic of the reading text. You can also ask the following questions:
  e.g. *Have you heard of any volcanoes either in your country or anywhere else in the world?*
  How destructive can volcanoes be?
- Discuss and elicit answers.

1 Aim: to help Ss understand text organisation

- Ask Ss to read through the text for gist, without worrying about the gaps.
- Ask Ss to try to guess what each of the missing paragraphs is about.
- Ask Ss to read through the removed paragraphs A-F and ensure that they understand them.
- Point out to Ss that they should always look for clues and / or key words / phrases which precede or follow the gaps. When there are no such cohesive devices, Ss should rely strongly on context.
- Ask Ss to read the first paragraph of the text and decide which of the removed paragraphs A-F best fits in the first gap.
- Check answers and ask Ss to provide justification by underlining the key words / phrases which helped them decide.

- Ask Ss to read the text paragraph by paragraph and do the rest of the activity.
- Point out to Ss that if they cannot decide what fits in a gap, they should move on and get back to it later.
- Check answers and ask Ss to provide justification.

Key

1 D

Text	Missing paragraphs
'I'm confident ... in my lifetime.' ... *will kill a million people ...*	*Not an unreasonable ... loss of life ...*

2 B

Text	Missing paragraphs
... *the eruptions of the last few hundred years ...*	*Many volcanic eruptions have taken place in the last two hundred years.* ... *three stand out ...* The writer goes on to talk about three eruptions.

3 E

Text	Missing paragraphs
	The paragraph begins by elaborating on the extent of the destruction caused by the eruption.

The eruption of Mount Tomboro took place in 1815+68=1883, 27th August when Mount Krakatoa erupted.

4 C

Text	Missing paragraphs
... *another huge volcanic explosion ...* ... *the ash was still causing such vivid red sunset afterglows ...*	*It refers to the huge volcanic explosion mentioned in the previous paragraph.* *The sun was blacked out ... volcanic ash fell over ships ...*

5 F

Text	Missing paragraphs
... *shot nineteen kilometres into the air ...* *However, the blast destroyed all wildlife ...*	*It was high enough to cause turbulence ...* ... *the loss of life was minimal as ... a sparsely populated national park.*

Extra paragraph: A

- When the activity is over, explain unknown words through definitions or example sentences.

optional post-reading activity

Ask Ss questions of personal response to the topic of the reading text.
e.g. *Have you heard of any other volcanic eruptions?*

words and phrases

1 Phrasal verbs

Aim: to give Ss practice in inferring the meaning
of the phrasal verbs in the reading text
through a matching exercise
- Refer Ss to the reading text.
- Ask Ss to do the activity.
- Check answers.

Key

a. called out   d. stand out
b. brought about   e. wiped out
c. put out   f. was blacked out

optional

If there is time, ask Ss to make their own sentences
using the phrasal verbs and check them.

2 Idioms

Aims: · to present idioms with *hot*
· to give Ss practice in inferring their meaning
through a multiple matching exercise
- Ask Ss to read through the sentences 1-5.
- Ask Ss to read through the meanings a-e.
- Have Ss do the exercise.
- Check answers.

Key

1. b   2. e   3. d   4. a   5. c

optional

If there is time, ask Ss to make their own sentences
using the idioms and check them.

Teacher's Notes

grammar

1 **Aim: to give Ss practice in inferring the meaning of *try* and *go* on when followed by different structures through a matching activity**

- Ask Ss to read through the sentences 1-4.
- Ask Ss to read through the questions that follow. Ensure that Ss understand the terms used.
- Have Ss do the exercise.

Key

- a) 2   b) 1
- a) 3   b) 4

- Elicit and check answers.
- When the activity is over, read out and explain the note. If necessary, provide Ss with further examples.

2 **Aims: • to elaborate and expand on the previous exercise**
    • to give Ss further practice in inferring the meaning of other verbs when followed by different structures through a matching activity

- Ask Ss to read through each set of examples.
- Ask Ss to read through each set of meanings given at the end of the sentences.
- Draw Ss attention to the first set of examples.
- Elicit and check answers.
- Do the same for the rest of the sentences.
- Elicit and check answers.

Key

1. a   5. a
2. b   6. b
3. b   7. b
4. a   8. a

3 **Aim: to give Ss practice in using the verbs presented above in context**

- Have Ss do the exercise.
- Check answers.

Key

1. to greet   4. talking
2. to buy   5. to buy
3. not studying

optional
If there is time, ask Ss to make their own sentences using the rest of the verbs presented in exercises 1 and 2 above and check them.

listening

Aim: to give Ss practice in listening for gist through a matching exercise

- Ask Ss to read through the list of natural disasters A-F. Explain any unknown words if necessary (e.g. a *tsunami* is a huge sea wave usually caused by an earthquake).
- Point out to Ss that they should listen carefully during the first listening, but should finalise their answers only after the second listening since there is one extra answer which could mislead them.
- Check answers.

Key

Speaker 1: E
Speaker 2: B
Speaker 3: F
Speaker 4: D
Speaker 5: A

Extra letter: C

optional post-listening activity
You may ask Ss further questions of personal response to the listening text.
e.g. *What other natural disasters have you heard of? How can we protect ourselves from natural disasters?*

Teacher's Notes

Lesson Three

Vocabulary

beauty spot	name after
chamber	one of a kind
come upon	overwhelmed
enhance	rest assured
faint-hearted	stalactite
feature (n)	stalagmite
handicrafts	steeply
illuminate	stretch (v)

speaking

1 **Aim: to generate discussion based on Ss' personal experiences and preferences**
- Ask Ss to look at the questions and generate discussion.

Key

Suggested ideas:
- Open answers
- go sightseeing / visit galleries and museums / walk around the place / get to know the locals / taste the local cuisine / buy souvenirs
- the time of year and the weather conditions / the tourist attractions / the kind of holiday I like to have / the facilities available

2 **Aim: to give Ss practice in discussing in order to reach a consensus**
- Divide Ss into pairs.
- Tell Ss to look at the profiles of each member of the Norris family.
- Tell Ss to look at the map of Peru with all the marked locations that the Norris family can visit.
- Engage Ss in meaningful and realistic conversations.
- Point out to Ss that they may agree or disagree as long as they give a reason for their choices.
- Have Ss do the activity.
- Elicit answers.

Key

Suggested ideas:
- **A:** I think Mr Norris should definitely visit Lake Titicaca since he likes being outdoors and he would probably enjoy being close to nature.
- **B:** You've got a point there! As far as Mrs Norris is concerned, I suggest that she should visit Machu Picchu since she is an archaeologist.
- **A:** Absolutely! Plus, she likes adventure and she would be really interested in visiting the ancient city of the Incas. She can also go to Cuzco, the capital of the Inca empire.
- **B:** Now, let's see where Scott should go! I think he would like to visit Puerto Callao, which is famous for its local handicrafts.

- **A:** I don't think Scott would be interested in something like that because he doesn't like shopping. I think that he should go to the local festival which takes place in Trujillo because it would be a good opportunity for him to meet new people and listen to the locals playing the guitar.
- **B:** I suppose you're right!

3 **Aim: to elaborate and expand on the topic of the speaking activity**
- Ask Ss the questions and generate discussion.
- Elicit answers.

Key

Suggested ideas:
- to relax / to enjoy themselves / to recharge their batteries / to meet new people and places
- Open answers
- by learning about the history, culture, geography of a specific place / understanding different cultures / experiencing something different / meeting new people

Teacher's Notes

writing

1 **Aims:** • to activate Ss' background knowledge
       • to prepare Ss for the writing task
• Ask Ss to look at the questions and generate discussion.

2 **Aim:** to give Ss practice in using strong adjectives when writing an article describing a place
• Ask Ss to read through the article for gist. Explain any unknown words except the ones in bold and the ones in the box.
• Have Ss re-read the article more carefully and do the exercise.
• Elicit and check answers.

Key

one of a kind = unique
very big = huge
overcome = overwhelmed
nice = enchanting
interesting = fascinating
easily frightened = faint-hearted

3 **Aim:** to familiarise Ss with the stylistic features of an article describing a place
• Ask Ss to read through the article.
• Have Ss do the exercise.
• Elicit and check answers.

Key

• **GIVING PERSONAL OPINIONS**
In my experience, Crag Cave is an impressive sight!
As far as I am concerned ... / From my point of view ...
• **RECOMMENDING PLACES**
It is well worth discovering ...
I would strongly recommend / suggest ...
It is a must-visit place ...

4 **Plan**

Aim: to help Ss plan their writing and enable them to identify what information is relevant
• Ask Ss to read the article.
• Ask Ss to do the exercise.
• Check answers.

Key

b, c, e

5 **Writing task**

Aim: to give Ss practice in writing an article describing a place
• Assign the writing task for homework.

06 Let the fun begin!

Lesson One

Functions

Talking about celebrations and social gatherings

Structures

Passive Voice I

Vocabulary

Words and expressions

annual	granny
audience	hose
be treated for	knit
blast (v)	not have a clue
chunk	paramedics
contestant	request (n)
countdown	spectator
dairy product	the opposition

Prepositional phrases *(with / without)*

with a view to	without a doubt
with regard to	without delay
with respect to	without warning
with the exception of	

presentation

Aim: to present vocabulary and structures in the context of the narrations of three people about unusual festivals

1 **Aim:** to relate the topic of the narrations to Ss' background knowledge and personal experience
- Ask Ss the questions and generate discussion.
- Elicit answers.

2 **Aim:** to give Ss practice in listening for specific information by spotting the mistakes in the pictures
- Ask Ss to look at the first picture and listen at the same time.
- Play the CD and pause after the first speaker.
- Ask Ss to spot the mistakes in the picture according to what they have just heard.
- Elicit and check answers.
- Do the same for the rest of the pictures and the narrations.
- Elicit and check answers.

Key

Picture 1: The contestants should be chasing the chunks of cheese **down the hill** (not up the hill), **a team of paramedics** (not a TV crew) should be at the bottom of the hill.

Picture 2: Grannies should **be taking part** in the motor race (and not selling biscuits and sweets).

Picture 3: A plastic ball (not a football) should be used, each team should consist **of four** (not six) firefighters.

- When this activity is over, you may ask Ss some more questions.
  e.g. *Have you heard of any unusual festivals in your country or abroad?*
  Have you attended / taken part in any festivals?
- Elicit answers.

Teacher's Notes

words and phrases

1 Words easily confused

Aim: to give Ss practice in distinguishing between words that can easily be confused

- Ask Ss to read through the first set of words and the three sentences that follow them.
- Encourage Ss to work out the difference in meaning. Provide them with definitions and further explanations when necessary.

viewer = sb watching TV
audience = a group of people gathered to watch an event (collective noun)
spectator = sb who looks on at a show, game, incident, etc.

- Ask Ss to do the rest of the exercise, one set at a time. For each set, explain the difference through definitions and / or examples.

popular (with) = liked or admired by many people
famous = well known
favourite = preferred to all others

actual = existing in fact
real = not imagined or made up
true = in accordance with fact or reality

live = having life (here used as an attributive adjective)
alive = not dead (here used as a predicate)
lively = full of life, energetic

- Check answers.

Key

a. audience	b. spectators	c. viewers
a. popular	b. favourite	c. famous
a. true	b. actual	c. real
a. alive	b. live	c. lively

> **optional**
> If there is time, ask Ss to make their own sentences using the words presented above and check them.

2 Prepositional phrases

A Aim: to present nouns preceded by the prepositions *with* and *without*

- Ask Ss to read through the words in the box. Explain any words Ss might not know.
- Have Ss do the exercise.
- Check answers.

Key

with	without
regard to	a doubt
respect to	delay
the exception of	warning
a view to	

B Aim: to give Ss practice in using the prepositional phrases in context

- Have Ss do the exercise. Explain any unknown words in the sentences.
- Check answers.

Key

a. With regard to
b. without a doubt
c. without warning
d. with the exception of
e. with a view to

> **optional**
> If there is time, ask Ss to make their own sentences using the prepositional phrases above and check them.

Teacher's Notes

grammar

1 **Aim: to help Ss review the use and the formation of the Passive Voice**
- Ask Ss to read through the sentences a-i.
- Ask Ss to distinguish between the active and the passive structures.
- Elicit and check answers. Provide Ss with further explanations when necessary.

Key

Active Voice	Passive Voice
begins	is heard
follows	be described
end up	are treated
catches	was held
reaches	is blasted
	was started
	be kept

- <u>The verb in the passive voice consists of the verb *to be* + the past participle of the verb in the active sentence. The subject of the active sentence is usually turned into an agent.</u>

2 **Aim: to give Ss practice in using the active and the passive voice in context**
- Ask Ss to read through the text for gist, without worrying about the gaps.
- Have Ss do the exercise.
- Check answers.

Key

(1) visited
(2) was invited
(3) takes
(4) is played
(5) tries
(6) are allowed
(7) is considered
(8) break out
(9) had never seen

Lesson Two

Structures

Passive Voice II

Vocabulary

Words

adopt	grace	platter
alienate	haggis	poverty-stricken
amateur	harshly	prematurely
bad-mouth (v)	honour (n)	proverb
bard	introduce	recite
beggar	jolly	regional
building	kilt	retirement
constructor	leaking (adj)	ritual
chiefly	liberalism	ruling (adj)
dialect	liberty	verse
eldest	literary	volume
emigrate	manners	
enduring	ode	
evergreen	outspoken (adj)	
folk	peasant	
forbid	piper	

Phrasal verbs and expressions

drag sb down	keep the wolf from the door
dressed up	make one's mark
fall in love with	speak one's mind
get one's hands on	wee small hours

Idioms with *time*

be short of time
have a great time
have a lot of time on one's hands
have the time of one's life
it's about / high time
time drags
time flies

reading

Background Notes:
- A Piper is a person who plays music on the bagpipes, a musical instrument played especially in Scotland.
- *Selkirk* is a place in Scotland.

Translated extract from *"Ode to a Mouse"*
Small cunning cowering timorous beast
Oh, how your heart pounds quickly
You need not go away so quickly
Making so much noise as you walk away
I would hate myself to run and follow you
With murderous intent

---

optional pre-reading activity
- Ask Ss to read the title of the reading text and look at the picture accompanying it.
- Ask Ss to predict the topic of the reading text. Explain the word *bard*. You can also ask Ss the following questions.
  e.g. *Do you like reading poetry? Why / Why not?*
  Do you know of any English poets? If so, name some.
- Discuss and elicit answers.

1 Aim: to give Ss practice in reading for specific information through a multiple choice exercise
- Ask Ss to read through the reading text for gist without worrying about the unknown words.
- Ask Ss to read the stem of each question (not the options).
- Ask Ss to read the text again paragraph by paragraph and try to find the part of the text each question refers to.
- Point out to Ss that they have to pay close attention to specific details in the text in order to answer the questions since some of the options may be distracting.
- Ask Ss to read the options of each question and choose the answer that fits best according to the meaning of the text.
- Check answers and ask Ss to provide justification.

Key

1 D (... to have taught himself by studying the Bible and any other book he could get his hands on.)
2 A (... he was trying to provide financially for his family ...)
3 A (However, Jean's father forbade his daughter to marry the poverty-stricken poet ...)
4 B (... because he always spoke his mind.)
5 C (... what is probably his most enduring and famous work ...)
6 D (... tried to drag him down by focusing on the negative aspects of his lifestyle.)
7 C (Ss should refer to line 76)

- When the activity is over, explain unknown words through definitions or example sentences.

optional post-reading activity
Ask Ss questions of personal response to the topic of the reading text.
e.g. *What do you think of Robert Burns?*
Would you be interested in reading any of his poems? Why / Why not?

words and phrases

1 Phrasal verbs and expressions

Aim: to give Ss practice in inferring the meaning of the phrasal verbs and expressions in the reading text through a matching activity

- Refer Ss to the reading text.
- Ask Ss to do the activity.
- Check answers.

Key

1. e	2. d	3. f	4. c	5. b	6. a

optional

If there is time, ask Ss to make their own sentences using the phrasal verbs and expressions and check them.

2 Idioms

Aims: • to present idioms with *time*
        • to help Ss infer the meaning of these idioms from context

- Ask Ss to read through each sentence.
- In each sentence, encourage Ss to work out the meaning of the idiom in bold.
- Ask Ss to read through the two options that follow each one of them.
- Have Ss do the exercise and check answers.

Key

1. a	2. b	3. a	4. b	5. a	6. b

optional

If there is time, ask Ss to make their own sentences using the idioms and check them.

grammar

1 **Aims:** · **to present the passive personal and impersonal constructions as opposed the active equivalent through a matching activity**

· Ask Ss to read through the sentences 1-3 and the patterns a-c. Ensure that Ss understand the terms used.
· Have Ss do the exercise.
· Check answers.

Key

1. b   2. c   3. a

· When this activity is over, read out and explain the note. If necessary, provide Ss with examples.

2 **Aim: to give Ss practice in using passive personal and impersonal constructions**

· Have Ss to do the exercise.
· Check answers.

Key

1. He is believed to be a very well-read man.
2. It is said that she is extremely wealthy.
3. Maria is believed to speak Greek fluently.
4. Nicholas is thought to have set the building on fire.
5. Sebastian is said to be the smartest child in his class.

Teacher's Notes

listening

Aim: **to give Ss practice in listening for gist through a multiple choice exercise**

· Ask Ss to read through the six situations. Explain any unknown words if necessary.
· Play the CD twice.
· Check answers.

Key

1 C	2 B	3 C	4 B	5 B	6 B

optional post-listening activity
Ask Ss questions of personal response to the listening text.
e.g. *Do you make New Year's resolutions?*
     Have you ever been to a ballet performance or the opera?

Teacher's Notes

Lesson Three

Vocabulary

Words and expressions

altogether	emotional
banquet	fabulous
casual	festive
contribute	guest house
crack a joke	reunion
delay (n)	

speaking

1 Aim: to generate discussion based on Ss' personal preferences
- Ask Ss to look at the questions and generate discussion.

2 Aim: to give Ss practice in relating words / phrases to context
- Tell Ss to look at photographs a and b.
- Then ask Ss to look at the box and decide which words / phrases can be used to describe each photograph. Ensure that Ss don't have any unknown words. If necessary, provide them with explanations and / or examples.
- Elicit answers.

Key

Photograph a: formal clothes, dull, three-course meal
Photograph b: presents, crowded gatherings, decorations, highlight of the party, loud music, casual clothes, fabulous

3 Aim: to give Ss practice in comparing and contrasting two photographs
- Divide Ss into pairs.
- In each pair, tell one student to describe the photographs and talk about how the people taking part in each of the social events shown in the two photographs might feel. Encourage him / her to use some of the words / phrases from the exercise above.
- Now ask the second student the question: *Which of the two events best appeals to you? Why?*
- Elicit answers.

Key

Suggested ideas:
- In photograph *a*, four people are having a formal, three-course dinner. They probably feel relaxed and seem to be having a good time.
- Photograph *b* shows a party. Young people who are casually dressed are having a great time dancing and probably listening to loud music.
  The first one appeals to me more because I don't like crowded gatherings or loud music / The second

one appeals to me more because the social event in photograph *a* looks dull and boring.

4 Aim: to elaborate and expand on the topic of the previous exercise
- Ask Ss to read the questions and generate discussion.

5 Aim: to give Ss practice in relating words to context
- Tell Ss to look at photographs c and d.
- Then ask Ss to look at the box and decide which words can be used to describe each photograph. Ensure that Ss don't have any unknown words. If necessary, provide them with explanations and / or examples.
- Elicit answers.

Key

Photograph c: ceremony, wedding cake, guests, traditional, festive atmosphere
Photograph d: annual, award, stage, traditional, festive atmosphere, folk dances

6 Aim: to give Ss practice in comparing and contrasting two photographs
- Divide Ss into pairs.
- In each pair, tell one student to describe the photographs and talk about the importance of each celebration shown in the two photographs. Encourage him / her to use some of the words in the exercise above.
- Now ask the second student the question: *Which of the two celebrations would you like to attend?*
- Elicit answers.

Key

Suggested ideas:
- Photograph *c* shows a typical western wedding. Guests are formally dressed to attend the ceremony.
- Photograph *d* shows a group of people, probably on stage, performing folk dances.
- Both celebrations are important. The western wedding ceremony unites two people in marriage, while folk dances remind people of their culture.

7 Aim: to elaborate and expand on the topic of the previous exercise
- Ask Ss to read the questions and generate discussion.

writing

1 **Aim: to help Ss identify the stylistic features of a story beginning or ending with given words**

- Ask Ss to read through the story. Explain any unknown words if necessary.
- Have Ss connect the highlighted sentences using linking words. Discuss the example given.
- Elicit and check answers.

Key

b. The time came when we all arrived at the village from the four corners of the world. Some people stayed with relatives while the rest of us stayed in local hotels and guest houses.

c. We did all sorts of interesting things, like taking a boat trip to the island where my grandfather was born.

d. We were one hundred and sixty people altogether, who will never all be together again in the same place.

- When this is over, ask Ss the questions.
- Elicit and check answers.

Key

- The Past Simple and the Past Perfect.
- To make his / her story sound more realistic.

2 **Aim: to give Ss practice in paragraph organisation**

- Ask Ss to read through the checklist and ensure that they don't have any unknown words.
- Ask Ss to do the exercise.
- Check answers.

Key

a. 3, 5   b. 2   c. 1   d. 4   e. 5

3 **Aim: to give Ss practice in using narrative language**

- Ask Ss to read through the extract for gist.
- Before Ss complete the gaps, draw their attention to the uses of the tenses: the *Past Simple* is used when narrating a sequence of events in order, the *Past Progressive* is used when describing the background scenes to the story or when referring to interrupted events, and the *Past Perfect* is used when describing earlier events or situations earlier in the past.
- Have Ss do the exercise.
- Check answers.

Key

(1) went	(7) drove
(2) had planned	(8) had arrived
(3) were looking forward	(9) got
(4) were driving	(10) had
(5) remembered	(11) didn't miss
(6) was	

4 **Writing task**

Aim: to give Ss practice in writing a story beginning or ending with given words

- Assign the writing task for homework.

Teacher's Notes

Revision 04-06

reading

1 **Aim: to give Ss further practice in understanding text organisation**

- Ask Ss a few pre-reading questions related to the topic of the text and generate discussion.

  e.g. *When is New Year celebrated in your country? How do people usually celebrate New Year? What do you know about New Year's celebrations in other countries?*

- Ask Ss to read through the text for gist, without worrying about the gaps.
- Ask Ss to try to guess what each of the missing sentences is about.
- Ask Ss to look at the sentences A-F which have been removed from the text and ensure that they understand them.
- Point out to Ss that they should always look for clues in the sentences which precede or follow the gaps. To this end, Ss may be helped by determiners (*this, that*) and subject / object personal pronouns (*he / him, she / her*) which refer to things or people mentioned in previous or later sentences. When there are no such cohesive devices, Ss should rely strongly on context.
- Ask Ss to read the first paragraph of the text and decide which sentence best fits in the first gap.
- Check answers and ask Ss to underline the key words / phrases which helped them decide.
- Ask Ss to read the text paragraph by paragraph and do the rest of the activity.
- Point out to Ss that if they cannot decide what fits in a gap, they should move on and get back to it later.
- Check answers and ask Ss to provide justification.

Key

1 F **Text**
... begin on the 13th April and end on the 15th April.

Missing sentence
These three days are of great symbolic significance ...

2 B **Text**
... the Thais dress up on the night of the 12th to signal the coming new year.

Missing sentence
The colourful Songkran parade also takes place on New Year's Eve.

3 D **Text**
... water was sprinkled ...
... a full-scale, nationwide water fight!

Missing sentence
People use buckets, pipes, plastic cannons, squirt guns ... to drench just about anybody they come across!

4 C **Text**
Young people ask their elders to forgive them ... sprinkle the old people's hands with water ...

Missing sentence
Once all the family duties have been seen to, the water wars begin ...

5 A **Text**
There are some basic rules ...

Missing sentence
Firstly, it's considered disrespectful to ... Secondly, ... be sure not to ...

Extra sentence: E

- When the activity is over, explain unknown words through definitions or example sentences.

Teacher's Notes

Use of English

1 **Aim: to revise various language forms through a multiple choice cloze exercise**

- Ask Ss to read through for gist, without paying attention to the gaps.
- Ask Ss to read the text again, one sentence at a time.
- Ask Ss to read the four options carefully, before deciding which one best fits in each space.
- Have Ss do the activity.
- Check answers.

Key

(1) C
(2) B
(3) C
(4) B
(5) B
(6) B
(7) D
(8) B
(9) C
(10) A
(11) C
(12) D
(13) B
(14) D
(15) C

2 **Aim: to check structural accuracy through an open cloze exercise**

- Ask Ss to read through the text for gist, without paying attention to the gaps.
- Ask Ss to read the text again and fill in the gaps with one world only.
- Have Ss do the activity.
- Check answers.

Key

(16) I
(17) D
(18) A
(19) L
(20) E
(21) B
(22) H
(23) K
(24) N
(25) F

Use of English

3 **Aim: to check structural accuracy through an error correction exercise**
- Ask Ss to read the text for gist, without trying to correct anything.
- Ask Ss to read the text again, one sentence at a time and try to identify which of the lines are correct and which contain a word which should not be there.
- Have Ss do the activity.
- Check answers.

Key

26	very
27	which
28	through
29	had
30	✓
31	too
32	all
33	✓
34	it
35	was
36	✓
37	such
38	place
39	them
40	✓

Teacher's Notes

Use of English (continued)

4 **Aim: to translate into English the Chinese given in brackets through a translating exercise**

- Ask Ss to read the text for gist.
- Point out to Ss that before completing the gaps, they should decide on which phrases are needed for each blank.
- Have Ss do the activity.
- Check answers.

Key

41 therein lies the seed of many of our mistakes
42 induces us to commit everyday errors of judgment
43 tends to go up, not down
44 it's an illusion of control
45 In a well-known series of tests

listening

Aim: to give Ss further practice in listening for gist through a multiple choice activity

- Ask Ss to read through questions 1-6. Explain any unknown words if necessary.
- Play the CD twice.
- Check answers.

Key

1 B
2 C
3 B
4 A
5 C
6 A

Functions

Asking for information
Giving instructions

Structures

Subject / object questions
Question tags

Vocabulary

Vocabulary related to food and cooking

alligator	dish (n)	raw
bake	fry	roast (v)
barbecue	grate	sauce
bite (v)	grill	shell
bowl	gum	shovel (v)
cheese soufflé	heaped (adj)	slice (v / n)
chew	marinate	sprinkle
chilli	meal	steam (v)
chop	microwave (v)	
cuisine	mouth-watering	

Other words and expressions

be all ears	stuffy
cool down	whirlwind

Conversational English

It's a new one on me.
Then it hit me.
What's cooking?

presentation

Aim: to present vocabulary and structures in the context of a radio phone-in show about unusual experiences with food

1 **Aims:** • **to activate Ss background knowledge**
   • **to relate the topic of the radio show to Ss' personal experiences**
• Ask Ss the questions and generate discussion.

2 **Aim: to give Ss practice in listening for gist through a matching exercise**
• Ask Ss to look at the sets of pictures and describe what is happening in each one.
• Play the CD.
• Check answers.

Key

1 a   2 b   3 b

3 **Aim: to expand on the topic of the listening activity**
• Ask Ss the questions and generate discussion.

Teacher's Notes

words and phrases

1 Words related to cooking

Aim: to present words related to cooking

- Ask Ss to read the words in the box and match them with the pictures that follow.
- Have Ss do the activity.
- Check answers.

> **optional**
> If there is time, ask Ss to write their own sentences using the words related to cooking and check them.

2 Words easily confused

Aim: to give Ss practice in distinguishing words that can easily be confused

- Ask Ss to read the first set of words. Then, ask Ss to read through the first three sentences.
- Encourage Ss to work out the difference in meaning.

kitchen = the room where one cooks
cooker = the electrical appliance used for cooking food
cook = a person whose job is to cook

- Ask Ss to do the rest of the exercise, one set at a time. For each set, explain the difference through definitions and / or examples.

meal = an occasion where people sit down to eat food, especially breakfast, lunch or dinner
cuisine = a style of cooking, especially from one particular area
dish = food prepared in a particular way as part of a meal

bite (v) = use your teeth to cut into or through sth
chew = to bite food into small pieces in your mouth with your teeth to make it easier to swallow (e.g. chew gum)
swallow = to make food, drink, etc. go down your throat into your stomach

grate = rub food against a rough surface (grater) in order to cut it into very small pieces (e.g. Grate the cheese and sprinkle it over the pasta)
chop = to cut sth into pieces with a knife (e.g. chop the onions, chop the carrots up into small pieces)
slice = cut sth into thin pieces (slices) (e.g. slice onions, cucumbers, meat)

- Check answers.

Teacher's Notes

grammar

1 Aim: to present subject and object questions and have Ss work out their structure

- Ask Ss to read through the questions 1-4.
- Ask Ss to answer the questions a-d.
- Discuss answers.

Key

a. 1. have   2. do   3. is   4. is cooking

b. 3. ✔   4. ✔

c. 1. ✔   2. ✔

d. 1. we   2. you

2 Aim: to give Ss practice in distinguishing between subject and object questions

- Ask Ss to read through the questions and answers.
- Ask Ss to do the activity.
- Check answers.

Key

1. c   2. e   3. d   4. a   5. b

3 Aim: to present question tags and have Ss work out their formation

- Ask Ss to read through the questions and complete the rules.
- Have Ss complete the rules.
- Discuss answers.

Key

Question Tags

Question Tags are short questions placed at the _end_ of a statement. They are formed with an auxiliary or a modal verb and a pronoun. If the statement is positive, the question tag is _negative_. If the statement is _negative_, the question tag is positive.

> **optional**
> Give Ss slips of paper with questions and their question tags. Ss work in pairs to match them.

4 Aim: to present special cases of question tags

- Ask Ss to read through the two halves of the sentences.
- Have Ss to do the activity.
- Check answers. If necessary, provide Ss with further examples and / or explanations.

Key

1. b   2. a   3. d   4.c

- They don't follow the general rule of how question tags are formed.

5 Aim: to give Ss practice in using question tags in context

- Have Ss do the activity.
- Check answers.

Key

1. isn't she   5. doesn't she
2. isn't it   6. do they
3. won't you   7. can she
4. did you   8. was he

Teacher's Notes

Lesson Two

Structures

Wh-ever

Vocabulary

Vocabulary related to food and cooking

additive	knead	overheated
crave (v)	label (n)	preservation
deep-dish	long-life	procedure
dietary	low-fat	saucy
dough	love at first bite	savour
fat free	lust (n)	sink one's teeth into
flat (adj)	make one's mouth	storage
flavour (v)	water	stuffed
gobble down	mozzarella	taste (v / n)
herb	nutrient	topping
ingredient	nutrition	toss (v)

Other words

basic	guard (n)	seize
border	immigrant	startle
common practice	kingdom	station (v)
consume	misleading	stunned (adj)
estimate (v)	overseas	the court
evolve	patriotic	worldwide

Phrasal verbs and expressions

blow out	punch down
find one's way to	set down
it goes without saying	set the record straight
kick off	sooner or later
live on	

Expressions with *cake*

a piece of cake
have your cake and eat it
sell like hot cakes
the icing on the cake
want one's slice of the cake

---

optional pre-reading activity

- Ask Ss to read the title of the text and look at the picture accompanying it.
- Ask Ss to predict the topic of the reading text. You can also ask Ss the following questions.
  - e.g. *Do you like eating pizza?*
    How often do you eat pizza?
    Do you make your own pizza or do you order it?
- Discuss and elicit answers.

reading

1 **Aim: to help Ss identify the main idea of each paragraph through a matching exercise**

- Ask Ss to read through the text for gist, without worrying about the gaps.
- Ask Ss to read through the headings A-G.
- Before the second reading, point out to Ss that they should look for key words / phrases in the text which are related to those in the headings.
- Now ask Ss to read the first paragraph of the text and decide on the most suitable heading. Ask Ss to underline the key words / phrases which helped them decide. Check answers.
- Ask Ss to read the text paragraph by paragraph and do the rest of the activity.
- Point out to Ss that if they cannot decide on a heading for a specific paragraph, they should move on and get back to it later.
- Check answers and ask Ss to provide justification.

Key

1 E **Text**		**Summary sentences**
… the early Greeks who first baked … found its way to Italy.		… the neighbour's idea.
2 C **Text**		**Summary sentences**
… the poor … eating … round, flat bread … the queen ordered her guards to bring her one … she went so far as to order … a selection of pizzas … it wasn't common practice for a queen to eat peasant food!		… travelled a long way before it ended up on an aristocrat's plate.
3 G **Text**		**Summary sentences**
… it made its way to America with the first Italian immigrants …		… crossed the border … went overseas.
4 D **Text**		**Summary sentences**
… special attention … paid to the making of pizza … has set down rules …		Certain procedures must be followed …
5 A **Text**		**Summary sentences**
… many different kinds of pizzas … … an Ice Cream Pizza or even a Candy Pizza?		… not just tomatoes and cheese …
6 F **Text**		**Summary sentences**
can be a healthy … treat.		… a healthy snack.

Extra heading: B

- When the activity is over, explain unknown words through definitions or example sentences.

---

optional post-reading activity

Ask Ss questions of personal response to the topic of the reading text.
e.g. *What did you find most impressive about what you have learnt about pizza?*
Do you know the history of any other popular dish?

words and phrases

**Aim: to give Ss practice in inferring the meaning
of the phrasal verbs and expressions in the
reading text through a matching activity**

- Refer Ss to the reading text.
- Ask Ss to do the activity.
- Check answers.

Key

1. d	2. e	3. f	4. b	5. a	6. c

optional

If there is time, ask Ss to make their own sentences
using the phrasal verbs and expressions and check
them.

2 Idioms

**Aim: to give Ss practice in inferring the meaning
of idioms from context**

- Ask Ss to do the activity.
- Check answers.

Key

1. a	2. a	3. b	4. a	5. b

optional

If there is time, ask Ss to make their own sentences
using the idioms and check them.

Teacher's Notes

grammar

1 **Aim:** • **to present Wh-ever words**
 • **to help Ss infer the meaning of Wh-ever words**

- Ask Ss to read through the sentences and the definitions and ensure that they understand them.
- Have Ss do the matching.
- Discuss Ss' answers.
- Then ask Ss to complete the rule.
- Check answers.

Key

1. b   2. d   3. c   4. e   5. a

The word ever can be added after certain *question* words to mean that *it does not matter* who, _what_, when, _where_, _which_, as the result will be the same.

2 **Aim: to give Ss practice in using Wh-ever words in context**

- Ask Ss to do the exercise.
- Check answers.

Key

1. whichever	5. Whenever
2. Wherever	6. whatever
3. Whoever	7. Whoever
4. whatever	8. Whenever

optional
If there is time, ask Ss to make their own sentences using wh-ever words and check them.

Teacher's Notes

listening

Aim: to give Ss practice in listening for specific information through a multiple choice activity

- Ask Ss to read sentences 1-5 and their options.
- Explain any unknown words.
- Play the CD twice.
- Check answers.

Key

1 C   2 B   3 A   4 C   5 C

optional post-listening activity
Ask Ss questions of personal response to the listening text.

e.g. *What do you think of fat-free products?*
  Do you buy fat-free / sugar-free products?
  Do you agree with Dr May's views?

Teacher's Notes

Lesson Three

Vocabulary

Vocabulary related to diet and lifestyle

calories	light (adj)
diet	lose weight
dietician	nutritious
fattening	processed food
high in fibre	stay in shape
high in protein	vegetarianism
keep fit	

Vocabulary related to cooking

bring to the boil	peel (v)
brown (v)	pint
drain (v)	plain
fish stock	pound (n)
flake (v)	pour
flour	preheated
gas mark	saucepan
mash	spread (v)
moderate (adj)	stir (v)
ounce	stock (n)
ovenproof	tender
parsley	thicken (v)

Other words and expressions

evenly	reserve (v)
exhausting	seal (v)
get back to sb	sound like a broken record
gradually	

speaking

1 Aim: to generate discussion based on Ss' personal experiences

- Ask Ss to read the questions and generate discussion.

2 Aim: to give Ss practice in relating words / phrases to context

- Tell Ss to look at photographs a and b.
- Then ask Ss to look at the vocabulary box and decide which words / phrases can be used to describe each photograph. Ensure that Ss don't have any unknown words. If necessary, provide them with explanations and / or examples.
- Discuss answers.

Key

Photograph a: processed food, calories, unhealthy, fattening
Photograph b: light, nutritious, source of vitamins, high in protein, balanced diet, high in fibre

3 Aim: to give Ss practice in comparing and contrasting two photographs

- Divide Ss into pairs.
- In each pair, ask one student to talk about the advantages and disadvantages of each meal shown in the photographs. Encourage him / her to use some of the words / phrases in exercise 2.

- Now ask the second student the question: *Which of the two types of meals do you prefer?*
- Elicit answers.

Key

Suggested ideas:
Photograph *a* shows an unhealthy meal. Although a lot of people like eating processed or junk food, it is high in calories and fattening.
Photograph *b* shows a nutritious meal which is high in both protein and fibre. Eating this kind of food is good for you. It is not as mouth-watering as the meal in photograph *a*, but it is definitely healthier.

4 Aim: to give Ss practice in relating words / phrases to context

- Tell Ss to look at photographs c and d.
- Then ask Ss to look at the box and decide which words / phrases can be used to describe each photograph. Ensure that Ss don't have any unknown words. If necessary, provide them with explanations and / or examples.
- Discuss answers.

Key

Photograph c: healthy meals, measure body fat, expensive, dietician
Photograph d: work out, stay in shape, exhausting, fashionable, burn calories, monotonous, keep fit, gym

5 Aim: to give Ss practice in comparing and contrasting two photographs

- Divide Ss into pairs.
- In each pair, ask one student to talk about which of the two methods of staying healthy shown in the two photographs is more effective. Encourage him / her to use some of the words / phrases in exercise 4.
- Now ask the second student the question: *Which of the two methods suits you / do you prefer?*
- Elicit answers.

Key

Suggested ideas:
Photograph *c* shows a dietician who is probably talking to one of her patients. Seeing a dietician is a good idea, especially for people who want to lose weight and need support and guidance. A dietician measures your body fat and offers you advice on how to improve your eating habits.
Photograph *d* shows two people working out at the gym. Going to the gym is pretty fashionable these days. Although it can be a bit monotonous and exhausting, it helps you burn calories and keep fit. It is recommended for people who are energetic and active.

6 Aim: to elaborate and expand on the topic of the speaking activity

- Ask Ss to read the questions and generate discussion.

writing

1 **Aims:** • to activate Ss' background knowledge
• to prepare Ss for the writing task
• Ask Ss the questions and generate discussion.

2 **Aim:** • to familiarise Ss with giving instructions
in the context of a recipe
• to give Ss practice in using verbs
related to cooking
• Ask Ss to read through the words in the box.
• Explain any words if necessary.
• Ask Ss to read through the letter and find out why
Brenda is writing the letter (to give Scott a fish pie
recipe). Tell Ss to ignore the gaps at this point.
• Ask Ss to read the letter again and complete the
gaps with the words in the box. Point out that they
might need to change them.
• Check answers.

Key

(1) Boil
(2) melt
(3) Cook
(4) stirring
(5) Chop
(6) pour
(7) Peel
(8) mash
(9) Sprinkle
(10) bake

3 **Aim:** to give Ss practice in giving instructions
based on visual input
• Ask Ss to look at the pictures and read the verbs in
the box. Ensure that Ss don't have any unknown
words and that they understand the procedure. If
necessary, provide them with further explanations.
• Have Ss do the activity.
• Check answers.

Key

Chop the onions and fry them.
Add the chopped tomatoes.
Add salt and pepper and cook for an hour.
Boil the spaghetti in water and drain when it is ready.
Spread the tomato sauce over the spaghetti and
serve.

4 **Writing task**

Aim: to give Ss practice in writing an informal
letter giving a recipe
• Assign the writing task for homework.

Our four-legged friends

Lesson One

Functions

Expressing an opinion

Structures

Reported Speech

Vocabulary

Words

average (adj)	practice (n)
bandage	quarrel (v)
co-exist	separate
contact (n)	shrimp
cub	starfish
cunning	tamer
flap (v)	territorial
nail (n)	tranquillizer
pack (n)	wing
paw	wrap

Phrasal verbs and expressions

be in pain	jump to one's rescue
cry wolf	pass away
get along	turn on sb
go crazy	

Idioms with animals

a wolf in sheep's clothing
crocodile tears
curiosity killed the cat
fight like cat and dog
let the cat out of the bag
like a bear with a sore head
no room to swing a cat
when the cat's away, the mice will play

presentation

Aim: to present vocabulary, structures and functions in the context of the narrations of three people talking about their animal-related jobs

1 Aim: to introduce the topic of the unit by relating it to Ss' personal preferences
- Ask Ss the questions and generate discussion.
- Elicit answers.

2 Aim: to build on Ss' background knowledge by presenting them with some amazing facts about various animals
- Ask Ss to read through the statements a-g. Explain any unknown words if necessary.
- Discuss and elicit answers.

Key

a. T
b. T
c. F (a shrimp's heart is in its head)
d. F (it will eventually turn white)
e. T
f. T
g. T

3 Aim: to give Ss practice in listening for gist through a matching exercise
- Ask Ss to look at the five photographs which show five different people at work.
- Ask Ss to listen to the three narrations carefully. Play the CD.
- Check answers.

Key

Speaker 1: b
Speaker 2: a
Speaker 3: e

4 Aim: to expand on the topic of the unit by relating it to Ss' personal opinions
- Ask Ss the questions and generate discussion.
- Elicit answers.

Key

Suggested ideas:
- Yes, everybody should own a pet, because they can be people's best friends. / No, only people who really love animals and will take care of them should own pets.
- We need to make sure they have a loving home, food and medical care.
- I would take it home / to the vet / to an animal shelter.

words and phrases

1 Adjectives

Aim: to present adjectives used to attribute positive and negative qualities to animals

- Ask Ss to read through the adjectives in the box. Explain any unknown words if necessary.
- Discuss the examples given.
- Have Ss do the activity.
- Check answers.

Key

POSITIVE	NEGATIVE
friendly	noisy
handsome	territorial
intelligent	cunning
cute	dangerous
	aggressive

2 Idioms

Aims: · to present idioms with animals
· to give Ss practice in using these idioms in context

- Ask Ss to read through the idioms in the box.
- Discuss the meanings of the idioms presented here. You may ask Ss whether any of these idioms exist in their own culture or mother tongue as well.
- Ask Ss to read through the sentences a-h.
- Have Ss do the activity.
- Check answers.

Key

a. crocodile tears
b. a wolf in sheep's clothing
c. fight like cat and dog
d. no room to swing a cat
e. let the cat out of the bag
f. when the cat's away, the mice will play
g. curiosity killed the cat
h. like a bear with a sore head

grammar

1 **Aim: to enable Ss to identify the differences between Direct and Reported Speech**

- Ask Ss to read through the sentences 1-3.
- Ask Ss to read the sentences a-c. Ensure that Ss understand the procedure.
- Have Ss do the activity.
- Check answers.

Key

a. "What *happened*?" I *asked* the man, who turned out to be a lion-tamer.
b. "The lion *shouldn't perform* for a week or two," I *told* the owner.
c. "The birds *are* at each other's throat!" one of the visitors *told* me.

- Draw Ss' attention to the basic differences they notice between Direct and Reported Speech. It is advisable not to go into detail as Ss will revise these changes more extensively in exercise 2.

Key

In Direct Speech we use quotation marks to give the exact words somebody said whereas in Reported Speech we give the meaning of what somebody said without quotation marks. The tenses of the main verbs change as well.

2 **Aim: to review how verb forms and time expressions change in Reported Speech**

- Ask Ss to read through the two columns.
- Have Ss do the matching.
- Check answers.

Key

DIRECT SPEECH
- Present Simple
- Present Progressive
- Past Simple
- Present Perfect
- Present Perfect Progressive

REPORTED SPEECH
- Past Perfect Progressive
- Past Perfect Simple
- Past Simple
- Past Progressive

- can
- will
- must

- had to
- could
- would

- today
- yesterday
- last week
- tomorrow
- now

- the next day
- then
- the previous day
- that day
- the previous week

3 **Aim: to give Ss practice in using Reported Speech in context**

- Ask Ss to do the exercise.
- Check answers.

Key

1. Anne said (that) she had visited a tropical island the previous summer.
2. Tim said (that) he had had that painting since 1985.
3. The teacher told us to sit down and be quiet.
4. Jerry asked Tom who had won the previous week's game.
5. My friend asked whether / if I was going to finish my project on warm-blooded animals soon.

Teacher's Notes

Lesson Two

Reported Speech (Special Introductory Verbs)

Vocabulary

Words

bloodthirsty	lipstick
breed (v)	migrate
companionship	non-conclusive
compatible	origin
conduct (v)	partnership
descendant	primitive
domesticated / -ation	puppy
faithful	scrap (n)
fulfil	settlement
gifted	simultaneously
hint (n)	species
inborn	tap (v)
interpret	value (v)
laboratory	

Phrasal verbs and expressions

be in the dark	pick up on
cast light on	put down to
close the door on	put one's finger on

optional pre-reading activity

- Ask Ss to read the title of the reading text and look at the picture accompanying it.
- Ask Ss to predict the topic of the reading text and try to interpret its title. You can also ask the following questions.
  e.g. *Do you think dogs are intelligent animals? Why do people say that 'dog is man's best friend'?*
- Discuss and elicit answers.

reading

1 **Aim: to give Ss practice in identifying the main ideas of the paragraphs in an article through a matching exercise**

- Ask Ss to read through the text for gist, without paying attention to the gaps.
- Ask Ss to try to guess what each of the headings is about.
- Ask Ss to read through the headings A-G and ensure that they understand them.
- Before the second reading, point out to Ss that they should always look for key words or phrases in the text which are related to those in the headings. When there are no such cohesive devices, Ss should rely strongly on context.
- Now ask Ss to read the first paragraph of the text and decide on the most suitable heading. Ask Ss to

underline the key words / phrases which helped them decide.
- Check answers.
- Ask Ss to read the text paragraph by paragraph and do the rest of the activity.
- Point out to Ss that if they cannot decide on a heading for a specific paragraph, they should move on and get back to it later.
- Check answers and ask Ss to provide justification.

Key

1. **F** (*... all dogs ... are the domesticated descedants of wolves.*)
2. **E** (*Quite recently, three dog studies ... carried out ... This new theory ...*)
3. **G** (*... where or when dog domestication first began. ... the people in the settlements probably managed to tame a few* (dogs) *to help them* (the people) *with hunting and guarding the camp.*)
4. **A** (*... dogs showed an astonishing ability to interpret human behaviour ... a communicative talent that was inborn ...*)
5. **B** (*... an experiment ... tested the animals' ability to understand ... The dogs usually picked up on the signals and chose the correct box ...*)
6. **D** (*... it would take a lot more time to fully understand our faithful companions.*)

Extra heading: C

- When the activity is over, explain unknown words through definitions or example sentences.

optional post-reading activity

Ask Ss questions of personal response to the topic of the reading text.
e.g. *Do you know of any other highly intelligent animals?*

words and phrases

1 Phrasal verbs and expressions

Aim: to give Ss practice in inferring the meaning of the phrasal verbs and expressions in the reading text through a matching activity

- Refer Ss to the article.
- Ask Ss to do the activity.
- Check answers.

Key

| 1. d | 2. e | 3. f | 4. a | 5. g | 6. c | 7. b |

optional

If there is time, ask Ss to make their own sentences using the phrasal verbs and expressions and check them.

2 Word building

A **Aims:** · to introduce nouns formed with the suffix -*ship*
· to give Ss practice in noun formation

- Read and explain the introductory comment as well as the examples in the table.
- Have Ss do the activity.
- Check anwers.

Key

noun root	noun (noun+-*ship*)
owner	*ownership*
companion	*companionship*
relation	**relationship**
member	**membership**
leader	leadership
friend	**friendship**
partner	partnership

B **Aim:** to give Ss practice in using nouns in context

- Have Ss do the activity.
- Check answers.

Key

1. membership
2. owner
3. relationship
4. partnership
5. companion

optional

If there is time, ask Ss to make their own sentences using the rest of the nouns from exercise 2A and check them.

Teacher's Notes

grammar

1 Aim: to elicit the use of special introductory verbs in Reported Speech

- Ask Ss to read through the sentences in Reported and Direct Speech.
- Ask Ss to look at the questions a-c.
- Discuss and elicit answers.

Key

a. It is true / Because
b. They are called **special introductory verbs**.
c. beg, deny, apologise, refuse, threaten, suggest, promise, warn, agree, advise, accuse, admit, remind, etc.

2 Aim: to give Ss practice in using special introductory verbs in Reported Speech

- Ask Ss to read through the verbs in the box. Explain any unknown words if necessary. Before Ss do the exercise, you may need to draw their attention to the different verb patterns:

- *beg* sb + full infinitive
- *deny* (= say that sth, e.g. an accusation, is untrue) + -ing form
- *refuse* (= be unwilling to do sth) + full infinitive
- *apologise* (to sb) for + -ing form
- *threaten* + full infinitive
- *suggest* + -ing form

- Have Ss do the exercise.
- Check answers.

Key

1. Claire apologised to Matt for missing his party.
2. Gareth suggested ordering pizza and renting a video.
3. Victoria begged her parents to let her go to the party.
4. Oliver denied damaging / having damaged Mary's CDs.
5. Mr Davison threatened to fire Gwen / that he would fire Gwen if she was / were late again.
6. Harold refused to do the washing-up because he was tired.

listening

Aim: to give Ss practice in listening for specific information through a note taking activity

- Ask Ss to read through the sentences of the exercise. Explain any unknown words if necessary.
- Ask Ss to predict what kind of information is required.
- Point out to Ss that they should complete each of the sentences with a word or a short phrase from the listening text.
- Play the CD twice.
- Check answers.

Key

1. three / 3 seconds
2. the UK / Britain
3. in another country
4. support
5. BUAV
6. poisonous
7. killed
8. methods

---

optional post-listening activity

You may ask Ss further questions of personal response to the listening text.

e.g. *Do you think that animal testing should be totally banned or not?*

Teacher's Notes

Lesson Three

Vocabulary

Words

authorities	neighbouring
ban (v)	obedient
benefit (v)	pose (v)
(in) captivity	proposed (adj)
community	reservation
construction	resolve
council	satisfactorily
devaluation	site
disrupt	stray
establish	tracker dog
habitat	ultimately
income	viable
negotiate	

speaking

1 **Aim: to generate discussion based on Ss'
personal preferences and background
knowledge**

- Ask Ss to look at the questions and generate discussion.

2 **Aim: to give Ss practice in relating words /
phrases to context**

- Tell Ss to look at photographs a and b.
- Ask Ss to read through the two columns. Ensure that Ss
don't have any unknown words. If necessary, provide them
with explanations and / or examples.
- Have Ss do the matching and check answers.
- Ask Ss to decide which of these phrases best describe
each photograph.
- Elicit and check answers.

Key

1. d (photograph a)	4. e (photograph b)
2. c (photograph a)	5. f (both photographs)
3. a (photograph a)	6. b (both photographs)

3 **Aim: to give Ss practice in comparing and
contrasting two photographs**

- Divide Ss in pairs.
- In each pair, tell one student to describe the two
photographs focusing on the living conditions of the
animals shown in the photographs. Encourage him / her to
use some of the words from the exercise above.
- Now ask the second student the question: *Do you think
that animals should be used in circuses in order to
entertain crowds?*
- Elicit answers.

Key

Suggested ideas:
- Photograph *a* shows an animal in captivity. Animals in
captivity might be tamed or taught to perform tricks. They
don't have to worry about finding food, or protecting
themselves.
- Photograph *b* shows an animal in its natural habitat. This
animal (a cheetah) is an endangered species and may
become extinct. These animals have to look for food and
protect themselves.

4 **Aim: to give Ss practice in relating words /
phrases to context**

- Tell Ss to look at photographs c and d.
- Ask Ss to look at the vocabulary box and decide which
words / phrases can be used to describe each photograph.
Ensure that Ss don't have any unknown words. If
necessary, provide them with explanations and / or
examples.
- Elicit answers.

Key

trained (both photographs)	obedient (both photographs)
rescue (both photographs)	trapped (photograph d)
companion (both photographs)	caring (both photographs)
tracker dog (photograph d)	intelligent (both photographs)
pet (photograph c)	

5 **Aim: to give Ss practice in comparing and
contrasting two photographs**

- Divide Ss in pairs.
- In each pair, tell one student to describe the two
photographs focusing on the different role that each animal
plays in our lives. Encourage him / her to use some of the
words from the exercise above.
- Now ask the second student the question: *What kind of
animal makes an ideal pet?*
- Elicit answers.

Key

Suggested ideas:
- In photograph *c*, the dog is obviously the girl's pet. It is
her companion and a faithful friend.
- In photograph *d*, the dog is not a pet, but a tracker dog. It
helps rescue people who are trapped.
- Open answers.

6 **Aim: to elaborate and expand on the topic of
the speaking activity**

- Ask Ss to look at the questions and generate discussion.
- Elicit answers.

Key

Suggested ideas:
- No, because animals get love, food and care. / Yes,
because animals should be allowed to live in their natural
habitats.
- They should be taken to animal shelters / adopted.
- Watchdogs, for instance, can protect properties from
burglars.
- No, because hunters kill animals for food. / Yes, because
it is a cruel sport.

writing

1 **Aims:** · to activate Ss' background knowledge
· to prepare Ss for the writing task

· Ask Ss to look at the questions and generate
discussion.

· Elicit answers.

2 **Aims:** · to help Ss understand the
organisation of a report
· to focus on headings as a major
stylistic feature of a report

· Ask Ss to read through the report. Explain any
unknown words if necessary.

· Ask Ss to decide on the most suitable headings for
the three paragraphs of the main part of the report.

· Elicit and check answers. Ask Ss to provide
justification.

Key

1 b (… will not only pose a threat to the environment
… it will also disrupt the peace and quiet in the
area … cause a devaluation of property.)

2 e (… such a project can benefit the community - it
goes on to explain the possible benefits.)

3 d (… the local council has expressed a willingness
to negotiate … to ensure that this issue is
resolved satisfactorily.)

3 **Aim:** to familiarise Ss with the organisation of
ideas in reports

· Ask Ss to read through the sentences a-f. Explain
any unknown words if necessary.

· Have Ss do the activity.

· Check answers.

Key

a. I	c. C	e. C
b. M	d. M	f. M

4 Writing task

Aim: to give Ss practice in writing a report

· Assign the writing task for homework.

Where the heart is

Lesson One

Functions

Expressing quantity
Comparing
Making suggestions
Talking about houses and accommodation

Structures

Quantifiers

Vocabulary

Words

accommodate	housekeeping
carve	housework
contact (v)	jacuzzi
film crew	occupied (adj)
herring	pelt
home-made	select
homemaker	set (n)
homesick	suite
home town	tuck (v)
house guest	tuna
household	

Idioms with *home*

an Englishman's home is his castle
be a home from home
it's nothing to write home about
make oneself at home
there's no place like home

Other expressions

give sth a try
take a dip

presentation

Aim: to present vocabulary and structures in the context of a web page advertising an alternative type of holiday accommodation

1 Aim: to arouse Ss' interest in the topic by asking them to predict its content.

· Ask Ss to look at the title of the web page and discuss the questions.

2 **Aim: to give Ss practice in reading for specific information**

· Have Ss read the first paragraph and ask them question a.
· Elicit answers.
· Ask Ss to read the rest of the text without worrying about unknown words and answer questions b and c.
· Discuss answers.

Key

a. Yes, they do. (... *it's easy to make yourself at home at our Ice Hotel.*)
b. There are cosy rooms and theme suites and people sleep in sleeping bags on beds of ice that are covered with deer pelts.
c. There is *Comedy Night* on Thursdays, a *DJ* and *Happy Hours* on Fridays and *The Ice Band* on Saturdays. People can also go to the ice cinema, visit the two exhibition rooms, go for a ride on a snowmobile, or take a dip in the outdoor jacuzzi.

· When this activity is over, ask Ss some more questions.
  e.g. *How much snow and ice are used to build the Ice Hotel?*
  Where exactly is the Ice Hotel?
  Do all the rooms in the hotel look the same?
  What kind of food is offered at the hotel?
  What happens to the hotel in spring?
· Encourage Ss to guess the meaning of new vocabulary, such as *unique, home-made* and *catch a movie*. Provide explanations through definitions or example sentences.

Teacher's Notes

words and phrases

1 Compound nouns and adjectives

A **Aims:** · to introduce compound nouns with *home* and *house*
· to help Ss distinguish their different meanings

· Ask Ss to look through the article and find any examples of compound nouns with *home* or *house*.
· Ask Ss to infer the meaning of these compound nouns from context.
· Point out that in some compound nouns their parts are separate words while in others the two words come together in one.
· Have Ss do the activity.
· Discuss answers and elicit the meaning of each noun.

Key

housekeeping (n) = the work involved in taking care of a house
homemaker (n) = a person who works at home and takes care of the house and the family
homesick (adj) = a person who is far from home and misses family and friends
home-made (adj) = made at home
homework (n) = work that is given to students by teachers to do at home
housework (n) = the work involved in taking care of a home and family (e.g. cleaning and cooking)
household (n) = all of the people living together in a house
house guest (n) = a person who is staying in your house for a short time
home town (n) = the place where somebody was born or lived as a child

B **Aim:** to give Ss practice in using compound nouns and adjectives with *home* and *house*

· Ask Ss to do the activity.
· Check answers.

Key

a. hometown
b. homesick
c. homework
d. home-made
e. household

optional
If there is time, ask Ss to make their own sentences using the compound nouns and adjectives with *home* and *house* and check them.

2 Idioms

Aims: · to present idioms with *home*
· to give Ss practice in inferring the meaning of idioms from context

· Ask Ss to do the activity.
· Check answers. Provide Ss with explanations and further examples when necessary.

Key

1. b   2. a   3. b   4. b   5. a

Teacher's Notes

grammar

1 Aim: to revise words and expressions used to express quantity
- Ask Ss to read through the sentences. Ensure that Ss understand them.
- Ask Ss to answer the questions.
- Discuss answers.

Key
- large quantities: *lots of, tons of, many, plenty, all* small quantities: *a little, hardly any*
- a lot of (*much* is normally used in negative and interrogative sentences)

2 Aim: to revise the different meanings of *a little, a few, little* and *few*
- Ask Ss to read through the sentences. Ensure that Ss understand them.
- Ask Ss to answer the questions.
- Discuss answers.

Key
- 1. b   2. b   3. a   4. a
- 3, 4

3 Aim: to give Ss practice in using quantifiers in context
- Have Ss do the activity.
- Check answers.

Key
1. a	4. a
2. b	5. b
3. a	6. b

Teacher's Notes

English in use

1 Aim: to check structural accuracy through an open cloze exercise
- Ask Ss to read through the text for gist, without worrying about the missing words.
- Ask Ss to fill in the gaps with one word only.
- Check answers.

Key
(1) with	(6) few
(2) be	(7) before / if
(3) All	(8) on
(4) that / which	(9) and / or
(5) enough	(10) what

Teacher's Notes

Lesson Two

Structures

Comparisons

Vocabulary

Words

accustomed	manor house	rent
arch	mansion	request (v)
brood	master (n)	rural
cellar	meddle with	rush (v)
clatter (n)	misbehaviour	sense (v)
converse	mumble (v)	smooth
court (n)	mutter	squealing
flushed (adj)	offend	still (adj)
growl (v)	parlour	stride (v)
high-backed	pat (v)	tenant
indeed	path	threshold
instruct	pause (v)	wink (v)
leap (v)	pointer	
let	privacy	

Phrasal verbs

take to sb   tell sb off

Word pairs

back and forth	safe and sound
more or less	sick and tired
now and then	up and down
peace and quiet	

Other expressions

at one's expense	make faces
be on one's guard	pay sb a visit
come into contact with	take control of

reading

Background Note:
Emily Jane Brontë (1818-1848) wrote *Wuthering Heights*, which was set in Yorkshire, between October 1845 and June 1846. It was first published in 1847. However, it was only after her death that the book was recognised as one of the most important novels of the 19th century.

optional pre-reading activity

- Ask Ss questions that will prepare them for what they are about to read.
  e.g. *Do you like reading books?*
       Have you heard of Emily Brontë? Have you read any books by her?
- Discuss and elicit answers.

1 **Aim: to give Ss practice in understanding text organisation**
- Ask Ss to read through the text for gist, without worrying about the gaps.
- Ask Ss to try to guess what each of the missing sentences is about.
- Ask Ss to look at the sentences A-H which have been

removed from the text and ensure that they understand them.
- Point out to Ss that they should always look for clues in the sentences which precede or follow the gaps. To this end, Ss may be helped by determiners *(this, that)* and subject / object personal pronouns *(he / him, she / her)* which refer to things or people mentioned in previous or later sentences. When there are no such cohesive devices, Ss should rely strongly on context.
- Ask Ss to read the first paragraph of the text and decide which sentence best fits in the first gap.
- Check answers and ask Ss to underline the key words / phrases which helped them decide.
- Ask Ss to read the text paragraph by paragraph and do the rest of the activity.
- Point out to Ss that if they cannot decide what fits in a gap, they should move on and get back to it later.
- Check answers and ask Ss to provide justification.

Key

1 G Text		**Missing sentence**
... as I rode up. 'Walk in!' he interrupted.		He led me up the path that led to the main house ... to take my horse. *He* refers to Mr Heathcliff who takes Lockwood up to the house.
2 E Text		**Missing sentence**
... whispering and a great deal of clatter from deep within the kitchen.		... no signs of roasting, boiling or baking about the huge fireplace. (these activities usually take place in a kitchen)
3 A Text		**Missing sentence**
... a huge female pointer. ... to pat the dog.		She ... growled angrily. *She* refers to the dog.
4 D Text		**Missing sentence**
... the pointer, the puppies and a pair of slightly smaller dogs. ... they quickly grew ...		... their sharp teeth ... ... at the three of them. *Their* and *them* refer to the dogs.
5 F Text		**Missing sentence**
... the female pointer suddenly jumped up ...		... she remained there ... *She* refers to the female pointer.
6 H Text		**Missing sentence**
... take some water ... Your health sir!'		... I took the glass and raised it. Lockwood responds to Mr Heathcliff's toast.
7 B Text		**Missing sentence**
... converse with me ... He didn't seem very keen on the idea ...		... I so enjoyed our conversation ... ... decided to pay him another visit ... *He* and *him* refer to Mr Heathcliff.

Extra sentence: C

- When the activity is over, explain unknown words through definitions or example sentences.

optional post-reading activity

Ask Ss questions of personal response to the topic of the reading text.
e.g. *What kind of person do you think Heathcliff was? How would the atmosphere of the house make you feel?*

words and phrases

1 Idioms

Aim: to introduce different word pairs and give Ss
practice in using them in context

- Ask Ss to read through the extract again and find the
  word pairs *sick and tired* and *peace and quiet*.
  Discuss their meanings.
- Ask Ss to read through the rest of the word pairs in
  the box and discuss their meanings. Provide Ss with
  examples when necessary.
- Have Ss do the activity.
- Check answers.

Key

a. peace and quiet
b. sooner or later
c. up and down
d. sick and tired
e. safe and sound

> **optional**
> If there is time, ask Ss to make their own sentences
> using the word pairs and check them.

2 Words easily confused

Aim: to give Ss practice in distinguishing between
words that can easily be confused

- Refer Ss to the verb *rent* in the extract (*... a young
  man ...* **rents** *a house from ... / ... my decision to*
  rent *a manor house ...*)
- Encourage Ss to work out the difference in meaning.

rent = to pay money to sb to use sth that they own,
such as a house, some land, a machine, etc.
to allow sb to use sth that you own in exchange for
payment
hire = to pay money to borrow sth for a short time (e.g.
a car, room, video)
let = to allow sb to use a room, house, etc. in
exchange for payment

- Ask Ss to do the rest of the exercise, one set at a
  time. For each set, explain the difference through
  definitions and / or examples. You can also refer Ss
  to the extract whenever necessary.

guest = a person that you have invited to your house
(**Guests** *are so rare in this house ...*)
tenant = a person who pays rent to stay in a room,
house, etc. to the person who owns it (*'I'm Mr
Lockwood, your new* **tenant** *... / ... to offend a
potential* **tenant** *...*)
landlord = a man from whom you rent a room,
house, etc. (*... opposite my* **landlord** *...*)

comfortable = making you feel relaxed; pleasant to
wear, sit on, etc. (*... never have a* **comfortable**
home;)
convenient = useful, easy or quick to do
suitable = right or appropriate for a particular
purpose or occasion

room = a part of a building that has its own walls,
floor and ceiling and is usually used for a particular
purpose
(*... the family sitting* **room** *...*)
area = part of a place, town, etc. or a region of a
country or the world
space = an amount of an area of a place that is
empty or is available for use

stairs = a set of steps built between two floors inside
a building
step = a surface that you put your foot on, especially
to walk on a higher or lower level (*One* **step** *brought
us into ...*)
staircase = a set of stairs inside a building including
the posts and rails that are fixed on the side

- Check answers.

Key

a. hire	b. rent	c. let
a. guests	b. landlord	c. tenants
a. suitable	b. comfortable	c. convenient
a. area	b. room	c. space / room
a. staircase	b. stairs	c. steps

> **optional**
> If there is time, ask Ss to make their own sentences
> using the words presented above and check them.

Teacher's Notes

grammar

1 **Aim: to revise the comparative and superlative forms of adjectives and adverbs**
- Ask Ss to read through the sentences 1-4 and the functions a-b and ensure that they understand them.
- Have Ss do the exercise.
- Check answers.

Key

1. b   2. a   3 b   4. a

2 **Aim: to present Ss with adverbs grading comparative forms**
- Ask Ss to read through sentences 1-2 and functions a-b and ensure that they understand them.
- Have Ss do the exercise.
- Check answers.

Key

1. b   2. a

optional

If there is time, ask Ss to make their own examples using the adverbs grading comparatives above and check their answers.

3 **Aim: to present the structure *the+comparative, the+comparative***
- Ask Ss to read the sentence.
- Elicit what it means and what the structure is used for.
- Ask Ss to complete the rule.
- Check answers.

Key

The structure **the** + *comparative*, **the** + *comparative* is used to describe two actions or situations which are directly related to one another and happen at the same time.

4 **Aim: to give Ss practice in using comparisons in context**
- Ask Ss to do the exercise.
- Check answers.

Key

1. the most suitable
2. more comfortable than
3. more, better
4. faster than
5. the biggest
6. better than
7. colder than

listening

Aim: to give Ss practice in listening for specific information through a T / F activity
- Ask Ss to read through sentences 1-7.
- Explain any unknown words in the sentences.
- Play the CD twice.
- Check answers.

Key

1 T   2 F   3 T   4 T   5 F   6 T   7 F

optional post-listening activity

Ask Ss questions of personal response to the topic of the listening.
e.g. *Does the idea of living in a tree house / 'button house' / four-wheel home appeal to you?*
What things should be taken into consideration when building a house?

Teacher's Notes

Lesson Three

Vocabulary

be located	spacious
extension	suburb
hesitate	tool shed
neglect	workshop

Expressions

at one's earliest convenience
meet one's needs

speaking

1 Aim: to give Ss practice in speculating and making a decision
- Divide Ss into pairs.
- Explain to Ss that they have to look at the plan of the house and decide where each of the rooms mentioned above should be located.
- Engage Ss in meaningful and realistic conversations. Encourage them to use the expressions in the box.
- Elicit answers.

Key

Suggested ideas:
- I think that the room next to the bathroom would be ideal for Dean and Susan's bedroom.
- It would be a good idea if the girls' bedroom was next to their parents' bedroom.
- It would be a good idea if the playroom was next to the WC.
- It would be convenient if the dining room was next to the kitchen and the living room in the open space between the kitchen and the hall.

2 Aim: to elaborate and expand on the topic of the speaking activity
- Ask Ss to read the questions and generate discussion.

Key

Suggested ideas:
- Open answers.
- Open answers.
- Living in a house is more comfortable than living in a flat because a house is more spacious than a flat is. However, blocks of flats are ideal for accommodating people in big cities.

writing

1 **Aims: · to activate Ss' background knowledge**
· to prepare Ss for the writing task
· Ask Ss the questions and generate discussion.

2 **Aim: to help Ss identify the stylistic features of**
a formal letter giving information
· Ask Ss to read through the extract from Mr Wilson's letter and answer the first question.
· Discuss answers.
· Ask Ss to read through the letter of reply and answer the second question.
· Discuss answers.

Key

· Mr Wilson's letter is formal:
a. he uses formal letter layout (he has left a line between paragraphs which have not been indented) and a formal way of signing off (*Yours sincerely*, signature, full name).
b. the language he uses is also quite formal, with formal expressions and no contracted forms.
   (*I was wondering whether …*
   In addition, I would like to know …
   Furthermore, could you tell me whether ...
   Finally, I would appreciate some information…
   particularly with regard to ...
   Thank you in advance for your time and assistance.
   I look forward to a reply at your earliest convenience.)
· The information that shouldn't have been included in the reply is the following:
   He is now studying … to sell the house.
   (where Mrs Keaney's son is and why she wants to sell the house is not Mr Wilson's concern.)
   You see, … a garage.
   (Mr Wilson only needs to know if it is big enough to be used as a workshop. Its history does not concern him.)

3 **Aim: to give Ss practice in writing a formal**
letter giving information
· Ask Ss to read through the extract and the notes on it. Provide Ss with explanations if necessary.
· Assign the writing task for homework.

Revision 07-09

reading

1 **Aim: to give Ss practice in scanning a text to find specific information**

- Ask Ss a few pre-reading questions related to the topic of the text and generate discussion.
  e.g. *How do animals help people?*
  Have you heard of any animals that have performed heroic acts?
- Ask Ss to read through the text for gist.
- Ask Ss to read through the questions and ensure that they understand them.
- Before the second reading, point out to Ss that they should look for key words / phrases in the text.
- Ask Ss the first question and allow them some time to answer it.
- Check answers and ask Ss to underline the key words / phrases which helped them decide.
- Do the same for the rest of the questions.
- Check answers and ask Ss to provide justification.

Key

1. **B** (*… two courageous chimpanzees … were used to test the safety of space travel.*)
2. **A** (*Cher Ami was awarded the French 'Croix de Guerre' and a gold medal …*)
3. **C** (*Stubby was promoted to honorary sergeant …*)
   The answers to questions 2 and 3 can be given in any order.
4. **A** (*… pigeons are still used to deliver much-needed medication in remote areas …*)
5. **D** (*… a young girl's pet rat …*)
6. **A** (*… completed their missions, even when they were badly injured.*)
7. **C** (*He was also made honorary member of the American Red Cross.*)

- When the activity is over, explain unknown words through definitions or example sentences.

Teacher's Notes

Use of English

1 Aim: to revise various language forms through a multiple choice cloze exercise

- Ask Ss to read through the text for gist, without paying attention to the gaps.
- Ask Ss to read the text again, one sentence at a time.
- Ask Ss to read the four options carefully, before deciding which one best fits in each space.
- Have Ss do the activity.
- Check answers.

Key

(1) D	(9) D
(2) A	(10) C
(3) D	(11) D
(4) B	(12) A
(5) D	(13) B
(6) A	(14) A
(7) B	(15) C
(8) C	

2 Aim: to check structural accuracy through an open cloze exercise

- Ask Ss to read the text for gist, without paying attention to the gaps.
- Ask Ss to fill in the gaps with one word only.
- Have Ss do the activity.
- Check answers.

Key

(16) K
(17) N
(18) A
(19) O
(20) D
(21) M
(22) B
(23) E
(24) L
(25) J

Use of English (continued)

3 **Aim: to check structural accuracy through an error correction exercise**

- Ask Ss to read through the text for gist, without trying to correct anything.
- Ask Ss to read the text again, one sentence at a time and try to identify which of the lines are correct and which contain a word which should not be there.
- Have Ss do the activity.
- Check answers.

Key

26	it
27	than
28	will
29	✓
30	✓
31	other
32	might
33	✓
34	them
35	✓
36	all
37	only
38	about
39	✓
40	in

Teacher's Notes

Use of English (continued)

4 **Aim: to translate the Chinese given in brackets into English through a translating exercise**

- Ask Ss to read the text for gist.
- Point out to Ss that before completing the gaps, they should decide on which phrases are needed for each blank.
- Have Ss do the activity.
- Check answers.

Key

41 From a health perspective
42 establish a rhythm that is relaxing and peaceful
43 going for a walk is an invitation for surprise
44 commit to meet each week at a set time
45 picturesque but accessible

listening

Aim: to give Ss further practice in listening for gist through a matching activity

- Ask Ss to read through the statements A-F. Make sure they understand what they mean.
- Point out to Ss that they can note possible choices during the first listening, but should finalise their answers only after the second listening since there is one extra answer which could mislead them.
- Play the CD twice.
- Check answers.

Key

Speaker 1: E
Speaker 2: C
Speaker 3: F
Speaker 4: D
Speaker 5: A

Extra letter: B

10 Art works

Functions

Making suggestions

Structures

Relative Clauses - Participle Clauses

Vocabulary

Words and expressions

be full of oneself	define	point of view
brand	(dis)graceful	pottery
cause a stir	medium	promote
commercial (adj)	mentor	representative
(in)competence	papier-mâché	wood carving
conservative	picturesque	

Idioms with colours

be green with envy	in black and white
be in sb's black books	out of the blue
be tickled pink	see red
give the green light	till one is blue in the face

presentation

Aim: to present vocabulary and structures in the
context of a radio interview about the nature of art

1 **Aim: to relate the topic of the unit to Ss'
background knowledge and experience**
- Ask Ss to look at the questions and generate
discussion.
- Elicit answers.

Key

Suggested ideas:
- Open answers
- the making of works that express the artist's
feelings and inner world
- to express feelings and ideas / to educate / to make
people think / to deliver messages

2 **Aim: to give Ss practice in listening for specific
information with the aid of visual prompts**
- Ask Ss to look at the pictures a-d.
- Play the CD.
- Check answers.

Key

Picture *c* accurately represents Ripley's art (*Nothing
more than silly stick figures on the Internet ...*)

3 **Aim: to give Ss practice in listening for gist
through a matching exercise**
- Ask Ss to read through the statements 1-3. Explain
any unknown words if necessary.
- Play the CD again.
- Check answers.

Key

1. R   2. R   3. M

---

optional

Ask Ss questions of personal response to the topic of
the listening text.

e.g. *What do you think of Ripley's views on the
nature of art?*
Would you be interested in Ripley's work?

Teacher's Notes

words and phrases

1 Word building

A Aim: to introduce and practice the formation of concrete and abstract nouns related to art

- Ask Ss to read through the examples in the table and discuss them. Ensure that Ss don't have any unknown words.
- Have Ss do the exercise.
- Check answers.

Key

Artist	Art
sculptor	sculpture
painter	**painting**
musician	music
architect	**architecture**
designer	**design**
potter	pottery
dancer	dance
poet	**poetry**
actor / actress	acting

B Aim: to give Ss practice in using abstract and concrete nouns in context

- Ask Ss to do the exercise.
- Check answers.

Key

a. paintings
b. pottery
c. dancer
d. music
e. designer

> **optional**
> If there is time, ask Ss to make their own sentences with the rest of the nouns presented in ex. A and check them.

2 Idioms

Aims: · to present idioms with colours
· to give Ss practice in inferring their meanings through a matching exercise

- Ask Ss to read through the sentences 1-8. Ensure that Ss don't have any unknown words.
- Ask Ss to read through the meanings a-h. Ensure that Ss don't have any unknown words.
- Before asking Ss to do the exercise, discuss the meanings of the idioms in bold. Ss should rely on their background knowledge of the world. You may also ask Ss whether any of these idioms exist in their own culture or mother tongue.
- Have Ss do the exercise.
- Check answers.

Key

1. c	5. d
2. b	6. g
3. a	7. h
4. e	8. f

> **optional**
> If there is time, ask Ss to make their own sentences using some of the idioms and check them.

Teacher's Notes

grammar

1 **Aims:** · **to present relative pronouns introducing relative clauses**
· **to help Ss elicit the meaning of relative pronouns**

· Ask Ss to read through the sentences a-d and underline the relative pronouns in them.
· Ask Ss the questions.
· Elicit and check answers.

Key

(The following relative pronouns should be circled in sentences a-d:)
a. *which* b. *who* c. *where* d. *whose*
· where
· who
· whose
· which

2 **Aim: to help Ss distinguish between defining and non-defining relative clauses through a matching activity**

· Ask Ss to read through the two relative clauses.
· Ask Ss to read through the two explanations that follow. Ensure that Ss understand the terms used and, in particular, the difference between defining and non-defining relative clauses.
· Have Ss do the exercise.
· Elicit and check answers. If necessary, provide Ss with further examples and / or explanations.

Key

1. b   2.a

· Now tell Ss to read through the two sentences again.
· Ask Ss the questions.
· Discuss and elicit answers. If necessary, provide Ss with further examples and / or explanations.

Key

The relative pronoun can be omitted in sentence 2 because it is the object of the relative clause.

3 **Aims:** · **to present participle clauses by elaborating on relative clauses**
· **to help Ss elicit one of the meanings of participle clauses**

· Ask Ss to read though the example from the presentation.
· Ask Ss to read the question and the two options that follow.
· Ask Ss the question. Elicit and check answers.
· Read out and explain the note. Ensure that Ss fully understand what a present participle is. If necessary, provide them with further examples and / or explanations.

Key

The correct answer is b.

4 **Aim: to give Ss practice in using relative and participle clauses in context**

· Ask Ss to do the exercise.
· Check answers.

Key

1. My boss, who is from Canada, has been living here for 15 years. / My boss, who has been living here for 15 years, is from Canada.
2. That boy, who is talking to the teacher at the moment, obviously comes from Australia. / That boy talking to the teacher at the moment obviously comes from Australia.
3. Sarah, whose flat was burgled last week, decided to move out.
4. A man, who was wearing black clothes and a ski mask, attacked me yesterday. / A man wearing black clothes and a ski mask attacked me yesterday.
5. The village where we spent the weekend was very picturesque. / The village at / in which we spent the weekend was very picturesque. / The village we spent the weekend in / at was very picturesque.
6. The film, which won seven Oscars, was a great success.

Lesson Two

Determiners

Vocabulary

Words

abstract	incredible	random
acquisition	intellectually	relevant
ape	interpretation	restriction
appealing	literate	scribbles (n)
awareness	masterpiece	sign (n)
delicacy	observation	splattered (adj)
differentiate	obstacle	struggling (adj)
emotion	outperform	trace (v)
extraordinary	phenomenal	unlike
foundation	possession	
illustrate	profit	

Phrasal verbs and expressions

a standing joke	place a limit on
in question	put out
pick out	rumour has it

reading

Background Note:

Expressionism is a major artistic movement that strives to express people's feelings rather than show events or objects in a realistic way. It developed during the late 19th and 20th centuries.

optional pre-reading activity

- Ask Ss to read the title of the reading text and look at the photograph accompanying it.
- Ask Ss to predict the content of the reading text. You may ask Ss the following question:
  e.g. *What might the connection between gorillas and a gallery be?*
- Discuss and elicit answers.

Aim: to give Ss practice in understanding the structure of a gapped text through a matching activity

- Ask Ss to read through the text for gist, without worrying about the gaps.
- Ask Ss to guess what kind of information is missing in each paragraph.
- Ask Ss to read through the paragraphs A-F. Ensure that Ss understand them.
- Before the second reading of the text, point out to Ss that they should always look for key words or phrases in the text which are related to those in the missing paragraphs. To this end, Ss may be helped by paying close attention to what precedes or follows the gaps. Determiners such as *this, that* or subject / object personal pronouns referring to people or things mentioned in previous or later sentences may help towards this direction. Ss should also rely strongly on context, especially when there are no clear cohesive devices.
- Ask Ss to read the first paragraph of the text and decide

which of the paragraphs A-F best fits in the first gap.
- Check answers and ask Ss to underline the key words / phrases which helped them decide.
- Ask Ss to read the text paragraph by paragraph and do the rest of the activity in the same way as described above.
- Point out to Ss that if they cannot decide what fits in a gap, they should move on and get back to it later.
- Check answers and ask Ss to provide justification.

Key

1 D

Text	Missing paragraphs
... compare the work ... the ape world ...	*... do a better job ...* *... two gorillas ...* The names of the gorillas are also introduced.

2 B

Text	Missing paragraphs
	Their work ... refers to the work of the chimps mentioned in the previous paragraph of the text.
In the 1950s ... The Gorilla Foundation was established in 1976 *... (time sequence of the events).*	*... expressionism ... popular at the time.*

3 A

Text	Missing paragraphs
Koko ... drew a glass ... while Michael drew a picture of his friend ...	*... about Michael's and Koko's paintings ...*

4 E

Text	Missing paragraphs
The pictures they made to illustrate feelings ...	*... inspired by a bouquet of flowers ...*
... both Koko and Michael gave the paintings titles.	*... what he would call the painting, he signed ...*

5 C

Text	Missing paragraphs
.... these incredible animals ...	*... being successful artists ...* *... have also done exceptionally well in IQ tests ... can intellectually outperform a number of us.*

Extra paragraph: F

- When the activity is over, explain unknown words through definitions or example sentences.

optional post-reading activity

- Ask Ss questions of personal response to the topic of the reading text.
  e.g. *What do you think of Koko's and Michael's work? Have you heard of any stories about animals being as creative as Koko and Michael?*

words and phrases

1 Phrasal verbs and expressions

Aim: to give Ss practice in matching the phrasal verbs and expressions in the reading text with their meanings
- Refer Ss to the article.
- Ask Ss to do the exercise.
- Check answers.

Key

a. point out
b. rumour had it
c. pick out

d. in question
e. a standing joke
f. put out

> **optional**
> If there is time, ask Ss to make their own sentences using the phrasal verbs and expressions and check them.

2 Word building

Aims: • to introduce common negative prefixes of adjectives
  • to give Ss practice in forming the opposites of adjectives
- Read out and explain the introductory comment.
- Ask Ss to do the exercise.
- Check answers.

Key

adjective	opposite adjective
possible	**impossible**
appealing	**unappealing**
successful	**unsuccessful**
satisfied	**dissatisfied**
relevant	**irrelevant**
legal	**illegal**
appropriate	**inappropriate**
familiar	**unfamiliar**
believable	**unbelievable**
literate	**illiterate**

B Aim: to give Ss practice in using the opposites of adjectives in context
- Ask Ss to read through the sentences a-f and do the exercise.
- Check answers.

Key

a. familiar
b. illegal
c. irrelevant

d. impossible
e. appropriate
f. literate

grammar

1 **Aim: to help Ss infer the meanings of determiners through a matching activity**
- Ask Ss to read through the sentences 1-5.
- Ask Ss to read through the explanations a-e. Ensure that Ss understand the terms used.
- Have Ss do the activity.
- Check answers. If necessary, provide Ss with further explanations and / or examples.

Key

1. c   2. e   3. d   4. b   5. a

2 **Aim: to give Ss practice in using determiners in context**
- Have Ss do the activity.
- Check answers.

Key

1. Both ... and ...   6. Neither ... nor ...
2. All   7. all
3. neither ... nor ...   8. Both ... and ...
4. either ... or ...   9. All
5. none

— Teacher's Notes —

listening

Aim: to give Ss practice in listening for specific information through a multiple choice activity
- Ask Ss to read through the six situations. Explain any unknown words if necessary.
- Play the CD twice.
- Check answers.

Key

1 A   2 A   3 A   4 B   5 C   6 B

optional post-listening activity
You may ask Ss further questions of personal response to the listening text.
e.g. *Would you ever invest money in a piece of art? Why / Why not?*

— Teacher's Notes —

Lesson Three

Vocabulary

action-packed (adj)	fast-paced (adj)
age-old (adj)	predict
beneath	(un)predictable
bizarre	take on
box-office hit	unfold
convey	wannabe
desperate	

speaking

Background Note:
Stand-up comedy is a new form of entertainment involving one person on a stage trying to amuse the audience by telling jokes, doing imitations, etc.

1 Aim: to relate the topic of the speaking activity to Ss' preferences and background knowledge
- Ask Ss to look at the questions and generate discussion.
- Elicit answers.

2 Aim: to give Ss practice in prioritising in order to reach a consensus
- Divide Ss into pairs.
- Tell Ss to look at the festival programme and read through the events described in it. Ensure that Ss understand what each event is about.
- Engage Ss in meaningful and realistic conversations.
- Point out to Ss that they can agree or disagree giving reasons for their choices as long as they manage to reach a consensus on the three events they would most like to attend together.
- Have Ss do the activity.
- Elicit answers.

Key

Suggested ideas:
A: Here's the programme for the three-day arts festival I was telling you about the other day.
B: Let me have a look! Oh, there are so many interesting events taking place that I wish we could attend all of them!
A: I know, but since exams are quite soon and we have to study, I think we should choose the ones that we're really interested in!
B: Well, to begin with, I think we shouldn't miss the Film Festival for the world! Black and white films are so cool!
A: Yes, they are! I would also like to attend the Graffiti Exhibition. Have you seen that amazing graffiti on the wall opposite the railway station? It's incredible! Maybe, this is my chance to prove my creativity!
B: What about Stand-up Comedy Night? I heard that it's really funny.
A: With all this pressure at school, I think I could do with a good laugh!

B: Now, shall we go to the Contemporary Crafts Exhibition? We'll have a chance to test our D.I.Y. skills.
A: Well, to tell you the truth, I would much prefer to go to the concert. Good music and dancing will help recharge our batteries. Don't you think so?
B: Yes, you're right! I can't wait!

3 Aim: to elaborate and expand on the topic of the speaking activity
- Ask Ss to look at the questions and generate discussion.
- Elicit answers.

Key

Suggested ideas:
- cost of materials / artist's reputation / the age of the work of art / public opinion
- paintings / sculptures
- talent / need to express themselves
- feelings / ideas about the world around them
- Yes, because art gives students the chance to be creative, reveal hidden talents and broaden their minds / No, because not all students are equally talented / students should not waste school time on art / it is not a requirement for most jobs

Teacher's Notes

writing

1 **Aim: to prepare Ss for the writing task by relating it to Ss' preferences and background knowledge**

- Ask Ss to look at the questions and generate discussion.
- Elicit answers.

2 **Aim: to help Ss understand the structure of a book review by identifying the main ideas of each paragraph**

- Ask Ss to read through the review for gist. Explain any unknown words Ss might have.
- Have Ss do the exercise.
- Check answers.

Key

Introduction

para. 1: *The Time Machine*, written by H.G. Wells, was ... a hundred years ago.

Main part

para. 2: *The Time Machine* is a science fiction story ... and their gardens are overgrown.

para. 3: Then, a terrible thing ... this bizarre future world forever ...

para. 4: The book is very well written, ... and the story flows smoothly.

Conclusion

para. 5: If you haven't read ... to put down.

3 Improve your style

Aim: to elaborate on descriptive adjectives as a major stylistic feature of a film review

- Ask Ss to read through the review for gist. Explain any unknown words Ss might have. However, don't explain any of the words in the box. Ss should rely on context to make reasonable guesses.
- Have Ss do the exercise.
- Check answers.

Key

(1) action-packed
(2) desperate
(3) unpredictable
(4) frightening
(5) first-class
(6) impressive
(7) box-office hit
(8) hugely entertaining

4 Writing task

Aim: to give Ss practice in writing a film review

- Assign the writing task for homework.

Teacher's Notes

11 On the couch

Lesson One

Functions

Expressing time, reason and contrast

Structures

Causative Form

Vocabulary

Words

apologetic	fund (n)	seated
aware	indicate	self-control
bent	list (n)	stress (v / n)
branch (n)	outer space	subject (n)
clenched	picture (v)	superior
compelled	plumber	tackle (v)
co-worker	pole	tap (n)
crossed	potentially	tense (adj)
defence	provoke	timing (n)
defensive	re-launch (v)	transfer (v)
eager beaver	restrained	worthwhile
facial expression	reverse (v)	yawn (n)

Phrasal verbs and expressions

break through	ring off the hook
collect one's thoughts	sort sth out
cut sb off	strain at the leash
head up	tie up all the loose ends
look out for	'to-do' list
push one's luck	

presentation

Aim: to present vocabulary and structures in the context of an article about body language

1 **Aim:** to arouse Ss interest in the topic of the presentation by asking them questions that relate it to their personal experience

• Ask Ss to look at the questions and generate discussion.

2 **Aims:** • to give Ss practice in reading for gist
• to transfer from verbal to visual information through a matching activity

• Have Ss read the first paragraph and ask them which picture it refers to.
• Elicit answers.
• Ask Ss to read the rest of the text paragraph by paragraph and do the rest of the activity.
• Check answers.

Key

a. 4	b. 5	c. 1	d. 2	e. 3

• When the activity is over ask Ss some more questions.
e.g. *What should you do before you tell your dad about his crashed car?*
Why would you want to have your co-worker transferred to a branch in outer space?
• Encourage Ss to guess the meaning of new vocabulary such as *co-operative, ring off the hook* and *eager beaver*. Provide explanations through definitions or example sentences.

optional post-reading activity

Ask Ss questions of personal response to the topic of the reading text.
e.g. *Have you ever found yourself in a situation similar o the ones described in the text?*
If so, did the other person's body language give you a clue as to how they were feeling?

Teacher's Notes

words and phrases

1 Phrasal verbs and expressions

Aim: to give Ss practice in inferring the meaning of the phrasal verbs and expressions in the article through a matching activity

- Refer Ss to the article.
- Ask Ss to do the activity.
- Check answers.

Key

1. d   2. e   3. a   4. b   5. f   6. c

> **optional**
> If there is time, ask Ss to make their own sentences using the phrasal verbs and expressions and check them.

2 Idioms

Aims: • **to present idioms expressing feelings**
        • **to give Ss practice in inferring the meaning of idioms from context**

- Ask Ss to read through sentences 1-7 and the words in the box.
- Have Ss do the exercise. Ss should try to make educated guesses by relying on their background knowledge. You may ask Ss if they can relate any of the idioms to their mother tongue.
- Check answers.

Key

1. fear
2. anger
3. eagerness
4. eagerness
5. happiness
6. happiness
7. fear

> **optional**
> If there is time, ask Ss to make their own sentences using the idioms and check them.

3 Words easily confused

Aim: to give Ss practice in distinguishing between words that can easily be confused

- Refer Ss to the verb *indicate* in the article (*... this could **indicate** that she's feeling tense*).
- Encourage Ss to work out the difference in meaning.

indicate = be a sign of sth; to show that sth is possible or likely
reveal = make sth known (especially sth that was kept a secret)
express = show or make a feeling, an opinion, etc. known

- Ask Ss to do the rest of the exercise, one set at a time. For each set, explain the difference through definitions and / or examples. You can also refer Ss to the article whenever necessary.

transmit = to send an electronic signal, radio or television broadcast
transport = to take sth / sb from one place to another in a vehicle
transfer (sth / sb from ... to ...) = to move from one place to another (*... your co-worker should be **transferred** to a branch in outer space ...*)

cause = to make sth happen, especially sth bad or unpleasant (*... to pay for the damage you **caused**!*)
create = to make sth happen or exist
provoke = say or do sth that you know will annoy sb so that they react in an angry way

- Check answers.

Key

a. indicate
a. Transferring
a. provoke
b. expresses
b. transport
b. caused
c. reveal
c. transmit
c. create

> **optional**
> If there is time, ask Ss to make their own sentences using the words presented above and check them.

Teacher's Notes

grammar

1 **Aim: to help Ss infer the use of the causative form**

- Ask Ss to read through sentences a-c. Ensure that Ss understand them.
- Ask Ss to answer questions 1-3.
- Elicit and check answers. If necessary, provide Ss with further explanations and / or examples.

Key

1. c   2. b   3. a

2 **Aim: to give Ss practice in using the causative form in context**

- Read out and explain the rules. Ensure that Ss understand the difference between the two patterns.
- Have Ss do the exercise.
- Check answers.

Key

1. Have the students answered
2. 'll have my mother pick up
3. had the tap fixed
4. had the secretary type
5. had the candidate fill out
6. is having his hair cut / is going to have his hair cut
7. watered the flowers

English in use

Aim: to check structural accuracy through an open cloze exercise

- Ask Ss to read through the text for gist, without paying attention to the gaps.
- Ask Ss to fill in the gaps with one word only.
- Check answers.

Key

(1) had
(2) of
(3) have
(4) just / only / simply
(5) Apart
(6) when / if
(7) can / will / may
(8) too
(9) to
(10) have / take

Lesson Two

question refers to.

Structures

Adverbial clauses I (time, reason, concession)

Vocabulary

Words

acknowledgement	optimistic
apparent	orphan
autonomy	outstanding
bankruptcy	panic attack
boost (v)	percentage
challenge (v)	pursue (v)
claustrophobia	reject (v)
cutback	resolution
despair (v)	reward (v)
energetic	rut
factor	steadily
goal	strive (v)
hierarchy	the basics
lack (v)	workplace
mega-achiever	

Phrasal verbs and expressions

breathe down sb's neck	hang around
come to light	last but not least
come to the conclusion	see sth through
fall into	set one's sights higher
fight a losing battle	statistically speaking
gain control over	the bottom line

optional pre-reading activity

- Ask Ss to read the title of the article and look at the picture accompanying it.
- Ask Ss to predict the content of the article. You can also ask Ss the following questions.
  e.g. *What makes you want to succeed in something? Is there anything negative about being ambitious?*
- Discuss and elicit answers.

reading

1 **Aim: to give Ss practice in reading for specific information through a multiple choice exercise**

- Ask Ss to read the text for gist, without worrying about the unknown words.
- Ask Ss to read the stem of each question (not the options).
- Ask Ss to read the text again paragraph by paragraph and try to find the part of the text each

- Point out to Ss that they have to pay close attention to specific details in the text in order to answer the questions since some of the options may be distracting.
- Ask Ss to read the options of each question and choose the answer that fits best according to the meaning of the text.
- Check answers and ask Ss to provide justification.

Key

1 **D** (*... once we've collected the basics, we set our sights higher.*)
2 **B** (*... a large percentage of successful people interviewed had lost a parent, been rejected by a parent or suffered some other tragic loss before the age of eighteen.*)
3 **D** (*... people who are successful on a more moderate level are usually motivated by a negative happening in their early lives.*)
4 **A** (*You have to be trusted in order to get on with your work without having your employer breathing down your neck.*)
5 **C** (*... most of us are not sufficiently motivated.*)
6 **D** (*... it's a good idea to define what you really want by writing it down.*)

- When the activity is over, explain unknown words through definitions or example sentences.

optional post-reading activity

Ask Ss questions of personal response to the topic of the reading text.
e.g. *Have you ever had a positive outcome from a negative experience?*

Teacher's Notes

words and phrases

1 Expressions

Aim: to give Ss practice in inferring the meaning of the expressions in the article through a matching activity

- Refer Ss to the article.
- Ask Ss to do the activity.
- Check answers.

Key

1. e	2. d	3. a	4. c	5. b

> **optional**
>
> If there is time, ask Ss to make their own sentences using the expressions above and check them.

2 Word building

Aim: to give Ss practice in word formation in context

- Ask Ss to do the activity.
- Check answers.

Key

1. achievement
2. conclusion
3. actions
4. acknowledgement
5. encourage
6. motivate
7. collecting

Teacher's Notes

grammar

1 **Aim: to help Ss identify different types of adverbial clauses and their uses**

- Ask Ss to read through sentences 1-6 and ensure that they understand them.
- Ask Ss to identify what type of clause each sentence is.
- Elicit and check answers.

Key

1. b   2. a   3. c   4. b   5. a   6. c

- Now ask Ss to read through the rules that follow. Ensure that Ss understand all the terms used.
- Have Ss complete the rules.
- Elicit and check answers.

Key

Clauses of time express time relations. They are introduced with _when_, _once_, _while_, _as soon as_, _before_, _since_, _after_, _until_, etc.

Clauses of reason express the reason for something. They are introduced with _because / as / since_ + subject + _verb_. To express reason we can also use _because of / due to_ + _-ing form_ and _noun_ or _the fact_ + _that clause_.

Clauses of concession express contrast or opposition. They are introduced with _although / even though_ + _subject_ + _verb_. To express concession we can also use _in spite of / despite_ + _-ing form_, _noun_ or _the fact_ + _that clause_.

optional

Give out to Ss separate slips of paper with adverbial clauses and the corresponding main clauses and ask them to match them.

2 **Aim: to give Ss practice in distinguishing between words introducing adverbial clauses**

- Ask Ss to read through the text for gist.
- Ask Ss to do the exercise.
- Check answers.

Key

(1) because
(2) although
(3) Once
(4) before
(5) In spite

listening

Aim: to give Ss practice in listening for specific information through a note taking activity

- Ask Ss to read through the sentences of the exercise. Explain any unknown words if necessary.
- Ask Ss to predict what kind of information is required.
- Point out to Ss that they should complete each of the sentences with a word or a short phrase from the listening text.
- Play the CD twice.
- Check answers.

Key

1. breathe
2. on the tube
3. heart attack
4. illness
5. twenties
6. car park
7. see a psychologist

optional post-listening activity

You may ask Ss further questions of personal response to the listening text.
e.g. _Have you got any phobias?_
Do you know of anybody who has?
What are your / their symptoms?
How do you / they try to get over it?

Teacher's Notes

Lesson Three

speaking

1 Aim: to generate discussion based on Ss' personal experiences and preferences

- Ask Ss to read the questions and generate discussion.

2 Aim: to give Ss practice in relating words to context

- Tell Ss to look at photographs a and b.
- Then ask Ss to look at the box and decide which words can be used to describe each photograph. Ensure that Ss don't have any unknown words. If necessary provide them with explanations and / or examples.
- Discuss answers.

Key

Photograph a: depression / depressed, despair, heartbroken, lonely
Photograph b: satisfied, uplifting, light-hearted, cheerful

3 Aim: to give Ss practice in comparing and contrasting two photographs

- Divide Ss into pairs.
- In each pair, ask one student to talk about how the people shown in the two photographs feel. Encourage him / her to use some of the words from exercise 2.
- Now ask the second student the question: *Would you rather spend time alone or with friends?*
- Elicit answers.

Key

Suggested ideas:
Photograph a: she looks sad / she could be feeling lonely / maybe she has a serious problem and she's in a state of despair / she might be suffering from depression / she might be heartbroken
Photograph b: the young people look cheerful / satisfied with what they have / they feel light-hearted

4 Aim: to elaborate and expand on the topic of the speaking activity

- Ask Ss to read the questions and generate discussion.

5 Aim: to give Ss practice in relating words to context

- Tell Ss to look at photographs c and d.
- Then ask Ss to look at the box and decide which words can be used to describe each photograph. Ensure that Ss don't have any unknown words. If necessary provide them with explanations and / or examples.
- Discuss answers.

Key

Photograph c: relaxing, relief, feel at ease, carefree
Photograph d: anxious, nervous, worry, stressed, stressful, tension

6 Aim: to give Ss practice in comparing and contrasting two photographs.

- Divide Ss into pairs.
- In each pair, ask one student to talk about what effect each situation has on the people shown in the photographs. Encourage him / her to use some of the words from exercise 5.
- Now ask the second student the question: *Which of the two situations are you most familiar with?*
- Elicit answers.

Key

Suggested ideas:
Photograph c: the people are relaxing at a lake and they feel at ease / they are carefree.
Photograph d: they are stressed / feel tension because of their tight schedules and stressful lifestyles / they are anxious to achieve / be successful.

7 Aim: to elaborate and expand on the topic of the speaking activity

- Ask Ss to read the questions and generate discussion.

writing

1 **Aim: to give Ss practice in using linking words / phrases in the context of a balanced essay**
- Ask Ss to read through the text for gist, without paying attention to the gaps.
- Ask Ss to read the linking words / phrases in the box and ensure that they understand them.
- Have Ss do the activity.
- Check answers.

Key

(1) Firstly	(5) In addition
(2) Furthermore	(6) Finally
(3) Although	(7) To sum up
(4) On the other hand	(8) As far as

2 **Aim: to identify the main idea of the essay in exercise 1**
- Ask Ss to read through the three headings and make sure that they understand them.
- Ask Ss to do the activity.
- Check answers and ask Ss to provide justification.

Key

b best describes the essay because it refers to both the positive and negative aspects of owning a pet.

3 **Aim: to identify the organisation of a balanced essay**
- Ask Ss to read through sentences a-e.
- Ask Ss to do the activity.
- Check answers.

Key

a. 2, 3	b. 3	c. 4, 5	d. 4	e. 2

3 Writing task

Aim:to give Ss practice in writing a balanced essay
- Assign the writing task for homework.

Teacher's Notes

12 Stop to shop

Functions

Expressing result and purpose

Structures

Adverbial Clauses II (Clauses of result)

Vocabulary

Words

battle (n)	consumer	sneaky
behavioural	mannequin	striking (adj)
bulb	pattern	tactics
catchy	pin	till (n)
cinnamon	rack	tilted (adj.)
clip	regardless of	wary
complexion	sentimental	

Phrasal verbs and expressions

at one's disposal	stop sb in their tracks
clear up	talk sb into + -ing form
go to any lengths	wise up
hang on to sth	

presentation

Aim: to present vocabulary and structures in the context of an article about methods shopkeepers use to make consumers spend more money

1 Aim: to introduce the topic of the unit by relating it to Ss' personal preferences and experiences

- Ask Ss to look at the questions and generate discussion.

2 Aim: to give Ss practice in identifying the main ideas of the paragraphs in an article through a matching activity

- Ask Ss to read through the text for gist, without paying attention to the gaps.
- Ask Ss to guess what each of the headings should be about.
- Ask Ss to read through the headings a-f. Ensure that Ss understand them.
- Before the second reading, point out to Ss that they should always look for key words / phrases in the article which are related to those in the headings.
- Now ask Ss to read the first paragraph of the article and decide on the most suitable heading. Ask them to underline the key words / phrases which helped them decide. Check answers.
- Ask Ss to read the text paragraph by paragraph and do the rest of the activity.

- Point out to Ss that if they cannot decide on a heading for a specific paragraph, they should move on and get back to it later.
- Check answers and ask Ss to provide justification.

Key

1 e (... window display ... gorgeous red dress ...)
2 a (... by paying more attention to you...)
3 f (... stimulate the senses ...)
4 d (... 50 per cent off rack ... low prices ...)
5 b (.... you suddenly look a bit slimmer and your complexion seems to have cleared up.)
6 c (... take your receipt and run!)

- When the activity is over, ask Ss some more questions.
  e.g. *What do you think of the methods used by shopkeepers to make consumers buy more and more?*
  Have you ever been persuaded to buy something that you didn't really need?
- Encourage Ss to guess the meaning of new vocabulary, such as *wary, striking* and *till*. Provide explanations through definitions or example sentences.

Teacher's Notes

words and phrases

1 Phrasal verbs and expressions

Aim: to help Ss match the phrasal verbs and expressions in the article with their meanings
- Refer Ss to the article.
- Ask Ss to read through the meanings a-f. Ensure that Ss understand them.
- Ask Ss to do the exercise.
- Check answers.

Key

a. stop you in your tracks
b. talk you into
c. wise up
d. go to any lengths
e. to have cleared up
f. at your disposal

> optional
> If there is time, ask Ss to make their own sentences using the phrasal verbs and expressions and check them.

2 Words easily confused

Aim: to give Ss practice in distinguishing between words that can easily be confused
- Refer Ss to the word *receipt* in the article (*... take your receipt and run!*).
- Encourage Ss to work out the difference in meaning of the first set of words.

receipt (n) = a piece of paper that proves that goods have been paid for
bill (n)= a piece of paper that shows how much you are charged for services you received
account (n)= an arrangement you have with a bank by which they take care of your money

- Ask Ss to do the rest of the exercise, one set at a time. For each set, explain the difference through definitions and / or examples. You can also refer Ss to the article whenever necessary.

price (n)= the amount of money that you have to pay for sth (*... regardless of the low prices.*)
cost (n)= how much sb needs to get by
value (n)= the quality of being useful or important

sale (n)= the act of selling sth (*... it can actually increase sales / ... you might find something on sale ...*)
offer (n)= sth sold at a lower price than usual or given for free when making a purchase
discount (n)= an amount of money that is taken off the usual cost of sth

spend (v)= give money to pay for goods or services (*... and encourage customers to spend, spend, spend ...*)

spare (v)= be (un)able to afford or give time or money *waste* (v)= use more of sth than is necessary
- Check answers.

Key

a. receipt	b. bill	c. account
a. cost	b. value	c. price
a. sale	b. discount	c. offer
a. spent	b. waste	c. spare

> optional
> If there is time, ask Ss to make their own sentences using the words presented above and check them.

Teacher's Notes

grammar

1 **Aim: to elicit the meaning of the structures** *so ... that* **and** *such ... that*

- Ask Ss to read through the first sentence and answer the first question.
- Do the same for the second set of questions.
- Elicit and check answers.

Key

- Because it is important.
- No, there isn't.
- You'd rather hang on to your money.

2 **Aim: to elicit the use and formation of the structures** *so ... that* **and** *such ... that*

- Ask Ss to read through the table. Ensure that Ss understand the terms used.
- Refer Ss to the examples above and ask them to complete the table.
- Elicit and check answers. If necessary, provide Ss with further explanations and / or examples.

Key

CLAUSES OF RESULT
Clauses of result are introduced with:
so + **adjective or adverb** + **that clause**
such + **(a / an)** + **(adjective)** + *noun* + **that clause**

3 **Aim: to give Ss practice in using clauses of result (so... that, such... that) in context**

- Ask Ss to do the exercise.
- Check answers.

Key

a. The traffic was so heavy on the highway that I missed my appointment. / There was such heavy traffic on the highway that I missed my appointment.
b. The book was so interesting that she finished it in a few hours. / It was such an interesting book that she finished it in a few hours.
c. Jack's job is so demanding that he spends most weekends working. / Jack has such a demanding job that he spends most weekends working.
d. The children were so excited about the trip that they weren't able to sleep the night before they left.

4 **Aim: to present** *too / enough* **structures expressing result**

- Ask Ss to read through the table. Ensure that Ss understand the terms used.
- Have Ss complete the rule.
- Elicit and check answers.

Key

To express result we use:
- *too* + **adjective / adverb** (+ for somebody) + *full infinitive*
- (not) **adjective / adverb** + *enough* (+ for somebody) + *full infinitive*

5 **Aim: to elaborate on clauses of result through an error correction exercise**

- Ask Ss to do the exercise.
- Check answers.

Key

a. He is **too** short to play basketball.
b. Sally was **so** cold that she wore two jumpers!
c. I have **so** many clothes that there's hardly any space in my wardrobe any more.
d. The car was **so** badly damaged that they decided not to have it repaired.
e. Mr Martin is too old **to** drive. He might have an accident.
f. It was **such** a beautiful day that we decided to go on a picnic.
g. Tom isn't old **enough** to drive.

Teacher's Notes

Lesson Two

Structures

Adverbial Clauses III (Clauses of purpose)

Vocabulary

Words and expressions

a click away	freelancer
aside (adv)	frustrating
assignment	go about sth
bring along	hire
browse	horde
client	observant
congestion	recruit
convention	retail / -er
delegate	scheduler
duty	senior
evaluate	submit
feedback	thrift shop
fluctuate	vital
freebies	work to one's advantage

Idioms with numbers

a hundred per cent
back to square one
from all four corners of the globe
in two minds
nine out of ten times
put two and two together
the number one

reading

optional pre-reading activity

- Ask Ss to read the title of the reading text and look at the picture accompanying it.
- Ask Ss to tell you what they understand by the term "mystery shopper".
- Brainstorm. However, don't correct Ss' guesses at this point.

1 **Aim: to give Ss practice in identifying the main ideas of the paragraphs in an article through a matching activity**

- Ask Ss to read through the text for gist, without paying attention to the gaps.
- Ask Ss to guess what each of the missing headings should be about.
- Ask Ss to read through the headings A-G. Ensure that Ss understand them.

- Before the second reading, point out to Ss that they should always look for key words / phrases in the article which are related to those in the headings.
- Now ask Ss to read the first paragraph of the article and decide on the most suitable heading. Ask them to underline the key words / phrases which helped them decide. Check answers.
- Ask Ss to read the text paragraph by paragraph and do the rest of the activity.
- Point out to Ss that if they cannot decide on a heading for a specific paragraph, they should move on and get back to it later.
- Check answers and ask Ss to provide justification.

Key

1 F (Ss should rely on context - The writer explains the 'mysterious' nature of the job)

2 D (*… senior citizens, university students and stay-at-home mums and dads … parents of small children …*)

3 A (*You don't need to have any previous experience … know how to use the Internet … Good communication skills … Any previous experience in retail, customer service or market research …*)

4 B (*… your income will fluctuate from month to month. How much you earn depends on … a reasonably regular income, another major bonus …*)

5 G (Ss should rely on context - The writer explains what somebody should do in order to find a job as a mystery shopper)

6 E (*It's important to … / Mystery shoppers should also make sure …*)

Extra heading: C

- When the activity is over, explain unknown words through definitions or example sentences.

optional post-reading activity

You may ask Ss questions of personal response to the topic of the article.

e.g. *Would you ever work as a mystery shopper? Why / Why not?*
Can you think of any disadvantages of working as a mystery shopper?

words and phrases

1 Idioms

Aims: • to present idioms with numbers
   • to give Ss practice in inferring their
      meanings through a matching exercise

- Ask Ss to read through the sentences 1-7. Ensure
  that Ss don't have any unknown words.
- Ask Ss to read through the meanings a-g. Ensure that
  Ss don't have any unknown words.
- Ss should try to make educated guesses by relying on
  their background knowledge. You may ask Ss if they
  can relate any of the idioms to their mother tongue.
- Have Ss do the exercise.
- Check answers.

Key

1. g	5. a
2. b	6. f
3. d	7. e
4. c	

optional
If there is time, ask Ss to make their own sentences
using the idioms and check them.

2 Word building

Aim: to give Ss practice in word formation
   through a word building exercise

- Ask Ss to read through the text for gist, without
  paying attention to the gaps.
- Point out to Ss that, before completing the gaps,
  they should decide on what part of speech is needed
  each time.
- Have Ss do the exercise.
- Check answers.

Key

(1) shopping	(4) happily	(7) increasing
(2) solution	(5) convenient	(8) pollution
(3) consumers	(6) delivery	(9) profitable

grammar

1 **Aim: to familiarise Ss with structures used to express purpose**
- Ask Ss to read the first sentence and find the structure that expresses purpose.
- Do the same for sentences b and c respectively.
- Elicit and check answers. If necessary, provide Ss with further examples and / or explanations.

Key

a. *in order to*   b. *so that*   c. *so as to*

2 **Aim: to help Ss elicit the formation of clauses of purpose**
- Ask Ss to read through the table. Ensure that they understand the terms used.
- Refer Ss to the sentences in the previous exercise and ask them to complete the table.
- Check answers. If necessary, provide Ss with further explanations.

Key

CLAUSES OF PURPOSE
Clauses of purpose are introduced with:
so that + **subject + modal verb** (can / may / will) + **base form**
in order to and *so as to* + **base form**

- Now read out and explain the note. If necessary, provide Ss with examples.

3 **Aim: to give Ss practice in using clauses of purpose in context through a key word transformation exercise**
- Ask Ss to do the exercise.
- Check answers.

Key

1. in order to finish
2. so as to teach / so that I can teach
3. so as not to catch
4. so that I can buy
5. in order not to miss / to catch

listening

Aim: to give Ss practice in listening for specific information through a T / F exercise
- Ask Ss to read through the statements 1-6. Explain any unknown words if necessary.
- Point out to Ss that during the first listening, they should listen carefully and only after the second listening should they finalise their answers.
- Play the CD twice.
- Check answers.

Key

1 F   2 T   3 T   4 T   5 F   6 F

---

optional post-listening activity
Ask Ss questions of personal response to the listening text.
e.g. *Are you influenced by advertisements?*
Have you ever bought something that you regretted buying afterwards?

Teacher's Notes

Lesson Three

speaking

1 Aim: to introduce the topic of the speaking activity by relating it to Ss' personal experiences
- Ask Ss to look at the questions and generate discussion.
- Elicit answers.

Key

Suggested ideas:
- age, gender, interests, cost, type of relationship
- Open answers

2 Aim: to give Ss practice in prioritising in order to reach a consensus
- Divide Ss into pairs.
- Tell Ss to look at the items shown in the photographs.
- Engage Ss in meaningful and realistic conversations.
- Point out to Ss that they may agree or disagree giving reasons for their choices as long as they decide on a present for their friend.
- Have Ss do the activity.
- Elicit answers.

Key

Suggested ideas:
A: Tomorrow's John's birthday party! We need to buy him a present.
B: What do you suggest?
A: Why don't we buy him a book? John likes reading, so I think a book would be the ideal present for him.
B: Well, I don't think so. Everybody's going to buy him a book for that very reason. Let's buy him a pair of trainers instead.
A: I don't think that's a very good idea. First of all, they're too expensive and secondly, John is not the sporty type.
B: You have a point! I think we should buy him a CD with all the latest hits. You know how much John enjoys listening to pop music!
A: I suppose you're right! Besides, he could play it at the party!

3 Aim: to elaborate and expand on the topic of the speaking activity
- Ask Ss to look at the questions and generate discussion.
- Elicit answers.

Key

Suggested ideas:
- I prefer buying presents because I like giving things to the people I love / it makes me happy.
  I prefer receiving presents because it shows that people care.
- I don't think that the price of a present determines its value. Less expensive presents are often of sentimental value which is more important than money / It's the thought that counts.

Teacher's Notes

writing

1 **Aim: to prepare Ss for the writing task by relating it to Ss' personal experiences and preferences**
- Ask Ss to look at the questions and generate discussion.

2 **Aim: to familiarise Ss with the stylistic features of a formal letter of complaint**
- Ask Ss to read through the phrases in the two boxes. Ensure that Ss don't have any unknown words.
- Have Ss do the exercise.
- Check answers.

Key

1. b   2. d   3. c   4. a

3 **Aim: to give Ss practice in using the stylistic features of a transactional letter of complaint identified above in context**
- Ask Ss to read through the advertisement and the notes on it. Ensure that Ss don't have any unknown words.
- Ask Ss to read through the model letter. Explain any unknown words if necessary.
- Have Ss do the exercise.
- Check answers.

Key

(1) your advertisement was misleading
(2) mentioned in your advertisement
(3) I believe I am entitled to a full refund
(4) I expect an immediate response

4 Writing task

Aim: to give Ss practice in writing a transactional letter of complaint
- Ask Ss to read through the advertisement and the notes on it. Explain any unknown words if necessary.
- Assign the writing task for homework.

Revision 10-12

reading

1 **Aims: to give Ss further practice in identifying the main ideas of the paragraphs in an article through a matching activity**

- Ask Ss a few pre-reading questions related to the topic of the text and generate discussion.
  e.g. Do you know any famous painters?
  Have you heard of Salvador Dali? What do you know about him?
- Ask Ss to read through the text for gist.
- Ask Ss read through the headings.
- Before the second reading, point out to Ss that they should look for key words/phrases in the text which are related to those in the headings.
- Now ask Ss to read the first paragraph of the text and decide on the most suitable heading. Ask Ss to underline the key words/phrases which helped them decide. Check answers.
- Ask Ss to read the text paragraph by paragraph and do the rest of the activity.
- Point out to Ss that if they cannot decide on the heading for a specific paragraph, they should move on and get back to it later.
- Check answers and ask Ss to provide justification.

Key

1 C *(... the most famous and successful artist ... Pablo Picasso ... the second most famous artist ... Salvador Dali)*

2 G *(... was the son of a wealthy notary ... the Dali family had a summer house ... built their son his first studio.)*

3 D *(As a young man, ... were recognised immediately ... He had a one-man show in Barcelona when he was just twenty-one years old!)*

4 F *(... he started painting in the style that was fashionable at the time, known as surrealism.)*

5 E *(... fell head over heels in love ... They were married in 1934 ... Ss should also refer to the last sentence of the paragraph.)*

6 A *(... illustrated books, designed jewellery and textiles and even produced a couple of films.)*

Extra heading: B

- When the activity is over, explain unknown words through definitions or example sentences.

Use of English

1 **Aim: to revise various language forms through a multiple choice cloze exercise**

- Ask Ss to read through the text for gist, without paying attention to the gaps.
- Ask Ss to read the text again, one sentence at a time.
- Ask Ss to read the four options carefully, before deciding which one best fits each space.
- Have Ss do the activity.
- Check answers.

Key

- (1) B
- (2) C
- (3) D
- (4) B
- (5) A
- (6) C
- (7) D
- (8) D
- (9) D
- (10) B
- (11) A
- (12) C
- (13) D
- (14) B
- (15) A

2 **Aim: to check structural accuracy through an open cloze exercise**

- Ask Ss to read through the text for gist, without paying attention to the gaps.
- Ask Ss to fill in the gaps with one word only.
- Have Ss do the activity.
- Check answers.

Key

- (16) G
- (17) E
- (18) I
- (19) D
- (20) C
- (21) B
- (22) A
- (23) L
- (24) O
- (25) K

Use of English (continued)

3 **Aim: to check structural accuracy through an error correction exercise**

- Ask Ss to read the text for gist, without trying to correct anything.
- Ask Ss to read the text again, one sentence at a time and try to identify which of the lines are correct and which contain a word which should not be there.
- Have Ss do the activity.
- Check answers.

Key

26	to
27	it
28	✓
29	is
30	the
31	✓
32	he
33	it
34	as
35	✓
36	being
37	up
38	✓
39	✓
40	very

Teacher's Notes

4 Aim: **to translate into English the Chinese given in brackets through a translating exercise**
- Ask Ss to read the text for gist.
- Point out to Ss that before completing the gaps, they should decide on which phrases are needed for each blank.
- Have Ss do the activity.
- Check answers.

Key

41	banished to the moon for delinquency
42	which means a crazy person
43	a popular romantic symbol
44	take your loved one walking by moonlight
45	as long as they have enough money

listening

Aim: **to give Ss further practice in listening for specific information through a note taking exercise**
- Ask Ss to read sentences 1-6 and predict what kind of information is required.
- Explain any unknown words in the sentences.
- Point out to Ss that they should complete each of the sentences with a word or a short phrase from the listening text.
- Play the CD twice.
- Check answers.

Key

1. basic
2. services/products
3. products/services
4. valuable
5. interested in
6. a low (monthly) cost

Listening transcripts

UNIT 01 LESSON 2

Speaker 1
Last month I travelled nine thousand miles to meet some new clients. I was determined to do things right, so, I memorised all of their names. Mind you, it was no easy job, as everybody in Hong Kong has three names. Anyway, I started the meeting by addressing the top man, called Lo Win Hao, as "Mr Hao". I soon realised what a huge mistake I had made. There I was calling the director of the company, a man I had just met, by his first name. Everyone thought that I was being really disrespectful. I completely forgot that in Chinese the surname comes first and the given names last. How stupid of me!

Speaker 2
My wife, Ethel, and I went to Europe last year. We stayed in the Netherlands for about a week. What a beautiful country! I must say we were quite surprised when we found out we didn't have to tip the taxi driver. Anyway, what was I going to say, Ethel? Oh yes … One day I made a complete fool of myself at the hotel. The receptionist was on the phone and she made a gesture at me, which in my country means "you're crazy". Of course, I was really upset. She tried to calm me down and explained that the gesture simply meant "I had a phone call".

Speaker 3
It was awful! I just wanted the earth to open up and swallow me. I was visiting Germany for the first time and I was invited to my client's house for dinner. I decided to buy a bouquet of flowers for his wife. So, I went down to the florist and got a dozen red roses. Big mistake! I found out later that in Germany it is considered bad luck to give somebody an even number of flowers. That explained the look on my hostess's face when I gave her the roses!

Speaker 4
Well, where I come from the service charge is included in the bill. So, you can only imagine the embarrassment I went through in France where it is customary to leave a 15% tip, be it for a meal, a taxi fare or a haircut. Anyway, as my taxi pulled up in front of the hotel, I paid the fare without leaving anything. The driver practically threw me out of the car! I was shocked! Can you believe the French even give small change to the person who shows them to their seat in the cinema or theatre!

Speaker 5
You'll hear people say that England and America are divided by a common language. I had no idea how true that was until I went to New York, where I attended a presentation on the newest advances in technology. I was so impressed that I decided to congratulate the guy on his wonderful presentation. I walked up to him and said, "your presentation was a bomb!", but he didn't look too pleased with what I had said. Turned out I had told him his presentation was a failure, not a great success. In America "bomb" is not a compliment! Talk about a misunderstanding!

UNIT 02 LESSON 2

Clark Waters: Good evening, dear listeners, and welcome to *The Clark Waters Show*. Cash cards, credit cards, supermarket cards, smart cards ... ladies and gentlemen, the future is plastic. Here with us today, to discuss the issue of cards versus cash and the usefulness of cards in general, are Giles Warburton, of the National Bank and Kathleen Arnold, of the Consumer Rights Union. Welcome to you both.

Giles: Thank you, Mr Waters.

Kathleen: Thank you.

Clark: Right. Ms Arnold, we're currently experiencing what I'd like to call a *plastic revolution*, any thoughts on this?

Kathleen: Well, firstly, I think that credit cards and cash cards are a clever technique that banks have come up with, simply to promote consumerism. We all know how easy it is to fall into the trap of spending too much, especially when we're short of cash. Very often, people spend freely without considering the consequences, and then wonder why they're always in debt.

Clark: But credit cards are necessities these days, Ms Arnold.

Kathleen: That's what banks want you to believe, I'm sure Mr Warburton knows what I mean ...

Giles: Now hold on a moment, Ms Arnold. Banks are not to blame. Credit cards eliminate the need to carry around wads of cash and people simply feel more secure. They also give you the choice of paying for your purchases in monthly instalments without interest. That's the bottom line. And cards are convenient, too, we now have supermarket cards, gas cards ...

Kathleen: Oh, don't even get me started on those! Those silly things are there simply to deceive you into believing that you're getting a discount on your purchases. The truth is, though, that you end up buying things you don't need just because you think you got them at a better price! Besides, personally, I have a real problem with the fact that some mysterious group are monitoring my every purchase.

Giles: Well, now that sounds ridiculous ...

Kathleen: Oh, really? You might like other people sticking their nose into your personal business, but I certainly don't! Next you'll probably tell me that smart cards are a brilliant invention.

Clark: Ah, smart cards, now for some controversy! I think ...

Giles: Hang on, Mr Waters. What could be more handy than a card that stores all your personal information on one microchip, Ms Arnold? Eventually we'll use smart cards to identify ourselves and even to open the front door.

Kathleen: And what if you lose your card? What if a thief gets hold of it? A smart card can be dangerous in the wrong hands. All your personal information can be accessed, from your medical records and financial status to your driving licence and passport. Not to mention the keys to your front door.

Giles: Hold your horses, Ms Arnold! Smart cards cannot be accessed by just anybody. Fingerprint and voice recognition will ensure that the card can only be used by its owner. Besides, it's the wave of the future. So, we'll all have to get used to it.

Kathleen: No, thank you! In fact, I've organised a petition to stop the production of smart cards in this country.

Clark: Well, I think it's time for another point of view. Ladies and gentlemen, please welcome our next guest, Simon Bradley of Bradley Electronics ...

UNIT 03 LESSON 1

Presenter: Tonight on *Face to Face* we have again Dr Martin Davis, Head of the Research Institute for Future Developments, whose presentation last week led us to a second show in a row. This time, however, he's here to answer some of your questions. Good evening, Dr Davis. It's a pleasure to see you again.

Dr Davis: Thank you. Good evening.

Presenter: OK. I think we're ready for our first listener. On the phone we have Larry Howards from Bristol. What's your question, Larry?

Larry: Hello, everybody. Dr Davis, many people believe that all these so-called technological wonders might have a negative effect on our future lives. What do you have to say about this?

Dr Davis: Well, I can see what you are trying to say. Let me reassure you, though, that the future won't look as gloomy as some might like to believe. What I mean is that man has definitely made some serious mistakes on the road to development. However, we can take advantage of this knowledge to serve the future.

Presenter: Hope we've answered your question! Next caller: Joan Lawrence from Lancaster.

Joan: Good evening. A few days ago I read an article on future working styles. What can you tell us about that?

Dr Davis: Well, for sure, they will be different! Technology will be available to everyone and this will create a new form of self-employment. This means people will be working from the comfort of their homes, which is the case already in many households. It is estimated that in the long run, home employment is also going to put an end to all these morning traffic jams!

Presenter: It sounds too good to be true! So, what will

we do with all that extra leisure time on our hands?

Dr Davis: Anything our heart desires! We could spend more time travelling, for example. By the year 2050 we estimate that travel will have improved to such an extent that it will become considerably safer and less time-consuming to get around. For example, new aircraft will hold more than 1 000 passengers on board!

Presenter: That's incredible, isn't it? This is definitely going to set new standards for aviation!

Dr Davis: Just imagine the kind of impact this will have on tourism as faraway exotic destinations become a realistic option for many people.

Presenter: Well, Dr Davis, the future does seem to have a lot in store for us. All we have to do is wait and see. Now, there's one more caller ... Oh, I'm afraid we'll have to stop for some breaking news. Football fans at Buggleton Stadium got involved in a fight, and the situation is getting out of hand. Now, live from the stadium ... (fade out)

UNIT 03 LESSON 2

1

Woman: That's so funny ...

Man: What is?

Woman: This article on science fiction films. Have you seen the one with the guy who memorises computer information and then has to download it somewhere before his head explodes?

Man: Yes, it's ridiculous. It's been classified as a really bad film. Generally, science fiction films are silly.

Woman: I see your point! But you must admit there are some really good ones.

Man: OK ... Name one!

Woman: Well, *E.T.* and *The Matrix*.

Man: OK ... They made money, but do you actually believe that we're not alone in the universe and that people will travel in time? It's impossible. Get serious!

Woman: I AM serious! I think that in a few years we will make contact with life forms from other planets AND I think we will be able to go back in time.

Man: Hmm ... Go back in time ... Now that's not a bad idea.

Woman: See? I knew you'd like it!

Man: What? Like it? Me? No way! I only wish I could go back in time and not start this conversation.

2

Sam: Have you read this article?

Hector: No ... what's it about?

Sam: It says that, in a few years, space travel, with these so-called *spaceplanes* will be a reality.

Hector: Really? Spaceplanes! I bet it will be expensive.

Sam: Let me see ... Well, it doesn't say ... I guess it probably will be ... but would you go? I mean would you travel at the speed of light in and out of the earth's atmosphere for fun?

Hector: Well, I'd probably have a go ... after thinking about it really hard! But I would definitely not be a frequent flyer! The idea of being away from my home, my planet for a long time doesn't really appeal to me. I want my feet on the ground!

Sam: Not even for a short trip?

Hector: Like I said maybe once!

Sam: Same here. There's no place like home!

3

Laura: I've always wanted to ask you this, Eugene. How did it feel being one of the chosen few?

Eugene: I was really excited! We knew it was a daring mission and we all wanted to be a part of it. You know, go down in history and all that.

Laura: Tell us about the moment you actually set foot on ...

Eugene: Oh! I can't even begin to describe it! Well, when I was out of the shuttle I had some difficulty adjusting to zero gravity, but when I started walking around it was a great experience.

Laura: Did you learn anything on your mission?

Eugene: Yes, many things.

Laura: Would you do it again?

Eugene: What? Another lunar mission? Any time!

4

Gertrude: Stanley, dear ... STANLEY! Wake up! Listen to this?

Stanley: What? What is it?

Gertrude: Well, this article says that in a few years we'll have the first thinking robot!

Stanley: You woke me up for THAT?

Gertrude: It says it will also walk, talk and look just like us!

Stanley: Can you program it to STOP TALKING?

Gertrude: Well, actually, there is a problem with the brain ...

Stanley: I'm sure there is, Gertrude ...

Gertrude: ... Says here human brains are about 1 000 times faster than the fastest computer! Goodness me! Can you imagine what the world would be like if robots could think like us? Just thinking about it gives me the creeps.

5

The future is filled with many exciting possibilities. One of the things scientists hope to achieve is the ability to predict natural phenomena, which more often than not result in catastrophes, leaving people homeless. Just think of the damage a flood or an earthquake can cause. Hopefully, we will be able to warn people in due time, thus preventing them from getting hurt. However, some people wonder if we will be interfering with the laws of nature. Actually, there is no ... (fade out)

6

Have you ever heard of *electrotextile*? Well, get used to the name as it's about to take over the fashion world. It's made of normal cloth and carbon-impregnated fibres that can conduct electricity. When the fabric is pressed, signals are sent to a computer chip which can work out whether the cloth has been touched or not. It's easy to wash and ironing won't be needed anymore. More and more industries ... (fade out)

REVISION 1 UNITS 01-03

Jimmy: Good evening everybody and welcome to another edition of *Rockin' Rollercoaster*. With us, tonight, we have famous musician and now author, Mick Rock. Welcome Mick.

Mick: Thanks Jimmy. It's great to be here!

Jimmy: Right. Now, Mick, everyone is talking about your book. Tell our listeners what *Fifty Years of Non-stop Music* is about?

Mick: Well, it's about the biggest moments in musical history and some of the legends that made it all happen.

Jimmy: I see. You say here that the 1950s were a turning point in the history of music.

Mick: That's right. It was in the mid 1950s that a new kind of music was born in the States. It was loud, fast and upbeat.

Jimmy: … and it became known as rock'n'roll.

Mick: Right. Rock'n'roll has its roots in the musical styles of Afro-Americans such as Little Richard and Chuck Berry. Later many white artists started copying them.

Jimmy: Like the one and only … Elvis Presley!

Mick: Ah, yes, the *King*. He conveyed an image of being *tough* and *dangerous* through his music. He was unlike any other artist of the time. He wasn't just a singer, he was a hero to many teenagers.

Jimmy: And then came the 1960s, bringing about major changes, right?

Mick: Yes, skirts got shorter, hair got longer and for the first time pop music became a major force, especially in Britain, home of the *Beatles*. Beatlemania soon spread across Europe and then the United States. Another hugely popular band at the time was, my all-time favourite group, *The Rolling Stones*. Their aggressive style of rock music is still popular these days.

Jimmy: But in the 1970s music became more diverse.

Mick: It sure did. While heavy metal took off in the US, elsewhere around the world, pop music evolved into many different forms, like glam rock, punk, disco and reggae. Bands from different countries burst on to the scene, too. Take ABBA from Sweden, for example. They became the most successful group of the decade. They started using hi-tech equipment to produce their music and they made music videos. The combination of technology and music videos soon turned music into a million-

Jimmy: dollar industry.

Jimmy: Yeah, I remember the lights and the glitter. What about the 1980s?

Mick: Well, in my opinion the music event of the decade was *Live Aid* and the man behind it all was Bob Geldof. He wanted to raise money for the starving children of Africa. In 1984, he recorded the song *Do they know it's Christmas* with other famous artists. And just a year later, Live Aid, the biggest concert ever, took place. More than 1.5 billion people watched the best that music could offer.

Jimmy: I remember that, 16 hours of non-stop music … Talk about music bringing people together! What happened in the 1990s?

Mick: New talents burst onto the scene. Many boy bands, as well as girl bands, were formed and gained in popularity practically overnight. There was a greater variety of music available, such as rap, techno, rave …

Jimmy: Music has come a long way since Elvis hasn't it? Now it's time for a short music break. Here's something from … (fade out)

UNIT 04 LESSON 2

J. J. Winters: Good evening and welcome to *Daredevils*. I'm J.J. Winters, your host. With us tonight we have Gary Jordan, a man who enjoys living on the edge. Welcome to the show, Gary.

Gary: Thanks. It's great to be here.

J. J. Winters: So, Gary, you are a Gravity Formula 1 racer.

Gary: That's right!

J. J. Winters: What on earth is *Gravity Formula 1* racing? I'm sure our listeners are dying to find out!

Gary: Well, think of it as a combination of Formula 1 racing, speedboat racing and go-karting.

J. J. Winters: So, what's the catch?

Gary: There's no engine, no fuel, no noise! And not a lot of control either!

J. J. Winters: Lethal stuff! So, what does a Gravity Formula 1 kart look like?

Gary: It looks pretty much like a normal go-kart, but it works like a skateboard actually. Climb into a GF1 kart and you'll be shooting down a mountainside faster than a shooting star, screaming your head off and wondering where the brakes are and what you're doing there in the first place.

J. J. Winters: Don't tell me there are no brakes!

Gary: Don't worry, they're there, alright. But there's no accelerator. There's not much need for it anyway, as there's no engine. Why build an engine and waste fuel, when you've got gravity working for you! Plus we don't have all those angry environmentalists breathing down our necks, as GF1 isn't a threat.

J. J. Winters: Let me get this straight, Gary, you tear down mountain roads, pulled by gravity, at a speed of what, 200 km/h?

Gary: 160. I know it's not quite Formula 1 racing, but it guarantees to keep your adrenalin flowing.

J. J. Winters: So, how do you drive the GF1 kart, or should I say control it?

Gary: Well, as I said earlier, there is not much control. To get around the bends in the road, you have the steering lever in your right hand and the brake lever in your left. Basically, you're taking your life in your hands. Skid turns are pretty much the order of the day.

J. J. Winters: You can say that again! Where do you get these GF1 karts?

Gary: You can't buy them, if that's what you're asking. There're home-built by their drivers, so if anything goes wrong, they have only themselves to blame. The cost of the vehicle is roughly speaking $1 000 … Mind you, for that amount of money you wouldn't be able to buy the wing mirror of a Formula 1 car.

J. J. Winters: True. Now, Gary, can you tell our listeners what happens on the big day?

Gary: The GF1 karts are brought to the race on the back of a truck and hauled to the top of a mountain. There's also a rule that the driver and his kart mustn't be heavier than 175kg!

J. J. Winters: What only 179kg?

Gary: No, five. Then the drivers climb into their karts, lie down on their backs with not much more than fresh air between them and the asphalt. They wait for the flag to go down. The race starts off slowly till the gravity kicks in. That's when you know you're running on luck! Another big difference between Formula 1 and GF1 is that everyone has the same power, the same vehicle … So, basically it all comes down to your driving skills.

J. J. Winters: Impressive. Well, listeners, you heard the man. If any of you out there are keen to lie down in a GF1 kart with no fuel and no engine and hit 160km/h, Gary Jordan is the person to talk to. And now for our commercial break … (fade out)

UNIT 05 LESSON 2

Speaker 1

It still makes me very sad when I think about it. That house on the beach was our dream house, and it cost us a fortune to build; our life savings to be precise. I mean, what better way to spend your retirement years than by the sea? We'd been living in the house for about a year when it happened. Fortunately, we weren't home that day ... We saw it all on TV, though. Most of the homes along the coastline, including ours, were simply swallowed up by this enormous wave. It was heartbreaking to watch ... our dream home was wiped out.

Speaker 2

I'm a freelance photographer and I was on an assignment in El Salvador for *Daredevil* magazine, you've heard of it, I'm sure. Anyway, there we were, quite close to the top, when we felt the ground move. My guide panicked and suggested we leave, pronto! I must admit, I was afraid, but I was sure I'd get some spectacular shots if we stayed a bit longer ... My guide, however, refused to stay with me so we made our way back down again. We were warned to leave the area as soon as possible ... The sky was so dark ... By the next day, ash and bits of solid lava were falling to the ground ... It was incredible! I got some excellent pics ... Pity I had to miss the big climax!

Speaker 3

It must've been about 3:30 a.m. when I woke up. Maisie was having an absolute fit. She was barking loudly and seemed very excited about something. Her behaviour was most unusual. I tried to calm her down, but it was no use. Then as I sat on the edge of my bed, wondering what to do, the rattling started. Rattling soon became violent shaking, pictures fell off the walls, vases fell to the ground ... it was terrifying! I picked Maisie up and dashed out of the house. Fortunately, the damage wasn't too bad. I heard later, though, that some of the buildings in the area had actually collapsed. I'm quite impressed with Maisie's predictive powers; I'll never doubt her again!

Speaker 4

Well, as you can see, the scene here is one of total destruction. Winds travelling at about 800km an hour swept through the quiet town of Winchester in the early hours of this morning, causing serious damage to property and loss of life. One witness reports that she looked out of her window and saw a 'big, brown funnel that just chewed up everything in its path'. Trees were uprooted and cars were lifted up into the air. Two people have been killed and at least 100 are seriously injured. This is Carrie Whittaker for WSBC News, Winchester.

Speaker 5

We weren't given any sort of warning at all. Perhaps we could've prepared ourselves ... saved some of the pieces ... I don't know. I was at work that day — I'm a curator at the museum — when some of my colleagues pointed out how dark the sky looked. Soon it started to rain heavily. I didn't really take much notice until I heard a report on the radio a while later that the river had burst its banks. I couldn't believe it. I looked out the window and saw that the water level was rising fast. We were told to evacuate the building. We did all we could to safeguard the pieces. Some artwork was destroyed ... It's such a shame, such a terrible shame.

UNIT 06 LESSON 1

1

Without a doubt, it's a real thrill to watch these people standing on top of Cooper's hill in Gloucester, ready to chase a huge chunk of, believe it or not,... cheese down the hill! The fun begins the moment the countdown is heard. What follows cannot be described in words. Crazed dairy product fans roll Double Gloucester cheeses down this steep hill, then hurl themselves after them, frequently right into the arms of waiting paramedics! It's no surprise, that contestants usually end up in hospital, where they are treated for broken bones and head injuries. The winner, if any, is the person who catches the cheese before it reaches the bottom. And the prize? Well, the winner gets to keep the cheese! As for the spectators, you can be sure they'll have quite a time cheering and laughing.

2

Well, ladies and gentlemen, here we are, live, in Norway for the annual Grandmothers festival. Yes, you heard right! For those of you who don't have a clue what this unusual, yet famous event is all about, here's a little background information: the first Grandmothers festival was held in Bodo in 1992 and gave brave grannies the opportunity to take part in a number of extreme events. The star of that show was 79-year-old Elida Anderson, also known as the world's oldest bungee-jumper! Since then the festival has gained in popularity, as more and more adventurous grandmothers ride motorbikes, take part in horse races, scuba-dive and even skydive! And you thought grannies just baked biscuits and knitted scarves. Now, without further delay, we cross to the motorbike race. They're in their positions, engines are roaring ... and ... off they go!

3

It's the 3rd of August and a very special day for us firefighters here in Tewkesbury, Gloucester. We're preparing for our annual competition called hose-balling, where a huge, plastic beach ball is blasted into the air using high-powered water hoses. Hose-balling was started by local firefighters in the 1960s to help them practise their aim. After all, practice makes perfect. Anyway, there are two teams of four firefighters each. With regard to the rules of the game, the ball must be kept in the air with the hoses. The teams then have five minutes to move the ball closer to the opposition's side of the field to win. And that's all there is to it. Everyone is welcome to watch and join the picnic afterwards.

UNIT 06 LESSON 2

1

Tiffany: OK, I wrote out my new list last night ... Listen: *one*, lose weight, *two*, learn how to speak Spanish, *three*, do more charity work, *four*, climb Mt. Everest ...

Marlene: Oh, please! You do this every year, Tiffany.

I really don't know why people make these silly lists anyway! Believe me, three weeks into January, you'll have forgotten everything.

Tiffany: That's not true!

Marlene: Oh, come on! Need I remind you what you said last year?

Tiffany: Alright, I remember what I said, but this year is going to be different.

Marlene: I've heard that one before!

Tiffany: Oh don't be so negative, Marlene. Making these lists is tradition; it's part of the fun … Anyway, *five*, learn how to scuba-dive, *six*, take up ballroom dancing …

2

Lloyd: Wake me up when it's over, Grace.

Grace: Oh, Lloyd. You do this every time. You should learn to appreciate culture, you know.

Lloyd: I don't think a bunch of people in tights, who, in my opinion, look as if they're really in need of a good meal, jumping about on a stage equals 'culture'.

Grace: Oh, I forgot. Your idea of culture is a Chinese take-away and an Arnold Schwarzenegger movie marathon!

Lloyd: And yours is this awful classical music and these people dancing …

Grace: Oh, just pay attention, will you?

Lloyd: I am paying attention ... Oh my, did you see that, Grace? How do they stretch like that ...? Ouch! That must have hurt!

3

Dj Dirk: Listen up, everybody! The *Jojo Karaoke Club* will be hosting a contest on Sunday, 8th November. Here's your chance to show everyone how talented you are! Amaze your friends, surprise your family – this is your chance to shine! The club will provide you with everything you need. All you have to do is show up and let everybody hear that great voice you've got! Choose any tune you want. A grand prize of C1 000 will be awarded to the lucky winner! Doors open at 8 pm and entrance is free to all performers! So, what are you waiting for, pick up the phone and enter now!

4

Olivia: Yes... that's right. No, I've taken care of everything; the invitations, the catering, the dress ... Oh yes, they're bringing the flowers tomorrow. Of course I'm excited! I can hardly wait! Yes, Barry's excited, too! ... Yes, at the Plaza. The reception will be held in the garden. It'll be lovely! Nervous? Why? ... Oh, I hadn't even thought of that, to be honest ... What? When did you hear that? ... Do you think it'll be that bad? ... Oh dear, we'll have to have the reception indoors, otherwise we'll all be soaking wet. I'd better call up the Plaza and make other arrangements. Oh no, and I've already sent out the invitations. Oh my

goodness! I'd better go, Liz. I have some phone calls to make. =

5

Joseph: Wow, that was fantastic! Singers, dancers ... I especially enjoyed the poetry! I mean, that fellow that just stood on the stage for ten whole minutes without saying a word ... Brilliant, I tell you! Just brilliant!

Theodore: Brilliant! I thought he was a bit weird, actually. I really enjoyed watching the mime, you know the one outside the coffee shop? He was excellent. He reminded me of a puppet! Anyway, I can't wait to go back again next year.

Joseph: Me neither. But right now, I'm starving. Let's get something to eat.

6

Mr Ballantine: ... This is some cake you've got here, I must say. Anyway, I'm just so pleased that you are all here to share this moment with me. When I first started working here, forty years ago, I didn't imagine for a minute that I'd be running this place one day ... Bradley, my boy, all I can say is, your time has come. I'm sure you'll make us all proud. I wish you the best of luck, but I'm quite sure you won't need it! Once again, thank you all for your support through the years and for the lovely gift. So, what are you all standing here for, go and enjoy the party!

REVISION 2 UNITS 04-06

Joey Lambert: Next up on *To your health*, we have an interview with dietician, Julia Campbell, who's going to talk to us about why people should seriously consider becoming vegetarians. Welcome Julia.

Julia Campell: Thanks, Joey. It's great to be here!

Joey: Well, I'm sure that most of you out there in radioland couldn't imagine saying *no* to a juicy piece of steak. But, these days, vegetarianism is becoming the more fashionable choice. Julia, could you explain to us why that is?

Julia: Well, it's true, more and more people, myself included, are opting for a vegetarian lifestyle, but meat consumption around the world is actually at an all-time high. One reason for this is the rise in popularity of fast food restaurants. In fact, it's been estimated that Americans spend at least $110 billion a year on processed food alone!

Joey: That's incredible!

Julia:	And surprising when you consider the number of meat-borne diseases that are out there! Remember the outbreak of mad cow disease? Well, it's not over yet, not by a long shot. In fact, it's still considered a threat in some parts of the world.
Joey:	So, aside from the possibility of contracting a disease, why else would you recommend that people give up meat?
Julia:	Well, for one thing, giving up meat can actually decrease world hunger.
Joey:	What? How?
Julia:	I'll give you an example. In order to produce a pound of beef, you need 4.8 pounds of feed. You could fill about 50 bowls with cooked cereal grains for the same amount of money that's required to purchase the feed. That's fifty meals!
Joey:	Unbelievable!
Julia:	Then there's also the environment to consider. Meat production has been linked to the erosion of millions of acres of farmland and to the destruction of rainforests. Deforestation is necessary to create grazing land for the animals – a single vegetarian actually saves an acre of trees each year.
Joey:	Wow, Julia! You've certainly given us some food for thought, if you'll pardon the expression. What about the dangers to our health?
Julia:	Well, the human digestive system is not designed to process meat. This leads to heart disease and a number of other disorders. Plus, factory-farmed, chickens, cows and pigs are fed huge amounts of antibiotics and other types of medication. Not exactly my idea of healthy eating.
Joey:	No, not my idea of healthy eating either. OK, so what sort of diet should a vegetarian follow to stay healthy?
Julia:	A varied diet is important and vegetarians should consume enough calories to maintain their weight. Good sources of protein include, rice, broccoli, spinach, peanut butter, peas and meat substitutes like soya-based products. Supermarkets are full of healthy meat substitutes ... Just shop around.
Joey:	Well, Julia. It's been a pleasure having you with us today and thank you for your insights.
Julia:	Thank you, Joey.
Joey:	And now ... (fade out)

UNIT 07 LESSON 1

Sheryl Maloney:	Well, folks I'm back after my whirlwind visit to Japan where I ate, you guessed it, raw fish! It wasn't so bad, but I think I'll stick to cooked food. That brings us to today's theme which is 'Strange experiences with food'. The phone lines are open and we're all ears!
Sheryl:	Who do we have on line one?
Mervin:	Hi Sheryl, this is Mervin Hodges from Lee-on-Sea.
Sheryl:	Welcome to the show Merv. You definitely have an interesting story to tell us, don't you?
Mervin:	You bet! I've just got back from Mexico. It was my first time there and I had no idea what the food was like.
Sheryl:	Very hot, am I right?
Mervin:	Yeah! There was this small bowl full of what looked like chopped tomatoes on the table. I shovelled a heaped spoon of the stuff into my mouth and chewed.
Sheryl:	Oh no! That was chilli sauce, wasn't it?
Mervin:	Yes, it was. My mouth was burning! I felt like I needed at least half a dozen fire engines to cool me down!
Sheryl:	Well, that was Mervin and now on to line two, where Magda is waiting with her story. Hi there, Magda.
Magda:	Hello, Sheryl.
Sheryl:	OK, we're all ears!
Magda:	Well, I just got fed up of cooking and thinking up different dishes to prepare. So, I went with Regina, a friend of mine, to her favourite restaurant for a change. I told her to order for me, too, as she knew the menu well.
Sheryl:	Which wasn't a good idea, was it?
Magda:	You can say that again. She ordered these shells cooked in white sauce with lots of garlic. After I had popped a few of them into my mouth, Regina said that her mother also collects them in her garden. Then it hit me. I was eating ...
Sheryl:	SNAILS! What did you do?
Magda:	Nothing! I actually quite enjoyed them.
Sheryl:	Well, thanks for your offering of the French cuisine Magda and now, who is our final caller for today?
Daryl:	Hi Sheryl, it's Daryl Walters here. I'm the chef at the new restaurant on Spratt Street called *Novelty Bites*.
Sheryl:	Hi there Daryl. What's cooking?
Daryl:	Alligator steaks all this week.
Sheryl:	You are kidding, aren't you?
Daryl:	No. Best alligator meat marinated in garlic and chilli, then fried in butter.
Sheryl:	It's a new one on me. So, tell me Daryl ... (fade out)

Gary: This is Gary Hughes coming to you live on WBC radio. Well, listeners, we see them all the time; low-fat food, sugar-free drinks, organic fruits and vegetables and the list goes on. But what does it all mean? More importantly, is it true? Can we really trust the food companies? To answer all these questions and to find out what exactly that label means, is Dr Esther May, nutrition scientist. Good evening Dr May and welcome to our show.

Esther: Thank you for inviting me.

Gary: Now Dr May …

Esther: Esther, please.

Gary: All right Esther, let's begin with a question I've often asked myself. Can a product really be, let's say, 94% fat free? You see it on yoghurts, biscuits, ready-meals … Is it really true?

Esther: That's a very good question. When we see the label 94% fat free, we tend to think it's low in fat and therefore we can eat plenty of it. Well, it might be 94% fat free, but that still leaves 6% of fat. That's 6g of fat per 100g of food, which is twice the amount that would classify it as a low-fat food.

Gary: Twice the amount! So, it's not as innocent as it sounds.

Esther: I'm afraid it isn't. That's why the Government's Food Advisory Committee or GFA for short, is against these x percent fat free labels, claiming that they do more harm than good. Still many manufacturers persist in using them on their products and by doing so …

Gary: … they pull the wool over our eyes.

Esther: That's right. So, all you dieters out there, you'd better rethink what you're eating! And if you want to stay fit, stick to foods that are naturally low in fat, like fresh fruit and veggies, cereal, wholemeal bread, fish and lean meat.

Gary: I see … what about sugar-free products?

Esther: Now that's a fantastic example of how manufacturers throw dust in our eyes. Surely everyone knows that almost all those so-called sugar-free drinks and products are sweet. How do they do that? Well, instead of sugar, they use artificial sweeteners.

Gary: But aren't manufacturers required to state that on their products?

Esther: That's where the trick is. Although it's a legal requirement to do so, it's often printed in tiny letters which are difficult to see.

Gary: Are these sweeteners bad for us?

Esther: High levels of sweeteners can be a concern especially for children as they are more sensitive to the effects of chemicals than adults are. That's why it's better to cut down on commercially-made drinks altogether and give children milk and pure fruit juices instead.

Gary: So, I guess we have to keep our eyes open next time we buy a fizzy drink or a yoghurt with the label no sugar added.

Esther: Now that you've mentioned yoghurt, I'd like to explain some things about dairy products.

Gary: We're all ears!

Esther: Let me begin with long-life milk. Long-life products have both advantages and disadvantages. On the one hand, you don't have to run to the supermarket every day to buy a carton of milk. On the other hand, though, prolonged shelf life is often achieved through ultra-heat treatment that can destroy certain vitamins, like vitamin B. Plus, in order to increase the shelf life manufacturers add preservatives.

Gary: So, what's the bottom line in your opinion?

Esther: If you can't go to the shops regularly for fresh foods, buy in bulk and freeze until you need them.

Gary: Well Esther, the phones are ringing like crazy! Fiona from Essex wants to know what manufacturers mean by labels such as strawberry or vanilla flavour on their products.

Esther: Well, if you see the words strawberry flavour on a food product, it's quite possible it doesn't contain any fruit at all, just artificial flavouring. However, by law, a strawberry product such as a strawberry yoghurt must contain real fruit. Also, if there is a picture of the food on the label, for example oranges on a chocolate wrapper, then the flavour must come mainly from that source.

Gary: There you go Fiona … and now our next caller is John Bingham … (fade out)

UNIT 08 LESSON 1

Speaker 1

This happened years ago when I first started my practice. It was quite late and I was getting ready to go to bed when I heard the doorbell. You can imagine my surprise when I opened the door and saw a man and … a LION standing next to him. I couldn't believe my eyes! A huge growling lion right on my doorstep! Being new to this profession at the time, I was used to dealing with cats and dogs, not lions if you know what I mean! The poor lion seemed to be in great pain. The man, who turned out to be a lion-tamer at the local circus, explained that the lion had stepped on a nail during that night's performance. Anyway, when the lion entered the examination room, it took up so much space there was hardly any room to swing a cat! I gave the lion a tranquillizer, removed the nail and wrapped its paw in a bandage. I told the owner that the lion shouldn't perform for a week or two.

Speaker 2

Well, we set up camp quite near the pack so that we could observe them closely. We noticed that the males were quite aggressive towards one another and extremely territorial. The females never let the little ones out of their sight, not even for a second. Anyway, the wolves knew we were close by, but didn't seem to care until we threw a piece of meat in their direction. One of the females, we called her Leila, snatched the piece of meat and ran off. That was our first contact. We thought that the wolves would soon be eating out of our hands … that's what we hoped anyway! One day, Leila wandered off, so we decided to approach her cubs. The moment I got close enough to touch them, Leila lept out of the bushes.

I cried wolf … and I meant it! That day curiosity killed the cat, or should I say almost killed the cat! If it wasn't for the rest of the team who jumped to my rescue, I would have been dinner for sure!

Speaker 3

This here is a cockatoo – cockatoos belong to the parrot family and they're very intelligent. We named him Frederick, he's a handsome one, isn't he? Quite noisy, too! You don't want to be around cockatoos when they start quarreling, trust me. The moment we brought Frederick in, our other cockatoo, Wanda, went crazy! In all the years I've been working here, I had never seen anything like it before! It was impossible for the two of them to co-exist peacefully! They were constantly fighting. In fact, there were usually feathers all over the place by feeding time! Just the other day, one of the visitors told me that the birds were at each other's throats! They were fighting like cat and dog! Wings flapping, feathers flying … Anyway, we had no other choice but to separate them yesterday. Now things are back to normal.

UNIT 08 LESSON 2

Danny: This is *Animal Print* coming to you, live, on FM 100. I'm Danny Thomas, your host. Well, ladies and gentlemen, there has been a lot of talk in the press recently about animal testing. So, we decided to invite Brenda Ryan, an animal rights activist, on to the show to explain to our listeners what really goes on in those laboratories. Good morning Brenda and welcome to the show.

Brenda: Good morning Danny and thank you for giving me this opportunity to speak about some of the appalling practices that go on when so-called scientists test products that most of us use every day.

Danny: Is it that bad? I was under the impression that a lot had already been done to stop animal experimentation.

Brenda: It's true that some steps have been taken, but it's still not enough, not by a long shot. Did you know that every three seconds an animal dies because of scientific research somewhere in Europe?

Danny: Really? I thought animal testing was against the law in the UK.

Brenda: It is, but that doesn't mean very much, unfortunately. You see, the manufacturers just have the product tested in another country and then ship it over here to be sold.

Danny: But, products not tested on animals usually advertise the fact on the label, don't they?

Brenda: Right, but that's also not a guarantee. You see, the product itself may not have been tested on animals; however some of the individual ingredients may have been.

Danny: Well, that makes it very difficult for consumers to know for sure that they are not supporting animal testing.

Brenda: Good point, Danny. That's why the British Union for the Abolition of Vivisection, BUAV for short, published a book called *Little Book of Cruelty Free* which lists all products that are animal friendly.

Danny: Really? How can our listeners get hold of this book?

Brenda: Well, you can write to BUAV or call them for a free copy.

Danny: Did you hear that, listeners? Stay tuned, we'll give you the address and phone number at the end of the show. Now, we come to the most crucial question. What actually happens to these animals, Brenda?

Brenda: Okay, let's take lab rats as an example. They're force-fed lipstick, which causes painful cramps or breathing difficulties. Some get so sick that they die.

Danny: Why is that done?

Brenda: To test that the product is not poisonous. Liquids such as shampoo are dripped into their eyes, causing many of them to go blind. At the end of these tests all the animals are killed.

Danny: That's shocking!

Brenda: To say the least. It's cruel and it's immoral. Just because laboratory animals aren't people's pets, it doesn't mean it's okay to treat them inhumanely. And secondly, there's really no point in these experiments.

Danny: What do you mean?

Brenda: Well it's quite obvious. There's a big difference between bunnies and us, so there's really no guarantee we'd find the same things harmful. The bottom line is that animal testing must be banned. Besides, scientists have already come up with new methods to test cosmetics, like using human cells or hi-tech computers. There's no need to use animals.

Danny: Well, that was Brenda Ryan on *Animal Print*. Thanks again for joining us, Brenda. Now get your pens ready. The address is … (fade out)

UNIT 09 LESSON 2

Professor Youngberry: Right then, I want you to imagine your dream home for a minute. Think carefully about where it would be located, what materials you would use to build it and so on ... OK. Now, I'm pretty sure that most of you imagined a four-walled structure, that stands on the ground, with a door, windows, etc. Am I right?

Students: Yes … that's right … yeah!

Professor Youngberry: Well, you'll be surprised that these days more and more

Susan: people are building houses that are rather unusual and, in some cases, quite bizarre! What do you mean by bizarre, Professor?

Professor Youngberry: In Japan, for instance, a fair number of people have chosen to live in houses made entirely of glass! Several Japanese homeowners have also decided to bring nature into their homes ... or on to their homes, to be more precise! Pine Tree House in Hakata, for example, has a live tree on its roof! These ideas may sound peculiar to us, but they are basically just another way to look at space, light and nature. And the result is often quite extraordinary. Yes, Arnold?

Arnold: Uh, Professor, earlier you said we'd probably all imagined a dream house that 'stands on the ground'. Why? Is there any other sort?

Professor Youngberry: I'm glad you asked that, Arnold. Yes, there are houses that are built on stilts. You usually find these kinds of houses on water. For obvious reasons, like flooding. Then, there are houses that are built in trees. Remember tree houses from your childhood years?

Arnold: Tree houses? You mean there are people who actually *live* in tree houses?

Professor Youngberry: Yes, and they're becoming quite popular these days. People use tree houses as offices, holiday homes and residences. This is not a new idea, though. People have been building tree houses throughout history. In the 1800s, there was a town in France that became quite famous for its tree house restaurants. You all look quite surprised! Well, prepare yourselves, I have some slides to show you of very unusual homes I've come across in rural parts of Canada and the United States. Eileen, please dim the lights ... Thanks ... OK. This first slide is of a house in Ontario made of screws. The owner must have had a loose screw! This next slide is of a

button house. No, your eyes are not playing tricks on you. You see the owner is an insomniac and stays up all night sewing buttons on things, including his house! All those crazy, little things people do! Now, this man, here, has goats living on his roof! The next ... Yes, Pamela?

Pamela: Professor, I thought that there were 'rules' regarding where and how houses are built; are these people allowed to do these crazy things?

Professor Youngberry: Good question. There are certainly laws that determine what houses should look like, but, in rural areas, they are far more relaxed. Now, these slides show people who have converted various means of transport into homes ... this family lives in a bus, this man, in British Columbia, lives on a converted ferry and this family lives in a converted aeroplane. Did you know that there's even a company that will convert planes into private homes for a fee of $290 000?

Arnold: Wow, that's quite a sum!

Professor Youngberry: Well, you're right, but when you think about it ... (fade out)

REVISION 3 UNITS 07-09

Speaker 1

I'd always wanted to visit Austria, so when I won a trip for two to Vienna last year, I was absolutely delighted! I arranged for the kids to stay at my sister's and off we went. The tour included a visit to the beautiful Schonbrunn Castle, which was the home of the Hapsburg royal family. The castle was named after a nearby spring called *schoner brunnen* (*lovely spring*). The castle is truly extraordinary ... the architecture is magnificent and there's even a lovely park to stroll through. I had a fantastic time, though I think Paul was a little bored!

Speaker 2

The first time I went to Leeds Castle was on my birthday, three years ago. I've made a point of going there every year since. The castle was originally the home of the Saxon royal family – it is lovely, but, being a keen gardener, I prefer to spend as much time in the garden as possible. The flowers are exquisite; they're the types you'd find in a typical English country garden ... Roses, poppies, pinks ... they're just marvellous to look at! But, my absolute favourite part is the maze; it consists of 2 400 yew trees and it's quite a challenge finding your way out of it!

Speaker 3

I had a fantastic time when I went to France a couple of weeks ago, but the highlight of my trip was definitely the Palace of Versailles. The palace was originally built as a hunting lodge in 1624 and became the official residence of the French kings in 1682. I was most impressed by the French classical architecture and the gardens are incredible!

I must've taken about a thousand photos and I can't wait to have them developed! Versailles is now a national museum and well worth a visit if you happen to be in that part of the world ...

Speaker 4

My sister, Priscilla, insisted that I join her on her tour of the castles of the Rhine Valley in Germany. I wasn't too keen on the idea, though ... I told her that I'd rather spend my holiday lying on a beach on some remote tropical island, rather than walking through some dank, old castles. Actually, it turned out to be quite interesting. The castles were awesome and the little towns and villages in the area were delightful! Still, I think my next holiday will be in the Bahamas!

Speaker 5

My friend, Elizabeth, and I had been planning a sightseeing trip to Rome for ages. So you can imagine how upset I was when she cancelled at the last minute! Then I did something I never thought I'd do ... I went on my own! It was great ... I chatted to some of the locals ... learnt a bit of Italian and visited all the sights. I especially enjoyed my tour of the Castel Sant'Angelo; it's named after the Archangel Michael, who apparently appeared at the castle during a plague in AD 590. The view from the castle is quite spectacular; you can see the entire city of Rome!

UNIT 10 LESSON 1

Harland Jones: Good evening, listeners, it's time for your daily dose of *The Harland Show* ... The show that gets you talking! With us tonight, we have Maurice Farnsworth of *The Truth in Art Society* and the hot, young artist, Ripley. As I'm sure you are all aware, Ripley's latest works are currently being exhibited at the Waterman Gallery and causing quite a stir ... In fact, some people are seeing red, isn't that right Mr Farnsworth?

Maurice Farnsworth: Yes, exactly right, Harland. *The Truth in Art Society*, which works to promote art and culture, strongly disapproves of Mr Ripley's art works. If you can call them that ...

Jones: Ripley, would you like to describe your exhibition to our listeners? Give them an idea of what all the fuss is about?

Ripley: I'm not quite sure what all the fuss is about either. My current exhibition is called *The Modern Caveman* and consists of a number of sketches, drawings and paintings that resemble cave paintings. But the theme is life in the modern world, so, for example, one of the cave paintings shows a man talking on his mobile phone.

Farnsworth: Yes, and it's absolutely ridiculous. You're exhibiting a collection of cartoon strips, in my opinion, Mr Ripley. Nothing more than silly stick figures on the Internet or watching satellite TV. Is that really art?

Jones: Good question. How would you classify your works of art, Ripley? Are you an artist in the traditional sense?

Ripley: Yes, I am because I offer the public my own perspective on the world. That's what artists are supposed to do. I like using different mediums and I have produced a number of works ranging from paintings and wood carvings to sculptures and pottery in the past. Right now, I'd classify myself as a painter, but I think labels and definitions are so limiting.

Jones: Who would you say are your influences, Ripley?

Ripley: Hmm... Rudolph Monk, who is famous for his papier-mâché sculptures, is my mentor and probably my greatest influence. Music is also a tremendous inspiration. You know, music really encourages the creative process.

Farnsworth: Creative process? My foot! Any fool could come up with the things you do! Picasso, Matisse, Michelangelo, those were great artists! After visiting your exhibition, I was shocked! I've seen more impressive art work at my niece's nursery school! And I'm very surprised that the Waterman Gallery, where more conservative pieces of art are usually exhibited, actually gave your *collection* the green light.

Jones: Any comment, Ripley?

Ripley: The people at the Waterman know good art when they see it. *The Modern Caveman* compares the modern world with the primitive world. You're just jealous of my unique vision, Mr Farnsworth.

Farnsworth: Yes. Jealous. I'm positively green with envy. That's exactly what it is ...

Ripley: Look, art is a form of self-expression, Farnsworth. There aren't any rules. Do you really think that you and your society can define art, can succeed where great thinkers and philosophers have failed?

Farnsworth: You know, Harland, I could talk till I'm blue in the face, but it won't do any good. This man, who is obviously extremely full of himself, will never understand my point of view and ...

Jones: Have to stop you there, I'm afraid, Mr Farnsworth. It's time for a commercial break ... (fade out)

1

Woman: Some people say it's boring, others don't understand what's going on. But I adore it. The scenery, the costumes, the choreography and of course, the music. The performers are always so synchronized, it's amazing. They know exactly what to do, where to go and when to step in. My favourite part is the *solo part*, the so-called *Aria*. You'll hear people say it's too loud for their liking, but I think it's breathtaking. It must take a lot of practice to achieve such perfection.

2

Man: Ladies and gentlemen, the next item is a genuine painting by Van Ross, *The Master Bedroom*. If you take a closer look, you'll notice he has used vibrant colours to convey mood and emotion. This painting, which represents his own room, is considered an absolute masterpiece. Please observe how he depicts the bed and the pictures he has on the walls. An excellent choice for any collector. Of course, since this painting is an original, the starting bid will be $1.5 million. Yes, do I hear another offer? Yes, $1.7million. Excellent sir, anyone else? Yes, the man in the back. $1.8 million. Going once … going twice…

3

Woman: Ahhh… Excuse me sir, do you work here?
Man: Yes, Madame.
Woman: Can you tell me where Picasso's painting is?
Man: Right here, in front of you Madame. This is the famous *Guernica*.
Woman: What, this mess?
Man: MESS! Madame, Picasso was moved to paint *Guernica* shortly after German planes bombarded the Basque town of Guernica on 26th April, 1937. It was completed in less than a month and is considered an artistic masterpiece!
Woman: Really? And this?
Man: THIS is an El Greco.
Woman: Is that what it's called?
Man: No Madame. It's the *Burial of Count Orgaz* BY El Greco!
Woman: Oh! Well, its not a happy subject, but at least I know what's going on.
Man: Yes, Madame. If you will excuse me now. I can't believe what I have to put up with every day!

4

Man: I think it's outrageous. They go around destroying public and private property and then have the cheek to call it art.
Woman: Well, I disagree. I think that some spray paint, a bit of imagination can really help brighten up the city. Some of those kids' creations are just incredible.

Man: We'll see how incredible you think they are when they decide to spray-paint your wall one day. Imagine coming home to find your front wall covered in strange designs or pictures of super heroes, or whatever those youngsters think is fashionable. What's next? Finding your car in a different colour!

5

Critic: So, tell us about this new creation of yours, Gary. It looks so real, just like a photograph. I'm impressed.
Gary: Thank you. I wish everybody shared your opinion. I've had some pretty negative feedback. Anyway, I was inspired by the fields near my village, the picturesque scenery, the magnificent colours of Autumn and the cloudy skies above. I've used short brush strokes and red and orange shades to add to the atmosphere and give it a more lively appearance. The final touch was the sharp contrast between the darkness of the sky and the bright sunlight streaming through the clouds.

6

Woman: Well, I think that it was a complete waste of time. Everything! I've never seen anything like it before either! I was expecting a better exhibition.
Man: Come on Liz, give the guy a break. It's his first exhibition. So, he didn't accurately represent his subjects. Some of his works aren't very realistic. So, what?
Woman: Give the guy a break! What about that statue called *Young Boy*? It was simply awful.
Man: Oh, all right! The arms were a bit uneven. But …
Woman: So, you noticed that, too. I knew my eyes weren't playing tricks on me.
Man: Anyway, as I was saying, the face was very detailed and expressive.

UNIT 11 LESSON 2

Babs: What's going on Paul? You look …
Paul: I'm a nervous wreck, Babs. I don't know what's happening to me. I feel awful.
Babs: Calm down, Paul. Whatever it is, it can't be *that* bad.
Paul: No, it's worse! You can't imagine what I've been going through for the last few months. I've been getting these … panic attacks. Sometimes it's so bad I feel like I'm going to suffocate. I can't breathe and I just want to get out. I feel like I need to escape from something.
Babs: Oh my, I had no idea! How often do you get these panic attacks?
Paul: Almost every day. When I'm walking to my office which is at the end of this long, narrow corridor, when I'm on the tube, in a lift …The worst one was a couple of days ago.
Babs: What happened?
Paul: Well, my friend had a party to celebrate his

wedding anniversary and it turned out to be a nightmare. Not that the party was bad, don't get me wrong. It was me, I just couldn't stay inside the house. I felt like the walls were closing in on me. I broke out into a sweat and my heart was pounding. I felt like I was going to faint. I thought I was having a heart attack or something!

Babs: What did you do?

Paul: I spent the entire night in the garden. I just couldn't go inside. Can you believe it?

Babs: Do you feel like that now?

Paul: No, not really. There are lots of windows in this room. I feel fine.

Babs: Seems to me you're claustrophobic, Paul.

Paul: Claustro … what?

Babs: Claustrophobic. Judging from what you've just described, it sounds like claustrophobia to me.

Paul: Oh no! Is it serious? Am I going to die?

Babs: Relax, Paul. You're not going to die. It's not an illness, it's a condition. It's a fear of confined spaces or of not having an easy escape route. That's why you've been getting those panic attacks on the tube.

Paul: How do you know so much about claustrophobia?

Babs: My aunt Mary has it.

Paul: When did she become claustrophobic?

Babs: In her twenties, I think.

Paul: So, how did it happen?

Babs: She got stuck in a lift at a car park for two days. It happened over the weekend and they didn't find her till Monday. Ever since then she's been scared of enclosed places.

Paul: Did she get professional help?

Babs: At first she tried to organise her life around it. Then, some years ago, she decided to see a psychologist.

Paul: I see. Well, maybe it's time I did something about it, too. I can't live like this anymore. (fade out)

UNIT 12 LESSON 2

Rex Partridge: Good morning ladies and gentlemen and a warm welcome to today's seminar which is called *Advertising – Let's fight back*. I'm Rex Partridge and I'm here today to tell you how to protect yourselves against the dangers of advertising. We're under attack, ladies and gentlemen, yes, you heard me, under attack. Every time you open a magazine or switch on the television or listen to the radio you are bombarded with hundreds of advertisements that are intended to persuade you to buy something you don't need. You think you're in control, you think you have a choice, but you are a victim!

OK, that's the bad news. Now, what can we, as responsible consumers, do about this? How can we fight back against advertising? First things first, increase your awareness. Count how many advertisements you are exposed to every day – that includes everything from newspapers and magazines to billboards and even people's T-shirts. Work out how many advertisements you're likely to come across in one year – the figure is shocking! Then, evaluate the ads. Try to become aware of the psychological techniques the advertisers use to sell products. People buy things for a lot of different reasons, like fear or greed or the desire to compete with others ... And advertisers are quick to take advantage.

Another thing you can do as conscientious consumers is keep track of your buying habits. If you find yourself about to purchase a particular product, ask yourself why. Did you see an advertisement for it somewhere? Do you really need it? The answers may surprise you. Next, do away with brand loyalty. Don't buy things simply because of the name. If you feel, for example, that you just have to wear a particular brand of trainers that everybody else is wearing, that could mean you're more concerned with fitting in than with expressing your own personality.

Which brings me to my next point – fashion trends.

Don't be fooled into thinking that you have to change your wardrobe each season. You really shouldn't allow a handful of greedy designers to determine how you look and how you feel about yourself. Forget about what's in and what's out. Just be yourself!

If you really want to battle with the advertisers, you may have to resort to more extreme tactics ... For one thing, stop buying things that are advertised. Companies can't make money if people don't buy their products. You might think this is a bit radical, but in practice, it's easier than you think. If you've seen an item of clothing at a famous brand store that you really like, why not look for it at a thrift shop? It'll be cheaper to buy and you'll be supporting the thrift shop, not the brand.

Finally, do away with the media altogether. Don't buy newspapers or magazines; read them at the newsagent's or the library, but don't buy them. If you must watch your favourite show on TV, then don't buy any of the products advertised during

the programme.
Well, I hope that I've inspired you all to take on the advertising industry. It's time to stand up for your rights as citizens and consumers ... together, we can make a difference!

REVISION 4 UNITS 10-12

Andy: So, Sheila, more and more companies are choosing to advertise their services or products on the Net. Does it really work?

Sheila: Yes, it does, Andy, but companies have to know how the Web works, and what the Internet audience wants to see. The Net is an excellent advertising medium if used correctly.

Andy: What exactly do you mean by that?

Sheila: Let me give you an example of a common mistake. Many companies advertise their services using *billboard-type* web pages; these are basic pages that feature the company logo, a few paragraphs about what they do, some contact info, and that's about it. This can be moderately effective, especially if the company offers a unique product or service and has no competition. But it's not enough because the Web is much more than a yellow pages of services and products.

Andy: What else should an effective web site include?

Sheila: Well, people browse the Internet to find products and services, but they also browse to explore, to search for information, and to entertain themselves. It's important to remember that the audience's time is valuable and they will not wait for pages that take too long to download. And they'll obviously ignore pages that are boring to look at, or that are poorly written. The best way to satisfy the Internet audience's need for raw information is with a clean, fast-loading design that sells the product or service at the same time.

Andy: You mentioned earlier that the Net offers excellent advertising opportunities. How is advertising on the Net more effective than, let's say, advertising in magazines or newspapers?

Sheila: A web site *hit* is far more significant than a passive consumer who sees an ad in a magazine, because the person who found a company's site on the Internet didn't just come across it by chance. He or she found it after entering a keyword into the search engine, or they followed a link to that page from another web site. Unlike traditional advertising, each visitor to a web site is part of a pre-selected audience. They're already interested in some aspect of what you do, or they wouldn't have arrived at your web site.

Andy: And I guess you can reach more people through the Net, right?

Sheila: Absolutely. Traditional advertising cannot match the global reach of the Internet. For a very small sum of money you can reach everyone on the planet who is connected to the World Wide Web. That's tens of millions of people and the number is growing. Unlike print advertising, your costs are exactly the same whether you reach someone across the street, or someone in Hong Kong.

Andy: But isn't it more expensive to create and maintain a web site than to use more traditional methods of advertising?

Sheila: Quite the opposite, actually. It would cost thousands of dollars to place a single colour ad for just one month in a national magazine. On the Web, you can post many pages of colour material, entire catalogues if you want, at a low cost. This means that you can afford to experiment with different approaches, and allow time for consumer interest in your site to develop. Besides, another advantage of Web advertising is that you can get immediate feedback from your audience, with customer surveys and online product or service orders. This is the kind of thing that you just can't do with other forms of advertising.

Andy: Well, thank you Sheila for joining us today. And now ... (fade out)

UNIT 01

Culture Notes

1. **drive-through, drive-in**
   a restaurant, bank, etc. where people can buy food or do business without getting out of their cars

2. **ATM**
   a machine outside a bank that people use to get money from the accounts

3. **espresso**
   a strong concentrated black coffee

Language Points

Lesson 2

1. **... you will be amazed — among other things — by the number of cars on the street.**
   among other things: This expression is used to say that there are more facts, things, etc. like the one or ones mentioned but that the speaker chooses not to discuss them in detail.
   e.g. At the meeting they discussed, among other things, recent events in Eastern Europe.
   Mr. Green, among other things, has shown us a new approach to the problem.
   amazed: adj. greatly surprised
   e.g. Tom was amazed by the news.

2. **(It's) no / little / small wonder**
   used to express that something is fully anticipated
   e.g. It's no wonder there is no picture on the screen, I didn't plug in the TV.
   Little wonder Jimmy and Robert asked so many questions, they were greatly confused.

3. **vehicle**
   n. a machine with an engine which can carry people or goods from one place to another (such as a bicycle, car, truck, or bus)
   e.g. On Sundays, there are all kinds of vehicles on the street.
   "Is this your vehicle, sir?" asked the policeman.

4. **run out of**
   use up all of something; have no more of something
   e.g. They ran out of gasoline.
   We're running out of time.

5. **be short of**
   not enough
   e.g. Amy was short of money, so she wanted to borrow some from me.
   Some areas in Africa are short of food.

6. **And if you feel that your life has become so busy that you don't even have time for some coffee ...**
   Here the "so ... that" structure tells readers the result of such a busy life.

7. **convenient**
   adj. close and easy to reach some place or suitable for sth.
   e.g. I find the most convenient way to the supermarket once a month.
   Is three o'clock convenient for you?

8. **be used to**
   be accustomed to; have experienced something so that it no longer seems surprising, difficult, strange, etc.
   e.g. Tim is not used to the weather here.
   She is used to getting up early in the morning.

9. **There are hundreds of drive-through fast food outlets and burger bars in the city, where you can grab a bite to eat.**
   ..., Las Vegas has been famous for its wedding chapels, where you can get married quickly and at a low cost.
   In these two sentences, unrestricted attributive

clauses modify "drive-through fast food outlets", "burger bars" and "wedding chapels".

10. **similarly**

adv. in a similar way

e.g. This idea is similarly expressed in his most recent book.

Men must wear a jacket and tie. Similarly, women must wear a skirt or dress but not trousers.

11. **date back to**

date from; have lasted since a particular time in the past

e.g. The custom dates back to the time when men wore swords.

12. **in that / this case**

used to describe what you will do, or what will happen, as a result of a particular situation or event

e.g. They might not offer me much money. In that case, I won't work for them.

Robert won't go there. In this case, I'm not going either.

13. **out of the ordinary**

unusual, uncommon

e.g. Nothing out of the ordinary had happened.

Chairman Mao is a great man out of the ordinary.

14. **catch on**

become popular and fashionable

e.g. It was a popular style in Britain but it never really caught on in America.

The new song caught on very quickly.

15. **needless to say**

of course; as was to be expected

e.g. Needless to say, this visit will certainly increase our friendship and draw close our economic ties.

Needless to say, it rained when I left my window open.

16. **weird**

adj. strange; unusual and not sensible or acceptable

e.g. He has some weird ideas.

Mike's got a really weird sense of humour.

17. **means**

n. a method or way (of doing) or achieving something

e.g. What would be the most effective means of advertising our product?

Use whatever means you can to solve this problem.

18. **depend on/upon**

1) trust or have confidence in someone or something

e.g. You can depend on Jane — She always keeps her promises.

I depended on the map, but it was wrong.

2) need the support, help or existence of someone or something else

e.g. My wife and my children depend on me.

The country depends heavily on its tourist trade.

3) change according to ...

e.g. The success of a person depends on many things.

Whether the game will be cancelled depends on the weather.

19. **vast**

adj. extremely large

e.g. A huge palace was constructed at vast public expense.

The vast plains stretch for 700 miles.

20. **routine**

n. the regular fixed ordinary way of working or doing things

e.g. Mark longed to escape from the same old familiar routine.

Please do it according to the routine.

Translation of the Text

Lesson 1

国家不同，习惯不同

如果你认为国内有一些风俗习惯非常奇特，那么你应该重新思考这个问题。当你了解到世界其它地方的人的行为习惯时，你可能会感到惊讶。

西班牙

今天是新年除夕，你正在西班牙参加一个舞会。你会忘记唱"友谊地久天长"，忘记玩扑克，或者忘记做任何能给你带来好运的事。这是为什么？很简单！因为这些在西班牙都不灵。当午夜钟声敲响时，生活在西班牙的人会吃掉12颗葡萄，希望来年能为自己带来好运。对，这并不是一个玩笑。这样做是不是奏效，很难说，除非你自己试一试。它的确值得一试。

泰国

在泰国，有几件事要铭记于心。到泰国人家里做客时一定要脱鞋，毕竟你不想表现出对主人的不敬，对吧？同样，泰国人不喜欢别人摸自己的头。他们把这种行为视为非常无礼。如果在社交聚会上观察泰国人，你会发现年轻人努力保持自己的头低于长者，由此来避免给人留下轻视长者的印象。当然，不可能总能做到，只要努力就行了。

玻利维亚

玻利维亚和世界其他地方一样，人们相互间候时常常握手。即使碰巧手脏时也没有问题，可以伸出胳膊代替。另外，在晚餐聚会上，玻利维亚人希望客人吃完盘子里的所有的食物。所以，要确保你盘里的食物别像小山一样多！玻利维亚人喜欢客人在用餐时恭维他们菜做得好。所以，如果希望再要一份，你最好称赞他们一两次。

赞比亚

离开玻利维亚，我们来到赞比亚。这里的人们总是提前约定见面时间，但约定并不起多大作用，因为不能保证如期见面。所以，拉把椅子坐，因为你可能会等很久。还有，到了晚餐时间，客人应该要求吃饭。对，就是这样！由主人先提出请吃饭会被认为没有礼貌。而且，别想拒绝吃饭，这也是赞比亚人不赞成的。

Lesson 2

生活在快行线上

当你造访美国时，有件事情是毋庸置疑的：暂不论其他的事，你将惊讶于街上汽车的数目之多。

当然，这是有原因的：美国人几乎做什么事都以汽车代步，因此也就难怪到处都有如此之多的车辆。

想像一下：你的牛奶喝光了而你身上的现金又不足，你会怎样做？你会坐车到免下车自动提款机去取现金，然后就能立即开车到免下车便利店购物。当你无法找到地方停车而后座上还有一个哭喊不停的小孩时，这种免下车服务的确是很有用的。如果你觉得你的生活忙碌得甚至没有时间喝咖啡，不要担忧！你随时可以在免下车的意大利咖啡厅喝上一杯。很方便吧？你认为如何？

全家人聚在桌旁，在家里享受一顿正餐，这当然是大部分人所期望的，但如今大部分美国人都习惯在他们的车里吃东西。城市里有成百上千家免下车快餐店和堡吧，在那儿你可以快捷而又轻松自在地吃上一顿。这一行生意现在仍然十分兴隆。事实上，这些地方在高峰期的时候外面总会停着长长一溜的汽车，特别是在中午12:30和下午2:30左右。

那些免下车餐馆的渊源要追溯到20世纪50年代的那些免下车即可享受服务的地方。同样免下车影院也不是什么新鲜事，它们可追溯到20世纪30年代，最初是为那些想去看电影的家庭设计的，他们不必盛装打扮，也不必找临时照顾婴儿的人。这些地方特别受那些不能去迪斯科或是夜总会的未成年青少年的欢迎，他们总在附近逛来逛去。如今，大约有1 000家免下车影院，人们经常去那儿看电影，同时在车里就餐。

除了吃、喝、玩，还有更多你不必下车就可以做的事情。比如你计划结婚，但想要避免所有的繁文缛节并节省下发邀请函以及为结婚作准备的费用。假如真是那样的话，拉斯维加斯就是适合你的地方。很长时间以来拉斯维加斯就以其婚礼小教堂而闻名，在那儿你可以迅速结婚，而且花费很少。现今，甚至有免下车结婚小教堂，在那儿，结婚的夫妇不必下车，他们只需驾车而来、停车、通过车窗举行仪式即可。这种事情似乎不同寻常，但在美国却越来越流行。

不用说，这种"忙碌的生活"对大部分人来说听起来不可思议，但对于美国人来说，这是自20世纪50年代以来他们就开始习惯的一种生活方式。那时，汽车就不仅仅是一种交通工具，更是地位的象征和艺术品。现在也许不再是那种情况，但美国人仍然依靠他们的汽车去做所有的事情。可能这是因为各地方之间的巨大距离，也许是因为人们日常生活太忙碌而没有时间做日常常规的事情。谁知道呢？不管是什么情况，有一件事情是真实的：美国是一个"车轮上的国家"。

UNIT 02

Cultural Notes

1. **the Internet**
   a computer system that allows millions of computer users around the world to exchange information

2. **Satellite TV**
   television programs that are broadcast using satellites in space

3. **mobile phone**
   a telephone that people can carry with and use in any place

Language Points

Lesson 2

1. **get one's money's worth**
   get something worth the price that someone pay
   e.g. At that price you want to make sure you get your money's worth.
   We enjoyed the film so much that we felt we'd got our money's worth.

2. **outrageous**
   adj. very offensive or shocking
   e.g. I can't believe he's been allowed to spread such outrageous lies.
   It is outrageous that the poor should have to pay such high taxes.

3. **trade**
   v. buy and sell goods, services, etc.
   e.g. These companies trade mainly in furs and animal skins.
   Salesmen traded the new products all over the country.

4. **The money used in these transactions didn't just come in a variety of forms, ...**
   In this sentence, the past participle phrase used in these transactions is an attribute, modifying the subject "the money".
   transaction: n. a business deal; the process of doing business
   a variety of: a lot of a particular type of things that are different from each other
   e.g. The girls come from a variety of different background.
   The box contains a variety of toys.

5. **tribal**
   adj. connected with a tribe or tribes
   e.g. a tribal dance
   tribal music

6. **dare**
   v. be brave or rude enough (to)
   e.g. I didn't dare to ask.
   The others used to steal things from stores, but I would never dare to.

7. **value**
   n. the worth of something in money or as compared with other goods for which it might be changed
   e.g. Because of continual price increases, the value of the dollar has fallen in recent years.
   The thieves took some clothes and a few books, but nothing of great value.

8. **In fact, it was not until the 7th century BC in the kingdom of Lydia that the first real coins were made.**
   Here "it" is the formal subject, indicating the actual subject, that-clause "that the first real coins were made".

9. **circulate**
   v. (cause to) move or flow along a closed path; move from place to place or from person to person

e.g. Blood circulates around the body.

A lot of false information has been circulated.

10. **In actual fact, people had been using coins for about 1600 years until banknotes made their historic appearance.**

In this sentence, "had been using" is the past perfect progressive form of the verb "use" in its active voice, indicating that the process of using coins was on all the way before banknotes appeared.

11. **fixed**

adj. fastened; not movable or changeable

e.g. The tables are firmly fixed to the floor.

He has very fixed ideas on this subject.

12. **spread**

v. (cause to) open, reach, or stretch out; make or become longer, broader, wider, etc.

e.g. The news soon spread through the whole of the town.

Let's spread the map out on the floor.

13. **issue**

v. bring out for the notice of the public

e.g. Silva issued a statement denying all knowledge of the affair.

I bought the book the day when it was issued.

14. **Credit cards originated in the United States in the 1930s, but they didn't become popular until the 1950s.**

The pattern "not ... until" is used to say that something happens or someone does something at a particular time or when something else happens.

e.g. We won't start until Jane comes.

John didn't go to bed until 12 o'clock.

originate: v. (cause to) begin.

e.g. a custom originating in Chinese culture

Her book originated in a short story.

15. **perception**

n. clear and natural understanding; something noticed and understood

e.g. Parents' views influence their children's perceptions of the world.

Ross shows unusual perception for a boy of his age.

16. **emergency**

n. an unexpected and dangerous happening which must be dealt with quickly

e.g. Ring the bell in an emergency.

He called an emergency meeting of the governors.

17. **undoubtedly**

adv. definitely truly or known to exist

e.g. That is undoubtedly true.

Undoubtedly, he is of wealth.

18. **It is widely believed that 'smart money' in the form of 'smart cards' will revolutionise financial transactions one day.**

In this sentence, "it" is formal subject, indicating the actual subject "that 'smart money' in the form of 'smart cards' will revolutionise financial transactions one day".

19. **capacity**

n. the amount that something can hold or produce; ability, power

e.g. The seating capacity of this theatre is 1 000.

Her capacity for remembering is very useful to her.

20. **take care of**

be responsible for; look after

e.g. Take care of the baby while I'm out.

Her secretary always took care of the details.

Translation of the text

Lesson 1

分类广告

1. 神奇磁拖鞋

又找不到您的拖鞋了？我们磁石公司已经找到了一个方法，帮助您解决寻找鞋子的难题。现在就向您介绍……神奇磁拖鞋！这种拖鞋拥有特殊的磁性，可以将两只鞋子粘在一起，且款式多样，色彩繁多。各大鞋店均可以买到。但是要注意，谨防假冒哦！

现在订货！电话 7963028

2. 电话哑铃

您必须得承认，您一直想要在繁忙的日常工作中抽出时间来做点锻炼，但是可怜的您一直未能如愿。那么，电话哑铃将为您解决这个问题！它决不会让您失望！它看起来就像个普通电话，但它的电话听筒里却附置了一个5公斤重的哑铃。这个绝妙的发明使您既可以锻炼身体，又可以同时保持与外界的联系。为办公室里也添置一个吧，您就会立刻拥有强壮的，线条优美的手臂！电话哑铃的售价令人难以置信的低廉，仅售£29.99。请记住，如果您对所售商品不是很满意，我们将全额退款！

致电8524430订货。

3. 狗狗自动洗浴器！

宠物爱好者们注意了！如果您心爱的雷克斯（Rex）总是在园子里打滚撒欢，不必担心！有了狗狗自动洗浴器，狗狗就又会干干净净了！这项神奇的发明就像是把狗狗当车来洗：你幸运的四条腿的朋友会被洗净、烘干，而您不必动一个手指头！还不想买？以下是萨里郡的Rory Thorpe 想要告诉您的："我试了各种方法来洗狗狗，但是全都不好用。直到我找到了狗狗自动洗浴器。它是我看到的最了不起的发明！"

现金付款，信用卡付款均可。我们甚至还会附赠您的狗狗朋友一件免费的皮夹克！不要错过这个一生一次的难得机会！现在就订货吧！

更多信息请查询5556700。

4. 随身小书桌

想像一下这样的情况：您暂时离开了一下你的办公桌，您的老板为此暴跳如雷。您该怎么办？很简单：您就买一个随身小书桌！这款精致的小东西包括一个书桌和固定在上面的一条很厚的吊带。您可以把它挂在脖子上。结果会怎样？您就会立刻拥有一个便携式办公室，可以携带它到几乎任何地方。详细信息请查询3797222。不要再迟疑了！赶紧拨打电话，立即订货吧！

Lesson 2

从石头到塑料

如果你去市场用苹果换得一打鸡蛋，你是否觉得物有所值？这听起来有点不可思议，是吗？这对你来说可能很奇怪，但在古时候人们确实就是这样交易的。在那些农业发达的地区，各种各样的农产品被用作支付的手段。

用在这些交易中的货币不仅是以各种各样的形式出现，而且也以各种大小不同的体积出现。例如，公元前13世纪时，中国人就使用贝币、刀形币，甚至铲币来购买物品。信不信由你，大约就在此时，一些部落群体就使用"石头货币"。太平洋上的一个岛屿——亚普岛上的人们使用宽达4米（12尺）的石头。像那样的钞票，谁还敢到处乱扔？

中国人发明了最早的硬币。这些硬币呈圆形，是由几乎没有什么价值的金属制成的。实际上，直到公元前7世纪吕底亚王国才制造出第一枚真正的硬币。这些硬币也是用金属制成的，其价值是由它们的重量所决定的。那时，货币已经非常重要，一些发展中的社会群体开始流通他们自己的印有可识别防伪标记的硬币。

事实上，在纸币问世前，人们使用硬币已经大约有1 600年的历史了。直到公元9世纪，纸币首先在中国出现，人们很快接受了纸币这个新生事物。起初，人们使用简单的手写收据，但到11世纪早期，这些收据被赋予了固定的价值，成了正式的货币。这种新的流行的东西在东方很快传播开来，然而，直到16世纪它才传到西方，而且直到17世纪末叶，英国才发行了第一批印刷的纸币。

但时过境迁。如今，现钞不再是我们唯一的支付方式，以信用卡的形式出现的塑料货币已经必不可少。信用卡源自于20世纪30年代的美国，但直到20世纪50年代才流行起来。这些卡片已经改变了我们对货币的概念，因为人们不必再提前支付现金。另外，在紧急情况下，信用卡很便利，而且很容易使用。

毫无疑问，货币的发展将不会停滞不前，可以确信，总有一天，以"聪明的卡片"形式出现的"聪明的货币"将会引起金融交易革命。"聪明的卡片"将包含微型集成电路片，它们能储存个人资料，有能力担负你所有的财政责任，而你毋需动一下手指。货币确实已经经历了漫长的历程，但又有谁知道未来和技术又会怎样掌握我们的个人财务呢？

UNIT 03

Culture Note

1. **A conventional TV set** has a two-dimensional (2-D) screen, while a holographic TV set projects three-dimensional (3-D) images.

2. **Hypersonic travel** occurs when you travel faster than the speed of sound.

3. **Infrared** involves the use of electromagnetic waves which are longer than those of red light in the spectrum and cannot be seen.

4. **Magnetic levitation** involves the use of powerful electric magnets which raise the train just above the track. The massive reduction in friction results in a faster, more efficient train.

Language Points

Lesson 2

1. **Several well-known electronics companies are currently in the process of developing ... battled it out in 3-D!**
   well-known: known to many people, familiar or famous
   currently adv. at the present time
   e.g. Our director is currently in London.
   in the process of doing sth: performing a particular task
   e.g. We're still in the process of moving house.
   　　The house is still in the process of being built.
   battle out: try hard to achieve sth difficult

2. **However, holographic TV is bound to revolutionise our concept of TV in the future.**
   be bound to do sth: be certain to do sth
   e.g. The weather is bound to get better tomorrow.
   　　You've done so much work that you're bound to pass the exam.

3. **... come up with an experimental microchip.**

come up with: find or produce (an answer, a solution, etc.)
e.g. She came up with a new idea for increasing sales.
microchip (chip): very small piece of silicon or similar material carrying a complex electrical circuit

4. **When this device has been installed in a television set, ...**
   install sth in sth: fix equipment, furniture, etc. in position for use, esp. by making the necessary connections with the supply of electricity, water, etc.
   e.g. He installed a heating or lighting system in a building.
   　　I'm having a shower installed.

5. **Though not recommended for dieters, the microchip is sure to be a hit when it becomes available!**
   be sure to be a hit: be sure to become very popular
   a hit: a person or a thing that is very popular, success
   e.g. He is a hit with everyone.
   　　Her new film is quite a hit.
   　　They sang their latest hit.

6. **... as soon as all the kinks have been ironed out.**
   kinks: difficult problems in technology
   iron out: get rid of/solve the difficulties

7. **If your washing machine is about to break down, for example, it sends a warning message to the computer link and inform you in time to take action. Handy, huh?**
   break down: cease to function because of a mechanical, electrical, etc. fault
   e.g. The telephone system has broken down.
   　　Our car broke down on the motorway.
   take action (on): do sth in order to deal with a problem
   e.g. The Government has promised to take swift action on the energy crisis.
   　　The Party would not be able to take action

on all the proposals now.

handy: adj. convenient to handle or use; useful

e.g. A good tool-box is a handy thing to have in the house.

Always keep a first-aid kit handy.

8. **So, you still think that e-mail is the ultimate in quick correspondence?**

This sentence means that you may still think that e-mail is by far the quickest communication method in the world.

ultimate: that cannot be surpassed or improved upon; greatest

e.g. The ultimate luxury of the trip was flying in Concorde.

9. **Provided that users have suitable decoders, they will be able to send messages directly and quickly and if the idea takes off, ...**

provided /provided that / providing / providing that ...: conj. on the condition or understanding that ...

e.g. I will agree to go provided / providing / (that) my expenses are paid.

Provided we get good weather it will be a successful holiday.

take off: (of an idea, a product, etc.) suddenly become successful or popular; (of sales of a product) rise very quickly

e.g. The new dictionary has really taken off.

Sales of home computers have taken off in recent years.

10. **... to stay in touch with ease**

to get the time information easily

Translation of the Text

Lesson 2

Reading

顶级发明

未来电视

如果你是电视迷，肯定会喜欢这一创意的。几家知名电子公司目前正在开发一种立体电视机，在这种

电视里，你可以看到你最喜爱的动作片英雄在三维空间里打斗。虽然这种技术在目前既不成熟，而且成本也是高得惊人，但却无疑会革新我们对未来电视的观念。未来电视的先进性，还远不止于此。研究人员已经研制出一种尚处于实验阶段的芯片。在电视机中装入这种芯片后，电视机将根据节目的内容，同时释放出相应的气味。因此，在观看你喜欢的烹饪节目时，你还能闻到诱人的烤鸡、土豆、苹果馅饼、巧克力苏芙哩的香味。无须赘述，你已经知道未来电视是一番怎样的前景了。这种芯片一旦被研制出来，肯定会轰动一时。但对于节食者来，这种技术却毫无推荐的价值。

能说话的家用电器

科学家预言：家用设备，像烤面包机、冰箱、茶壶将有一天能与你沟通交流。这听起来似乎有点不可思议。各种家用设备将通过计算机网络被相互连接在一起，只要所有的技术难题解决之后，这种专门的技术便可问世。你也许会问，那又如何？问得好，打个比方，如果你的洗衣机即将出问题，它会向计算机网络发出预警信息，通知你及时采取行动，很方便，是不是？

电视邮件的诞生

到目前为止，你也许仍然认为，电子邮件是最快的通讯方式，仔细想一想，它比寄信要快多了。但电子邮件还存在一些问题。因为电子邮件总是不能很安全地到达目的地，且发电子邮件还得首先解决一台计算机。几家美国公司正在开发一种通过电视传送信息的技术，这种技术被称为电视天线方式，简称为"a-mail"，用户只要有合适的解码器，就能直接而迅速地发送信息了。如果这一创意得到实现，电视邮件将会比电话更受欢迎，

手表将被淘汰

还有一种新颖的发明有望出现。老式单调的手表将被改造成一种便携式的微型可视电话。它可使你很容易得知时间信息。这种手表里面有一个能被声音激活的微型话筒。如果你经常幻想成为詹姆斯·邦德，听到这个消息，你一定会非常高兴的。

交友

是不是觉得有点孤独？好啦，振作起来吧！"发光的徽章"会迅速拓展你的社交圈。这个讨人喜欢的小设备可以储存你所有的个人信息，诸如最喜欢的食物、电影、音乐等。仅需在公共场所戴上此"徽章"，它就会将你的个人信息传送到他人的"徽章"里。如果你的个性和爱好与他人一致，双方的"微章"都会发光。你们两人便可以开始交谈了。

Revision 01-03

Reading

奢华的生活方式

千岛群岛除了指闻名世界的沙拉美味外，还指加拿大一侧的圣·劳伦斯河从金士顿到布罗克维尔这一段和位于美国一侧的亚历山大湾这一带散布着众多大小不一的岛屿的水域。千岛群岛因19世纪晚期和20世纪早期的大实业家们奢华的生活方式而闻名。他们在岛上大兴土木，建造了为数众多、极尽奢华的消夏别墅，还特地为自己建立了一个俱乐部——千岛俱乐部。

在群岛上所有的房产中，最为宏伟和豪华的别墅的主人是乔治·鲍兹，一个"从布衣到富豪"的经典范例。乔治·鲍兹1851年出生在波罗的海一个隶属于德国的小岛，汝根。在他13岁的时候，鲍兹来到纽约，在那里他开始在饭店厨房干活。几年之后，他攒了足够多的钱，随后来到德克萨斯开始自己创业。结果，他的这个尝试被证明是一个错误：他所经营的牧场在经历了接连不断的自然灾害后一蹶不振——他失去了一切。

1871年鲍兹年仅20，重返纽约。在那里，他供职于服务业，并开始平步青云，担任了一系列的职务。5年后，鲍兹担任费城著名的三叶草俱乐部的管家。在那里他第一次见到了他未来的妻子，三叶草俱乐部老板的女儿，路易斯·奥古斯塔·凯瑞尔，而且也获得了他后来在私人岛屿上建造童话城堡的灵感。1877年，鲍兹和凯瑞尔结婚。

1881年，鲍兹在费城开了一家名为贝拉维的饭店，其服务品质达到了前所未有的水平。他也因此在利润共享的基础上同时负责纽约市最负盛名的饭店沃尔多夫·埃斯托利亚的管理工作。

当鲍兹全家第一次到千岛群岛旅游时，鲍兹就已经是百万富翁，而且正在向千万富翁的目标努力。1895年，他从国会议员E.K.哈金手中购买了一处地产，一个名为哈特的小岛的一部分，随后将其更名为"心"。鲍兹对这个自然形状颇似心的小岛准备进行一番改造，并着手将岛上原有的建筑推倒，代之以魔幻城堡。鲍兹在2月14日这一天，既是情人节同时又是路易斯的生日，宣布了这项计划。

数百名工人来到岛上，在费城建筑师的指挥下来进行这项改建工程。到1904年的时候，城堡的外围建筑已经完工。正当内部装修从一楼开始进行时，一封来自纽约的写有"停止工程，鲍茨夫人去世"的电报宣告了城堡的停工。

直到鲍兹1916年去世，他再也没有造访过这个城堡。它在那里孤零零地伫立了73年，直到1977年千岛群岛桥梁工程管理处接管，并经过重新修缮，才得以恢复它往日的荣耀。

现在，对于每一位参加千岛群岛一日游的游客来说，魔幻城堡是一个必游项目。没有一个返回船上的游客不对鲍兹心中的童话景象唏嘘不已。

UNIT 04

Language Points

1. **... however, wasn't too thrilled about the idea.**

   thrill: v. cause sb to feel excited

   e.g. The film thrilled the audience.

   I was thrilled by her beauty.

   We were thrilled to hear your wonderful news.

2. **It was an opportunity I couldn't turn down.**

   turn down: reject or refuse to consider

   e.g. He tried to join the army but was turned down because of poor health.

   He asked Jane to marry him but she turned him down.

3. **... a pickup truck passed by and the driver offered to give us a lift**

   offer

   1) put forward sth (to sb) to be considered and accepted or refused; present

      e.g. The company has offered a high salary.

      She offered a reward for the return of her lost bracelet.

      I've been offered a job in Japan.

      We offered him the house for $500 000.

   2) show or express the willingness or intention to do or give sth

      e.g. I don't think they need help, but I think I should offer anyway.

      They offered no resistance.

      We offered him a lift, but he didn't accept.

4. **... as I was feeling a bit under the weather.**

   under the weather: feeling unwell or depressed

   e.g. be/feel/look under the weather

She's been a bit under the weather recently.

5. **After surviving an uncomfortable drive, the unbearable heat and the blinding sun, we finally reached ...**

   After doing ... sb do sth=After we had survived ..., we finally reached ...

   e.g. After working for a long time, she sat down to have a rest.

   the blinding sun: the sun is too bright, so it makes people temporarily blind

   e.g. a blinding flash/light

   He was blinded by the sunlight.

6. **... noise which had me on my feet in a split second!**

   on one's feet: standing

   e.g. I've been on my feet all day, so I'm terribly tired.

   in a split second: at once, quickly

   e.g. The accident happened in a split second.

7. **He tried to calm me down and offered to show me where the growling was coming from.**

   calm ... down: cause ... to become calm

   e.g. Just calm down a bit!

   Have a brandy — it'll help to calm you down.

8. **I still felt the need to take precautions.**

   precaution n. thing done in advance to avoid danger, prevent problems

   e.g. Take an umbrella just as a precaution.

   fire precautions / precautions against fire

   I took the precaution of locking everything in the safe.

9. **Suffering under the burning sun with wild animals on the prowl wasn't that bad, after all.**

   on the prowl: moving quietly and cautiously

   e.g. There was a fox on the prowl near the chicken coop.

that: so; very

e.g. I am not that foolish and I can tell the wrong from the true.

Translation of the Text

Lesson 1

"福尔摩斯先生，"圣·克莱尔夫人说道，当我们走进这明亮的饭厅，"我不想再拖延了。我要问你一两个问题，你必须给我一个明确的答复。"

"当然，夫人。"

"你不必考虑我的感受。我不会歇斯底里的。我只是想知道你真正的想法。"

"关于什么的想法？"

"在你内心里，你是否认为奈维拉还活着？"

福尔摩斯似乎对这个问题感到很尴尬。

"老实回答，就现在！"她说道，敏锐地注视着他，看他向后靠在柳条椅上。

"老实说，夫人，我不这样认为。"

"你认为他已经死了？"

"是的。"

"被谋杀？"

"我并没有这么说，但有可能。"

"他是在哪天死的？"

"星期一。夫人，您一连串的质问，有什么原因吗？"

"是的，我有，福尔摩斯先生。我今天收到一封奈维拉的信，你是否能解释一下是怎么回事吗？"

福尔摩斯惊讶地从椅子上弹了起来。

"什么？"他叫道。

"是的，就在今天。"她微笑着站在一旁，手里举着一片信纸。

"我可以看一看吗？"

"当然。"

他急切地从她手里拿过来，拉近灯仔细地检查。我已经离开坐椅，从他后面看那封信。信封非常粗糙而邮戳正是今天。

"字迹潦草，"我低声说道。

"我也这么想。华生。夫人，这不可能是您丈夫的笔迹。"

"是，但是地址是对的。"

"我认为任何人写这封信都会弄清楚地址的。"

"您凭什么这么说？"我问道。

"很简单，我亲爱的华生，"福尔摩斯说道。

"继续说…"我说道。

"你看，这个名字是用非常黑的墨水写的，其他的则发灰，这表示这张带墨渍的纸曾经用过。这个人先写下他的名字，然后便在他写地址之前停下来，这表明他对这个地址并不熟悉。让我们看一看里面…等一下，这是什么？一个戒指？"

Lesson 2

走进丛林，找回激情

1. 远离城市

有人向我提供了随团探索泰国kang kranchan 国家公园的绝好机会，我当时立刻接受了。然而我的朋友PATRICA对此却并不怎么激动。她说，"你不该去，太危险了。"可我没有理会。我知道这次Kang Kranchan探索我一定会有所收获。我需要的就是暂时离开车水马龙的街道、密集的人群及忙碌的生活。这种机会我是不能拒绝的。

2. 辛苦一天的补偿

旅行刚一开始，我们就意识到应该租一辆车而不是坐公交车，因为公交车只把我们送到公园的边缘。沿着一条泥泞小路步行了15公里后才来到了公园的主要入口。几个小时以后，我们都精疲力竭了，正好一辆小卡车路过，司机提出送我们一程，我们感激不尽。下午时分，四周一片寂静。我们都在与一只家养的巨型犀鸟戏耍。这只怪模怪样的鸟竟然让我们忘记了整个一天遇到的艰难。

3. 直面丛林的挑战

第二天就没有那么好了，我感觉身体不适。尽管我应该卧床休息，但我还是决定与其他人继续此次艰难之旅。烈日当空，炎热难当，我们的车一路颠簸后终于到达雨林的最高点，也就是我们开始步行的出发点。起初，路还比较好走，越到丛林深处，行程越是艰难，几乎看不见前面的路。只见猴子在树林里跳来跳去。途中跋涉了好几个小时，到达目的地以后，我只有一个想法，便是好好睡一觉。

4. 保持高度警惕

幸运地我们很快找到一个露营的地方。那天晚上我被安排值夜班。老实说，我并不真正知道晚上要当心什么。我非常沮丧，因为晚上不能好好地睡觉了。

但当我独自坐在野外时，立刻感觉到一种令人震撼的无垠的宁静。那是一种多么美妙的感觉啊！我几乎能听到自己的心跳声，整个世界好像属于我自己。突然一阵吓人的咕隆声使我惊跳起来，心中那无以言喻的宁静感顿时消失。

5. 虚惊一场

见我面带惧色地坐在火堆旁，向导试图使我平静下来，并且表示要告诉我咕隆声的来源。我有点犹豫，但还是跟在他后面，毕竟他很有经验。尽管如此，我觉得采取一些预防措施是必要的，于是随身带了一根大木棍，以防野兽窜到我们面前。走近灌木丛时，我几乎可以听到我的心在怦怦直跳。向导笑了，弯下腰捡起一片树叶，简直难以置信，树叶上有一只褐色的小青蛙，正是这邪恶的家伙吓了我一跳，我狠狠地瞪了它一眼，它却报之以深沉的咕隆声。回到营地时，我觉得自己实在是可笑之极。

6. 并不总是同一个选择

我们在这个区域探索了三天，已开始觉得营帐便是家。每天都有很多活动，拂晓就得起床。食物很简单，早餐是鱼和米饭，晚餐也是鱼和米饭，加上一点当地的鱼酱，谈不上丰盛却能使我们有能量走完每天的路。

7. 令人兴奋

此次旅行，最难忘的便是茂盛的植被、野生物以及与自然的亲近，对我来说，kang kranchan就是这个样子。毕竟，在探索中与野兽一道遭受炎炎烈日也并非就那么惨。此次经历使我兴奋不已，也许同样会激起任何一个冒险人心中的激情的。

UNIT 05

Culture Notes

1. **Mount Etna**

   It is the highest volcano in Europe, lying in the eastern coast of Sicily in Italy. The major crater is an elevation of 3 323 meters and 500 meters in diameter. The top of the mountain is covered with snow all the year. It has erupted for 200 times since the first record.

2. **Sumatra Island**

   It lies in the west of Indonesia covering 434 000 square kilometers. It is the sixth biggest island in the world. In the west of the island there exist many volcanoes, valleys and hot springs. This island abounds in oil, tin, rubber, palm oil, tobacco, pepper and coconut.

3. **Sumbawa Island**

   It is located in the east of Java Island in Indonesia covering 15 000 square kilometers. It is mountainous and quite developed in agriculture.

4. **Mount Krakatoa**

   It lies between Sumatra Island and Java Island in Indonesia. The volcano in Mount Krakatoa erupted in 1883, with the blast sound reaching beyond 5 000 kilometers and causing the deaths of 30 000 to 50 000 people.

Language Points

Lesson 2

1. **... and the end is nowhere in sight**

   in sight: where sth can be seen

   e.g. The end of this boring task is in sight.

2. **... coastal villages were wiped out.**

   wipe out: get rid of; remove; destroy completely

   e.g. It's time to wipe out the disgrace.

   All the enemies had been wiped out.

3. **... which increased the death toll ...**

   toll n. sth paid, lost, or suffered

   e.g. The toll of the roads are increasing.

   The war took a toll of the nation's manhood.

4. **... trying to come up with a way ...**

   come up with: produce; find (a solution, an answer)

   e.g. I'm on a diet. My wife came up with this idea to help me lose some weight.

5. **... of piping hot ash into the air ...**

   piping hot: (of liquids, food) hissing or steaming hot

   e.g. The soup is piping hot.

   He got his information while it was still piping hot.

6. **... brought about an ice age on Earth.**

   bring about: cause to happen

   e.g. The crisis in bilateral relationships brought about a war.

   The reform has brought miraculous changes about.

7. **A little extreme, to say the least, ...**

   to say the least: stating, describing less forcefully than one easily could

   e.g. It is a thoughtful and readable novel, which is, to say the least, a pleasant change from what is flooding the market.

8. **... to put out what they ...**

   put out: extinguish; cause to stopping burning

   e.g. The fireman soon put the fire out.

   She put out the lights and went to sleep.

9. **... the blast destroy all wildlife ...**

   blast n. strong, sudden rush of wind; strong rush of air or gas spreading outwards from an explosion.

   e.g. Thousands of windows were broken by blast

during the air raid.

10. **These facts are just the tip of the iceberg.**
the tip of the iceberg: the small, visible or measurable part of sth known to be much greater.
e.g. The million dollars involved in the tax evasion case was only the tip of the iceberg.

Translation of the Text

Lesson 1

Presentation

进入一个全新的世界——参观自然博物馆
狂暴肆虐的火山、骇人听闻的恐龙、噩梦般感觉的爬行动物…您从未经历过的令人震颤的自然奇观…
生物展厅
鉴于人们很少有机会解开生命之迷，我们推荐您参观蔚为壮观的生物展厅。首先进入引人入胜的恐龙陈列室。在那里您能了解到有关哺乳动物的一切、人类的进化以及人类的心理、生理机能。尽管各类虫子让你看得浑身发痒，但我们确信您一定会欣然漫步于一号爬行动物展室去一览曾遍布地球各处的各式爬行类动物。
您是否对流星、陨石坑感兴趣？
您现在有机会观看大约15 000颗从太空陨落的流星，科学家们因此有机会更好地了解遥不可及的宇宙部分。
地球展厅
地震、火山、狂风…您将在紧张刺激的地球展厅体验大自然的力量。电视录放设备的音响效果使参观者逼真地体验地震！调查各种火山间的差异又是另一种独特的经历！地球展厅中另有6 000颗珠宝和水晶石的展出，绝对使您一饱眼福。
引人入胜的其它部分
许多展室既好玩又有教育意义，值得一看。您肯定想在生态展示部分踏上一片巨大的树叶去探究植物是如何将太阳能转化成食物的吧？您还可以乘坐自动楼梯穿越一个巨大的地球雕塑去历游地球的中心。

关于我们
自然历史博物馆位于伦敦南堪森顿

开馆时间：星期一至星期六
上午10:00到下午5:50
星期日上午11:00到下午5:50

Lesson 2

Reading

沉睡的巨人
多年以来，科学家们积极寻求方法预测可能即将发生的火山喷发。但迄今为止，基本没有成功。火山问题专家斯坦利·威廉姆斯说；"我相信，在我有生之年火山喷发将会残忍地夺去100万人的生命。"
当你了解到在过去的一万年里有1 511座火山喷发，引起巨大的破坏和人员伤亡，这绝不是毫无根据的现象。即便如此，令人惊奇的是人们并没有对火山的存在更多地煞费脑筋、大光其火。
220万年前，在现在的美国黄石，世界历史上最大的一次火山喷发爆发了。2 500立方千米的炽热火山灰仿佛沿着管道一般喷向空中，改变了整个地貌。两万年前，在苏门答腊岛爆发了另一次火山喷发。此次喷发后，岛中心形成了一个巨大的洞，地球由此进入冰河时代。这样说可能有些极端，但至少，它使得近几百年的火山喷发显得无关紧要。
许多火山喷发都发生在近200年里，其中有三次异常突出，皆因火山喷发不仅引起巨大破坏，而且夺取了无数的生命。
到1815年的时候，印度尼西亚桑巴瓦岛的汤波洛山还是4 100米高，而近年来它却仅高于海平面2 821米，其原因在于现代最大的一次火山喷发。50立方千米的岩浆喷向空中，火山灰落向各岛，远达数千公里之遥。
火山喷发本身吞噬了上万的生命，但家畜、农作物的毁坏所造成的饥荒更使死亡人数上升至9万之多。同时火山喷出的大量残片散布在地球上空的大气层中而导致气温急剧下降，以致1816年成了众所周知的"无夏之年"。
汤波洛山喷发68年后，同样的地方又发生了一次巨大的火山喷发——柯拉喀托火山1883年8月27日爆发。
巨大的海啸使165处海岸村庄化为乌有，太阳在长达24个多小时的时间内完全失去光芒，火山灰落在6 000公里以外的船上。
同年11月，由于火山灰引起酷似夕阳余辉的"火烧"景象，纽约市市民警惕地叫来救火车去扑灭他们认为非常危险的大火。

最后，最近一次巨大的火山喷发发生在美国华盛顿州。1980年5月18日圣·海伦斯山骤然喷发，浓烟滚滚的火山灰和气体喷向19公里高的空中。

喷射出的火山灰和气体之高，竟然给飞过上空的喷气式客机带来巨大的湍流。所幸有山脉位于人口稀少的国家公园中央，生物伤亡降至最小程度。

但是，火山爆发破坏了距火山180平方公里范围内的所有野生生物。小规模的喷发仍持续不断，明天会怎样，不得而知。

以上事实只是冰山一角，但由此可以预知，火山会继续喷发，人类对此无能为力。也许不是在我们的时代，但有一天斯坦利·威廉姆斯的预言很可能会变成现实。

Lesson 3

Writing

岩洞

岩洞景色壮观，潜藏在爱尔兰凯利郡城堡岛区，直到1983年尚无人知晓。经一群当地探寻该地污染源的研究者偶然发现后，世界各地成千上万的人们才得以欣赏到这处地下美景。

岩洞是个地下王国，纵深4公里，包含以托凯恩《指环王》中出现的各个地名命名的隔室。一走进岩洞，你就会被这古老洞穴的美景吸引。洞内温度保持恒温10℃,这一温度在开始时可能会令人望而却步，但继续前行30步，深入陡峭的地下，映入眼帘的是一个神奇的梦幻世界。驻足片刻，你开始逐渐确信，跋涉中决定坚持下来真是明智！

历游中轻歌绕洞，主要播放的是爱尔兰歌手恩雅的歌曲。毫无疑问，岩洞最引人入胜的外观是其异乎寻常、甚至有些吓人的石笋、钟乳石，其形态、式样各异。蓝黄两色光照亮了洞穴，一种神秘气氛油然而生，使得整个洞穴倍显自然、美丽。

虽然历游岩洞对参观者来说绝对安全，但仍不适于那些胆小的人。真该去好好探索一番这个小而令人惊叹的自然景观。在我的经历中，岩洞是一处令人记忆深刻的奇观。

UNIT 06

Culture Notes

1. **Robert Burns**
   Robert Burns was born in a clay cottage at Alloway, Scotland in 1759. At 13, Robert was doing a peasant's full day's labor and at his early years, he had a little schooling. During his life, Burns did a great deal of work in collecting, editing, restoring and imitating traditional Scottish folk songs or writing verses of his own to traditional tunes. This was for Burns, a labor of love and patriotism.

2. **West Indies**
   It refers to the more than 1 200 islands in North America which lies in the enclosure of the Atlantic Ocean, Gulf of Mexico and the Caribbean. In 1492 Columbus first voyaged here, mistaking them for the islands near India. Later they were named "West Indies" for being located in the Western hemisphere.

Language Points

Lesson 2

1. **... come upon a crowd of Scots ...**
   come upon: encounter
   e.g. We came upon a group of man who were waiting for the public house to open.

2. **... all dressed up in their kilts ...**
   dress up: put on formal clothes, as for a party, ceremony, etc.
   e.g. There's an official reception next week. It will mean dressing up.
   Children often enjoy dressing up in their parents' clothes.

3. **... having the time of their lives ...**
   have the time of one's life: enjoy oneself greatly doing sth on a particular occasion or during a certain period
   e.g. You're as fit as a flea and having the time of your life.

4. **... certainly made his mark.**
   make one's mark: become successful and well-known in a certain circles
   e.g. Malcolm has now made his mark on the international show.

5. **... and keep the wolf from the door, but not very successful.**
   keep the wolf from the door: be able to buy enough food for oneself and or one's family
   e.g. The small wage couldn't make him keep the wolf from the door.

6. **... and fall in love with ...**
   fall in love with: become filled with love (for)
   e.g. He fell in love with an actress.

7. **... the poverty-stricken poet, ...**
   poverty-stricken adj. affected by poverty
   e.g. He was born in a poverty-stricken family.

8. **... because he always spoke his mind ...**
   speak one's mind: express one's views frankly or bluntly
   e.g. He just spoke his mind never caring whether others like it or not.

9. **... who tried to drag him down by ...**
   drag sb down: bring to a low physical or mental level
   e.g. Slander can never drag him down.
   The intense heat drags her down.

10. **... until the wee small hours of the following morning.**
    the wee hours: the hours after midnight
    e.g. He stayed up until the wee hours of the following morning.

Translation of the Text

Lesson 2

Reading

彭斯，苏格兰伟大的诗人

如果有外国人1月25日来到苏格兰，他也许认为当地的居民一定是疯了，或是时光倒流，令他重返古代。因为他很可能碰上一群穿短裙的苏格兰人在尽人生之乐来庆祝"彭斯之夜"。

对于一个仅有37年生命岁月的人来说，罗伯特·彭斯，这个苏格兰诗人，无疑在生命中记下了浓重的一笔。他于1759年1月25日出生在埃尔郡的艾勒威，是7个孩子中的长子。由于家境贫寒，彭斯没有受过多少正规教育，但据说，他通过学习《圣经》和阅读其他一些他能获到的书而自学成材。在父母亲的鼓励和引导下，他同时学习法语，并初步接触了苏格兰民歌、传奇故事和谚语。

1784年，彭斯的父亲去世，他从此成为家庭的顶梁柱。也正是这个时期，他意识到用苏格兰地方方言创作诗歌的可能。接下来的两年他创作了其最为著名的诗歌，包括《万圣节前夕》、《快乐的乞丐》、《老鼠颂》。创作诗歌的同时，他接济家用，虽能勉强度日，但仍不尽如人意。

1785年彭斯邂逅吉恩·阿默尔，一个建筑家的女儿，两人随即坠入爱河。吉恩的父亲不许女儿嫁给这样一位穷困的诗人，于是彭斯决定移居西印度群岛，但就在离开之前，他发表了诗集，取名《主要用苏格兰方言创作的诗歌》，诗集随即取得成功，彭斯也因此放弃了移居海外的计划，转而迁往爱丁堡。在爱丁堡他为当地上流社会的文人所接纳，但他们错误地认为，他不过是一个富有灵感，但缺乏教育的农民。彭斯对此心有不快，而且直言不讳。据说，当时他因总是直言不讳以至疏远他人而闻名于诗坛。

1787年他发表了另一册诗集，并取得成功。他因此挣了不少钱而去游历全国。期间他把诗歌带给各地的人们。从此以后，彭斯主要从事诗歌创作，作品包括其经久不衰、最为著名的《往昔的时光》。没有哪一个苏格兰新年除夕夜的聚会不是唱着这位苏格兰诗人的不朽之作欢乐而终的。

罗伯特·彭斯也是位法国大革命的支持者——他公开严正地支持自由与正义，因此和统治阶级格格不入。他们大肆攻击其生活中的消极方面，妄图使其身败名裂。但越是被人诽谤，他越是赢得普通百姓的爱戴。然而，早年艰苦的农活和食不果腹使他患上风湿性心脏病，并于1796年7月21日英年早逝。

我们又一次回到了"彭斯之夜"。庆祝之前的仪式正式庄严。全体就座后，人们开始饭前祷告，之后，一名风琴师口吹风笛引领厨师进入餐室。厨师头顶盘子，盘中是苏格兰的国菜——羊肉杂碎布丁。菜盘被放置在桌上最尊贵的位置，人们一起吟唱彭斯的《布丁颂》，唱至诗歌的第三节，主人郑重其事地切开布丁。晚餐一经开始，人们吟唱着彭斯的一首首诗歌，之后，音乐、舞蹈竞相开始。人们尽情享受这一良宵美宴，一直持续到第二天凌晨1、2点钟才告结束。

Lesson 3

Writing

我母亲出生在一个人口众多的大家庭。她有三个兄弟，三个姊妹，兄弟姊妹们都各自在世界各地成家立业。

几年前，依然住在家乡村子里的几个表兄妹决定组织一次历时三天的家庭聚会。届时，全家从天涯海角汇聚到了小村庄，一些人住在亲戚家里，其余的则住在当地的旅店和宾馆。

我已是多年没见过这些亲戚了，此次相见，机会难得。你相信吗？有些亲戚我还是平生第一次见面呢！

我们做了各种有趣的事情，譬如我们乘船去了我外祖父出生的那座小岛。每个人都开心得不得了，甚至连一向严肃的罗伯特舅舅都讲了一个笑话。他说："瞧，如果这时候突然发生海啸，那我们这个家庭就没有一个人了。"天哪，这样的笑话我可不敢恭维。

最后一天晚上，大家共进晚宴，之后一起跳舞。真是太感人了，160人齐聚一堂，以后可能再也不会有机会在此地重聚了。这是我参加过的最大的一次家庭聚会。

Revision 04-06

新年快乐

你是否曾有过手提水桶，穿街奔跑，泼洒无辜行人的冲动？

最好是预定4月中旬的泰国游，因为那时适逢泰国人用这种泼水的方式庆祝泰历新年。泰历新年庆祝活动于4月13日正式开始，15日结束。

全泰国人以极大的热情庆祝新年，节日期间，人们通常在喧嚣热闹的家中进行庆祝活动。4月12日又叫Wan Sungkharn Lohng，人们打扫房屋，为新年做准备。按照传统习俗，12日夜泰国人身着盛装以迎接新年的到来。

4月13日(Wan Nao),泰历新年活动集中在家里，人们精心准备新年大餐及腌制食品，在被称作Wan Payawan的14日，泼水仪式正式开始。最早的时候，人们把香水喷洒在长者和朋友的手上，但这一习俗现已发展成为全国范围内的泼水大战。

节日里另一项重要的活动叫作Rohd Nam Songkran。活动中，年轻人向年长者致以敬意，并恳请年长者原谅他们过去一年中的过失；同时将水喷洒在长者的手上，祝福他们新年快乐。

对于去泰国旅游的外国人来说，泰历新年无疑是内容丰富，令人难以忘怀：愉快、清爽。但切记，走出屋门，看起来似乎人人可泼，实际上是因人而异。如果你想在新年之际东游泰国，一些基本的规范必须铭记在心。

最后，按照常理，不要把水泼到开车人的身上。节日快乐！

UNIT 07

Culture Notes

1. **Queen Margherita of Italy**

   Throughout her life, Queen Margherita was known for her beauty, grace and charm. She was also a trend setter in fashion. Her gowns and jewels are still astonishing. Pizza became widely popular in 1889 because of the Queen Margherita.

2. **pizza**

   pizza is not an Italian invention, as is widely thought. The origins of pizza go far back to the ancient times. Greeks and Romans ate the bread, topped with vegetables, olive oil and native spices — but without tomatoes. Pizza became widely popular in 1889 because of the Queen Margherita. Originally, pizza was a poor man's food. In 1889, Italian King Umberto I and Queen Margherita gave visit to Naples. They saw many peasants eating large, flat bread. The Queen loved the bread, which made pizza even more popular among the Italian people. Thanks to Italian immigrants, pizza made its way to the whole Europe and America by the beginning of 1900's. But the real "pizza-boom" came after World War II, when American and European soldiers returned from Italy. They ate it there; it was love at first taste! Therefore, they demanded it at home as well.

Language Points

Lesson 2

1. **... enough to make your mouth water.**
   make one's mouth water: make one have a good appetite
   e.g. The smell from the kitchen made my mouth water.

2. **It's high time we set the record straight.**
   set the record straight: provide a correct account, explanation etc. of facts, events
   e.g. All in all, this is quite profound. It had to be written to set the record straight.

3. **... flat bread found its way to Italy.**
   find one's way to: reach a destination, or objective
   e.g. I'll be able to find my way to your house by myself.
   He determines to find his way to reality.

4. **... people were gobbling them down.**
   gobble down: eat fast, noisily and greedily
   e.g. Imperial powers throughout history have always tended to gobbled down their weaker neighbors.

5. **... the pizza business kicked off.**
   kick off: start
   e.g. The match is due to kick off at 2:15.

6. **It's actually a piece of a cake.**
   a piece of cake: a task that is very easy to carry out successfully
   e.g. Oxford was a piece of cake.
   Passing the exam is a piece of cake for me.

7. **... they practically live on pizza.**
   live on: feed and support oneself on a stated amount, or form a certain source
   e.g. I can't live on that wage.
   Don't you know how little they manage to live on.

Translation of the Text

Lesson 2

Reading

第一口便爱上它

圆的或方的，包馅的或焙烤的，不管哪种，一定能挑出你喜欢的口味。一想到酥软的奶酪配上辣椒、蘑菇、番茄便足以使你流涎欲滴。

你认为比萨饼最初起源于何地？意大利，对吗？错了！现在该是还其本来面目的时候了。最初是希腊人开始烤制一种又大又圆的扁平面包，上面铺上简单的几样，如橄榄油、大蒜、洋葱和香草。然而直到18世纪末这种扁平面点的制作才传入意大利。被叫做比萨饼的这种扁平面包，卖价便宜，上面没有浇料，在大街上卖给那些那不勒斯的穷人。

如果1889年意大利玛赫雷塔女王没有决定巡视全国的话，比萨饼可能永远都只是一种普通的小吃。巡游中，女王不禁注意到，穷人们吃着一种又大又圆的扁平面包。她惊奇地发现这种小吃像热蛋糕一样销售得很快，人们狼吞虎咽，如痴如醉。情动之下，她让侍卫买了一个。咬第一口，便觉香甜怡人。她太喜欢了，命令御厨拉菲利·埃斯伯西托制作各式比萨饼，以尽其兴。这一行动震惊朝廷，女王吃这种凡夫百姓的食物可真是件新鲜事。拉菲利厨师做成了一种极具爱国精神的比萨饼，颜色和意大利国旗一样：绿色（紫苏），白色（奶酪），红色（番茄），取名玛赫雷塔，以纪念这位女王，比萨饼也因此逐渐发展起来。

比萨饼如此美味，在意大利不胫而走，毫不奇怪。19世纪下半叶，伴随第一批意大利移民，比萨饼也来到美国。很快地，意大利移民开设自己的面包房，卖比萨饼及各种百货。比萨饼业从此在美国兴

起。但直到二战后比萨饼才令世人疯狂。二战中，盟国驻军意大利时，士兵们第一次吃这种饼。战争结束回国后，他们异常渴望这种汁浓欲滴的美味，比萨饼从此成为全球范围的需求。

当然还得说说制作比萨饼时需要注意的事项。不仅香草、大蒜、新鲜奶酪、番茄很重要，另外生面团也必须符合制作要求。那实际上是块大饼。制作中规定，面和好后，用手或搅拌器揉匀，使面团不至于过热。最后，再用手定型，放在柴火炉里微焙之前，必须捶扁面团并在空中抛甩。

现在的比萨饼种类各异，中空的，包馅的，炙烤的，不尽其数。你听说过冰激凌比萨饼或糖果比萨饼吗？不管你信不信，这样的比萨饼的确有。加上些薯条，有种薯条的风味，或在比萨饼上插生日蜡烛，再吹灭蜡烛如何？现在好像任何事情都可以和比萨饼扯上关系。

种类如此之丰富，难怪能赢得世界各地成千上万人们的青睐。据估算，普通的一个美国人一年要消费10.35公斤的比萨饼，听起来好像他们就靠比萨饼为食似的。别忘了，比萨饼不见得都是垃圾食品。用新鲜的蔬菜，低脂的奶酪的话，比萨饼不仅美味，而且健康。

下次你吃比萨饼，不管是自家做的，还是外卖，咬一口酥热汁浓的美味后，不妨想想玛赫雷塔女王和拉菲利厨师。嗨，今晚有谁吃比萨饼吗？

UNIT 08

Culture Notes

1. **Chihuahua**

a very small dog with smooth and short hair, originated from Mexico

2. **Great Dane**

also called the spot dog, Former antenatal Yugoslavia, not only more and more popular in a lot of countries, but also become pets of the advertising circle

Language points

Lesson 2

1. **domesticated**

animals or plants that are raised by people and are able to be used for work or food

e.g. The area is populated by domesticated birds such as geese and turkeys.

Tian Tian is a domesticated tiger and she won't hurt anybody.

People who enjoy being at home and taking care of a house and family.

2. **migrate**

(of animals, etc.) go from one place to another with the season, esp. to spend the winter in a warmer place

e.g. These birds migrate to North Africa in winter.

More than 2 million ducks migrate to the lake each fall.

3. **primitive**

of or at an early stage of social development

e.g. There are a lot of primitive straw huts in this village.

Mary's research is focused on three primitive New Guinea tribs.

4. **tame**

to train a wild animal to obey you and not to attack people

e.g. It is impossible to tame some animals.

Men are able to manage to tame some wild birds to deliver message.

5. **gifted**

having a great deal of natural ability or talent

e.g. Elaine is gifted with a super singing voice.

He was gifted at writing.

6. **interpret**

understand sth in a particular way

e.g. He interpreted the silence as a refusal.

7. **inborn**

existing in a person or animal from birth; natural

e.g. Some people seem to have an inborn talent for cooking.

Birds have an inborn ability to fly.

8. **faithful—loyal (to sb/sth)**

e.g. She was always faithful to her husband.

Mary's always been a trustworthy and faithful friend.

Translation of the Text

Lesson 2

Reading

英雄所见略同

1. 共同的源渊

近年来，人们进行了许多研究项目调查"人类最好的朋友"，狗，是如何赢得这个头衔的。很久以前，据研究报告称，所有的狗，从微型的吉娃娃狗到大型的大麦狗都是被驯养的狼的后代。可是，科学家仍然不知道究竟从什么时候开始狗不再是嗜血的野生动物而开始和人类和睦相处并赢得"人类最好的朋友"的这个称谓。

2. 新发现

最近，三项关于狗的研究同时在世界不同的地方进行，试图进一步弄清楚我们的四脚朋友的来源。根据这些研究，大量的驯养狗在9 000年以前就存在了。这意味着狗早已被看重，他们不但跟随人类迁移，还被大量买卖。此外，研究者还进行了关于遗传物质的基因测试，结果发现实际上人类和狗最早是在东亚地区开始发展关系的。这一新的理论显然推翻了所有的狗都来自欧洲或中东的说法。

3. 第一次和人类接触

然而，研究者们仍然不能准确地指出狗的驯养是在何时何地开始的。他们猜测，狼在远古人类的居住地附近徘徊，希望能偷到一些剩余的食物。久而久之，居住地的居民可能成功地驯服了一些狼以帮助他们狩猎和看守帐篷。下一步是选择最优秀的狼种进行培育。然而，狗是在什么样的情况下成为我们今天所知的宠物仍然不得而知。它不仅是人类的伙伴，而且也担当了许多其他的角色。

4. 生来就有非同一般的理解力

为了解释什么能够使狗和人类如此地和谐共处,科学家们进行了深入的研究。调查结果表明在首次进行的狗和黑猩猩的直接对比中，狗显示出令人惊讶的理解人类行为的能力。这种能力应归因于它们与生俱来的交流天赋而不是当它们还是小狗的时候从和人类的交往中学来的。这种天赋是其经过几个世纪的被筛选和喂养的结果，并基于它们对自己主人的能力的理解力之上的。

5. 成功运用于实验

这些结论是在一项涉及黑猩猩和狗的实验之后得出的。这两种动物都被施以两个不透气味的盒子，一个是空的，另一个装有食物。研究组测试了这两种动物是否具有理解人类暗示其哪个盒子有食物的能力。这些暗示包括轻拍装有食物的盒子，指着它，甚至是注视着它。狗通常可以对信号做出反应，选择正确的盒子，而猩猩没有任何反应的迹象。

6. 不是结论的结果

其中一名研究员将这一试验认为是如何理解狗的意识的一个良好的开端。他解释说，这类实验是很难设计完美的，而且有可能要花费更多的时间去完全了解我们忠实的伙伴。毕竟，关于人类大脑潜力的争论从远古时代就开始了，为什么对于狗来说就要有任何的不同呢？

UNIT 09

Culture Notes

Emily Bronte

Emily Jane Bronte,1818-1848, with pseudonym "Ellis Bea", British poetess, novelist; the second child of three sisters of Bronte, an author of Wuthering Heights.

Language Points

Lesson 2

1. **rent**

   pay for the occupation or use of land, premises a telephone, machinery, etc.

   e.g. We don't own our house, so we rent it.

   Do you buy or rent the video.

2. **indeed**

   used to emphasize a statement or answer

   e.g. Thank you very much indeed.

   We have very little information indeed.

3. **request**

   to ask for sth politely or formally

   e.g. All I request of you is that you should be punctual.

   We request him to help us.

4. **take to sb**

   to stand to like someone or sth

   e.g. When they saw him, they took to him at once.

   We took to each other right away.

5. **be accustomed to**

   to be used to sth

   e.g. I'm accustomed to this sort of work.

   I'm accustomed to getting up so early.

6. **instruct**

   to officially tell someone what to be

   e.g. He instructed them to start.

   Have you been instructed when to start?

7. **offend**

   to make someone feel angry and upset, by doing or saying

   e.g. I hope I haven't offended you.

   Some people are offended by swearing on television.

8. **converse**

   talk

   e.g. He can converse fluently in English.

   We conversed at the dinner-table.

Translation of the Text

Lesson 1

Presentation

"冰"馆

想像有这样一家大型宾馆，里面所有的床是用冰制成的，墙也是用整块整块的冰凿成的，当然门和天花板也是用大量的冰雪做成的！确切说，每年在加拿大魁北克省建造的这样一个富丽堂皇的建筑物需要用掉11 000吨雪和350吨冰。与你可能的想像相反，在这家"冰"馆中你很容易找到家的感觉。

欢迎光临！

房间

在此您可以尽情享受一般房间和主题套间的舒适。在鹿皮覆盖的冰床上，钻进睡袋中睡觉，您会感到非常温暖。天才艺术家的设计赋予了每个套间独特之处，无一雷同。

设施

我们保证您在这里决无想家的感觉。这里有各式各样的娱乐设施供您选择，而且会乐此不疲。主要项目有：周四的"喜剧之夜"、周五的"DJ和欢乐时光"和周六的冰乐队演出。即使室内温度已降至零下，但我们相信这些活动定会使一个冰冷之夜变成一个火热的盛会。您可以在冰影院里欣赏电影，在两个展室内观看展览，乘着冰雪摩托车兜风，在夜空下的温泉中浸泡，一天下来，我们的活动会使你感到乐趣无穷！

垂涎欲滴的美食

在这里我们提供给您的是一如家庭烹饪般可口的各种美食。种类之多，供您选择：熏鱼、金枪鱼、鲱鱼和鸭肉等，全部用冰制托盘盛奉。以上仅仅是我们这里的部分特色菜，我们保证这里令人垂涎的美味定会令您将其"一网打尽"的。

不幸的是，所有这些美妙的东西到了春天就会融化！但是要切记，当来年第一片雪花降落之时，又一座新的"冰"馆会诞生。因此，您一定要在明年冬天来临之前提前预订房间。毕竟，您不希望错过这个在我们美妙"冰"馆中享受的绝好机会吧，因为这里的确胜似居家！

Lesson 2

Reading

呼啸山庄
艾米莉·勃朗蒂

1801年，一名叫洛克乌德的年轻人从居住在呼啸山庄的富有的希斯克历夫先生那里租了一幢房子。洛克乌德要他的女管家奈莉告诉他有关呼啸山庄中奇怪的居民的逸事。他在日记中写下了她所讲的故事……

"希斯克历夫先生吗？"我下马走上前去问道，他点了点头。

"先生，我是洛克乌德，您的新房客。我希望您……"

"进来！"他打断了我的话。

他领我走上通往大屋的石路，在我们到了院子里的时候，他命令一个叫约瑟夫的老头把我的马牵走。呼啸山庄是希斯克历夫先生住宅的名字，的确，它是我所见过的令人印象最深的宅第。在跨进门槛之前，我停下来观赏房屋前面的雕刻，特别是正门顶部的那些雕刻。我本希望主人介绍一下这个地方的简短历史，但是我意识到他根本不喜欢我，而我也不想像先前那样再进一步惹恼他。我们径直进入起居室。房间比我想像的要大得多，包括厨房和大厅。我听到厨房深处有喋喋不休的低语声和厨房用具的磕碰声。但是，奇怪的是在大壁炉里我并没有看出烧煮或烘烤食物的迹象。地面由平滑的白石铺就；除了一两把笨重的黑椅子藏在角落外，其他的椅子都是高背的，并漆成了绿色。衣柜下面的圆拱里，躺着一条很大的母猎狗，它周围是一窝嗷嗷待哺的小狗。

我亲爱的母亲曾说过我永远不会有个舒服的家。我此刻突然惧怕起来，她的预言有可能是准确的。我坐在房东对面的椅子上。他情绪很糟糕…，使得我一时有点后悔决定从他手中租住庄园。希斯克历夫先生和我沉默地坐着，我只有去摸弄那只母狗，但它却抬起头来很生气地低吼。

"你最好别理这只狗，"希斯克历夫先生警告说。"它不习惯别人碰它的——它不是当作宠物养的。你越友好，它就会变得越愤怒。"他说了我一顿后，接着大步走到一个边门大叫道："约瑟夫！"约瑟夫在地窖的中嘟囔了一些什么，于是他的主人下到地窖去找他，留下我和那只母狗、一群狗崽和两只稍小一点的狗面面相觑。我并不想和锋利的犬牙打交道，就静坐着不动；但是我愚蠢地选择对其中的三只狗挤眉弄眼、做鬼脸来消磨时间。我猜想他们很快就对我感到厌倦了，因为那条母狗突然跃上我的膝盖。它的这一举动鼓舞了6只形状大小不一的小狗，一起窜到我面前。我不得不大声求援，让这家里的什么人来"重建和平"。

令人高兴的是，厨房里有人快步走来——一个健壮的女人。她两颊火红，挥舞着一个煎锅冲到我们中间，利用那个武器和她的舌头控制了现场的形势。谢天谢地，她一直待在那儿直到她主人回来。

"见鬼！到底是怎么回事？"当希斯克历夫先生返回时问到。

"是啊，真是见鬼！"我咕噜着。"您倒不如把我丢给一群老虎的好！"

"对于不碰它们的人，它们是不会多事的。"他说，"狗的职责就是应该保持警觉的。来杯水吗？"

"不，谢谢您。"我说到。

"狗没咬着您吧？"

"没有。"

希斯克历夫的脸上露出笑容。"好啦，好啦，您受惊啦，洛克乌德先生。喝点水吧。这所房子里客人极少，我和我的狗甚至都不知道该怎么接待客人。先生，祝您健康！"我举起杯，也回敬了他。

我开始觉得为了一群狗的失礼而坐在那儿生气，可能有点傻。此外，我也不再想让这个家伙再取笑我。也许他也并不希望得罪一个可能的房客，所以聊起了其他的话题。

事实上我对我俩之间的交谈颇感兴趣，因此我决定下一星期再来拜访。他似乎对我的想法并不感兴趣。但是不管怎样，我还是要去。

Revision 07-09

Reading

动物英雄

A 鸽子的功绩

尽管我们倾向于认为它们是满身疾病有害的动物，但在历史上，尤其是在战争时期，鸽子已被证明对于人类来说是必不可少的。数百年以来鸽子一直都被当做信使，而军鸽在两次世界大战中都被带到了飞机和军舰上。军鸽在最困难的时刻显示了惊人的勇气，即使在它们遭到重创时，95%的军鸽依然完成了赋予它们的使命。最有名的信鸽是在第一次世界大战时期执行任务的"亲爱的朋友"。尽管受了重伤，这只英勇的鸽子仍成功地传递了信息，结果营救了一营共194名士兵。"亲爱的朋友"后来被授予法国"战争十字奖"，并获得"美国赛鸽迷组织"颁发的一枚金质奖章。今天，在偏远地区，鸽子仍然被用来运输急救药品；在城市里，它们实际上被用来清理废物和野草种子。

B 猴子的责任

在内尔·阿姆斯特朗登上月球的几年之前，两只勇敢的黑猩猩汉姆和伊诺斯被用来测试太空飞行的安全性。汉姆被训练在闪烁的彩色灯的指示下来操控飞船，并在失重环境中存活。1961年1月，它被放在一个太空舱内从美国卡那维拉尔角发射升空。这项任务持续了17分钟，并获得成功。汉姆返回地球时有一点疲倦，但是非常高兴。后来它被送往美国北卡罗莱那的一所动物园并居住在那里，直到1983年去世。

1961年11月，另一只叫伊诺斯的猩猩成功完成了首次环绕地球轨道飞行，此次飞行共持续了1小时28分钟。遗憾的是伊诺斯在此次飞行结束几个月后死去了。这些勇敢的猩猩为未来人类宇航员安全地探索未知领域铺平了道路。

C 勇敢的军犬

不仅仅是鸽子在战时帮助了他们的人类战友，军犬也扮演着非常重要的角色。也许最出名的军犬是斯达比，它在一战服役的18个月期间，有过许多英勇的行为，包括在芥子气突袭中救出它的团队并照顾伤员。它甚至攻击了一名潜伏在营地外的间谍。斯达比被晋升为"荣誉中士"，从而成为在美军中服役过的军衔最高的军犬。他还是美国红十字会的荣誉成员。斯达比死于1926年。在美国它成为一个传奇，同时也是美国在二战中起了很大作用的"K-9"兵团成立的灵感。

D 老鼠的故事

它们也许是世界上最不受欢迎的"家中客人"了，但是老鼠——宠物鼠——据说也有其英勇的行为。在德国，一个小姑娘的宠物鼠，吉达，竟然在武装窃贼闯入家中时从窃贼手中救出了小姑娘的家人。吉达从它躲藏的地方，一个书柜，跳向窃贼，并且疯狂地攻击他们。其结果是未得手的窃贼被关进了警察局的拘留所。在英国，一个九岁小女孩的宠物鼠，费都，则在某天晚上家中突然发生大火时，从肆虐的火中挽救了主人的性命。当时，费都成功地冲上楼去，使劲地抓门，尖利的声音唤醒了熟睡中的家人。所有人都毫发无损地逃离着火的房子。

UNIT 10

Culture Notes

1. **Pablo Picasso (1881-1973)**

   He was born in Malaga, Spain. He was a very famous, controversial and important art icon. Pablo made many paintings; some are The Young Ladies Of Avigon, Old Man with Guitar, and Guernica. Picasso became famous by dazzling people with his artistic abilities. He went through many stages in his career, including The Blue Period, The Rose Period, and Pablo Picasso was the creator of Cubism. Pablo saw things out of order, backwards or upside down. Picasso also painted this way. Pablo influenced people to paint, and this type of influence could have only came from one person, Picasso.

   Picasso lived in many places including France and Spain. He created many beautiful works of art. Pablo Picasso was a great painter, but he expressed many controversial views. On April 8th, 1973 Pablo Picasso died, and he was 91 years old.

2. **A measure of a person's intelligence as indicated by an intelligence test; the ratio of a person's mental age to their chronological age**

   Intelligence testing is a form of psychological testing of an individual's capacity to learn and deal effectively with his/her environment. IQ (Intelligence Quotient) is the score of an intelligence test.

Language points

Lesson 2

1. **regard sb/sth as sth**

   think about someone or something in a particular way

   e.g. Paul seems to regard sex as sinful and immoral.

   Mary wore strange clothes and was widely regarded as eccentric.

2. **apart from**

   except for

   e.g. Apart from the occasional visit, what does Alan do for his kids?

3. **feel/be put out**

   to feel upset or offended

   e.g. We were a little put out at not being invited to the party.

4. **standing joke**

   something that happens often and that people makes joke about

   e.g. My spelling mistakes had become a standing joke in the office.

5. **in question**

   the things, people etc. in question are the ones that being discussed or talked about

   e.g. The goods in question had been stolen.

6. **pick out**

   to choose someone or something carefully

   e.g. Pick out all the words in the poem that suggest despair.

7. **on sale**

   available to be bought at a lower price than usual

   e.g. I could only afford to buy the CD player because it was on sale.

8. **end up**

   to come to be in a particular situation or a state

   e.g. He will end up in prison if he is not careful.

Translation of the Text

Lesson 2

Reading

博物馆中的大猩猩

让人觉得有点好笑的是，在现代艺术馆里，看过这些画的人中至少有一位会误解艺术家所要表达的内容并且将其比作是幼稚园中小孩的乱涂乱画。

你闻所未闻的是大猩猩可能会更出色地完成工作，这在那些勤奋而年轻的加利福尼亚州艺术家看来，却不觉得那么有趣。事实上，他们却因为两只名叫柯柯和迈克尔的大猩猩而一直深感忿忿不平。因为这两只西方低地大猩猩一直在艺术馆中占据着重要的地位。

猿类动物涉足艺术领域这已不是第一次。生物学家在20世纪50年代就曾鼓励黑猩猩作画，他们试图以此来探询艺术的根源。

两只大猩猩的作品被认为是当时十分流行的表现主义的抽象形式。实际上，他们的作品不过是一些简单的涂画，但价值不菲，其中一幅画甚至成了毕加索的收藏品，还有谣言说另一幅被一名政府官员偷偷买走。

其中一只大猩猩，柯柯，住在加利福尼亚州伍德赛德的大猩猩基金会。另一只，迈克尔，一直到2004年4月死去之前也住在那里。大猩猩基金会成立于1976年，旨在保护大猩猩并提高公众对大猩猩的关注。现在似乎基金会取得的成绩不止于此；柯柯和迈克尔学会了用美式符号语言来进行交流，而且都成功地成为了艺术家。

柯柯和迈克尔的绘画与其他动物的绘画的区别在于：他们似乎能画出自己所见的周围的物体，而不是在画纸或画布上随意涂画或是泼洒颜料。多数人认为是他们的语言习得能力帮助他们创造了绘画形式。

例如，柯柯画了一块玻璃，一根香蕉和一辆公共汽车，而迈克尔则给他的朋友——一只名叫"苹果"的狗——画了一幅画像。让人印象尤其深刻的是迈克尔是凭自己的记忆画出来的。而那些用来阐释情感的画作更让人觉得不可思议。这些画反映了他们理解的深度，对各种情感的诠释以及他们对于色彩的现象运用能力。 通过符号语言和对大猩猩日常行为的仔细观察，基金会研究人员发现：猩猩像人类一样有各种各样的情感。柯柯在画中用红色和粉红色来表达爱，用绿色和棕色表示恨。令人惊讶的是柯柯用以表达情感状态的颜色中有百分之八九十和人的选择是一致的。

这两只大猩猩的画作和其他各个研究中心的猩猩的画作的另一个区别是柯柯和迈克尔都能给他们的作品命名。

在迈克尔的作品中，其中一幅画的灵感来自于在基金会庭院所采摘的一束花。人们后来问迈克尔如何给他的作品起名，他以手势表示"stink、猩猩、更多"。在特别供大猩猩使用的美式语言符号中，"stink"代表的就是"花"。

不像其他黑猩猩的艺术品，柯柯和迈克尔的作品都不是用来买卖的。不过你可以买一件印有他们画作的T恤。这是因为人们简直难以阻止大猩猩将一完成杰作就将其吃掉的习惯。丙烯颜料被证明是大猩猩的美食。基金会的工作人员曾试图在颜料中添加辛辣物来阻止大猩猩的这一行为。但结果不但没有使画作失去诱惑，反而使大猩猩以更快的速度将画吞了下去了。

也许，迈克尔和柯柯的画最终归宿何处并不重要，首先应值得足够重视的是他们能够进行创作。我们应该牢记的是他们巨大的手掌限制了他们的创作，但这些身体上的制约对他们的创造力来说并不是一个障碍。

让人惊叹不已的是柯柯和迈克尔不仅是出色的艺术家，他们在IQ测试中也表现得异常出色。值得指出的是他们的智商在75至95分之间，而人类的平均智商是100，这就意味着在动物王国中猩猩的智力超出了我们中的相当一部分人。

令人惋惜的是我们也许没有更多的时间来研究这些令人不可思议的动物，因为全世界仅剩600只山地大猩猩和几千只低地大猩猩了。

UNIT 11

Culture Notes

1. **New Year's Day**

   The beginning of spring is a logical time to start a new year. After all, it is the season of rebirth, of planting new crops, and of blossoming. January 1, on the other hand, has no astronomical nor agricultural significance. It is purely arbitrary. Ways of celebrating differ as well, according to customs and religions of the world. People in Moslem societies, for example, celebrate the new year by wearing new clothes. Southeast Asians release birds and turtles to assure themselves good luck in the twelve months ahead. Jewish people consider the day holy, and hold a religious ceremony at a meal with special foods. Hindus of India leave shrines next to their beds, so they can see beautiful objects at the start of the new year. Japanese prepare rice cakes at a social event the week before the new year. Whatever the custom, most of people feel the same sentiment. With a new year, we can expect a new life. We wish each other good luck and promise ourselves to do better in the following year. In most cultures, people promise to better themselves in the following year. Americans have inherited the tradition and even write down their New Year resolutions.

2. **New Year's Eve**

   December 31. In the United States, the federal holiday is January first, but Americans begin celebrating on December 31. Sometimes people have masquerade balls, where guests dress up in costumes and cover their faces with masks. According to an old tradition, guests unmask at midnight.

   At New Year's Eve parties across the United States on December 31, many guests watch television as part of the festival. Most of the television channels show Times Square in the heart of New York City. At one minute before midnight, a lighted ball drops slowly from the top to the bottom of a pole on one of the buildings. People count down at the same time as the ball drops. When it reaches the bottom, the new year sign is lighted. People hug and kiss, and wish each other "Happy New Year!"

3. **New Year's Resolution Week**

   An annual event, which is observed during the first week of each New Year. It encourages people by providing them with the opportunity to make personal resolutions, set challenging goals, and develop detailed action plans for their accomplishment.

Language Points

Lesson 2

1. **deal with sb/sth**
   a) have relation with
      e.g. The man is easy to deal with.
   b) behave towards; treat
      e.g. How would you deal with an armed burglar?
   c) be concerned with
      e.g. These ideas are dealt with more fully in Chapter Four.

2. **be confident that**
   sure that you can do something or deal with a situation successfully
   e.g. We are confident that next year's profits will be higher.
   be confident about
   e.g. The boy is very confident about using computer.

3. **complain to sb**
   be dissatisfied about
   e.g. Neighbors complained to the police about the dogs barking.

4. **push your luck/push it**

   (informal) to stupidly do something again

   e.g. Look, just don't push it. I've had about enough of your criticism.

5. **on business**

   for the purpose of doing

   e.g. Are you here on business or for pleasure?

6. **look out for**

   be watchful (for)

   e.g. You have to look out for the earthquake.

7. **spot**

   see, recognize (one person or thing out of many)

   e.g. The boy spotted his mother in a crowd.

8. **let sb down**

   disappoint; fail to help

   e.g. Harry will never let you down, you can rely upon him to help you always.

Translation of the Text

Lesson 1

Presentation

心理分析

1. 长者

想像一下这一情景：你正在向兄长征求建议，怎样应付一个多次让你失望的不可靠的朋友。你不能确信他的建议是否可取，是吗？仔细观察他在听你讲话时的举动：他是不是背靠椅子并且双手从后抱头，看上去似乎是副高高在上的样子？那么他也许对将提供给你的解决办法非常有信心，因此你可以相信他的建议。

2. 紧张

你决定向你的上司诉苦：说你如何讨厌某个同事。很遗憾，你选择了一个很不合适的时机，因为她的秘书有事出去了而且电话响个不停。一开始，你列出一些原因以表明为什么你认为这个同事应该被调到另外一个部门…如果你老板的头略微低下并把一只手

放到脖子后面，这可能表明她感到些许紧张。她可能会用一些措辞来打断你的抱怨，例如"过一会儿再来见我"，或是"我将尽早处理这件事情"。你还是不要得寸进尺，尽快离开！

3. 克制

你在爸爸出差时借用了他的跑车，倒车时意外地碰到了电线杆。不巧的是你没有时间趁他不在的时候修理好车子。因此，你决定把事情经过和盘托出，并把车子损坏处指给他看。尽管怕得要命，你还是觉得有必要说出事情的真相。当爸爸查看车辆受损情况时，你可以观察一下他的反应。他是紧握手腕放在背后吗？这种举动表明他是在尽力控制自己不发脾气，因此你此时应尽可能地表示歉意并主动赔偿你所造成的损失。

4. 防卫

假设你是陪审团成员。你正在观察一位律师向一桩案件的目击证人提问。你该如何判断这位目击证人是否合作呢？这里有一些你需要特别注意的手势：目击证人双臂交叉双手紧握胳膊——这种姿势表明他很担忧；目击证人想尽力保护自己免受可能的攻击。律师可能会要求目击证人迅速回答一系列小问题来突破他的心理防线。

5. 渴望

你现在正在领导一个委员会，准备组织一场精彩的新年舞会。你在屋里和委员会的几名成员商讨一长串要做的事情。环顾屋子四周，你能判断出这里面谁有可能是最勤奋、工作热情最高的人吗？有以下姿势的人可确定为特别卖力的人：人坐在那儿，手平放在大腿上，肘尖朝外。这意味着她想迫不及待地投入到这件工作中去，而且她不会令你失望的。

Lesson 2

Reading

你有成功的动力吗？

关于动机，心理学家们提出了许多不同的理论，他们一直在忙于回答什么是动机、动机来自何处、为什么有人因缺乏动机而痛苦而有些人却"动力"十足等一系列问题。

当我们拥有房子、食物、衣服、电视等生活必需品之后，为什么我们仍然不满足？从20世纪40年代开始就对动机进行研究的心理学家兼理论家亚伯拉罕·马斯洛认为，当人们衣食无忧后，他们的目标就会更

高。此时，他们开始追求同事的认同感、成就感和归宿感，此乃人类本性使然。否则，你就会发现生活毫无意义。

当然，工作岗位是最能体现人们动机的地方。我们大部分人都有成功地做好工作的动机，但是，那些仅仅想在公司中平步青云的人和那些想取得辉煌成就的人相比，两者之间有着天壤之别。由麻省理工学院心理学教授凯里·库珀率领的研究组发现，在接受访谈的成功人士中，大部分在18岁以前要么失去了父亲或母亲，要么被父母所遗弃，要么遭受这样或那样的人世挫折。库珀认为，他们追求成功的动机不是获得领导他人的权力，而是想征服发生在他们身上的不幸。

库珀同时也声称，即使是那些在顺境中取得成功的人士，他们早期经历过的某些不幸也会使他们产生某种动机。例如，小时候，老师认为某些学生不是好学生，正是这种刺激所产生的动机使他们在大学里取得了成功。当然，成功并不总是因受到刺激而产生。那些给予孩子鼓励而不是压力的家长，也能促使其子女产生成功的动机。不过，库珀认为这种比率极低。

库珀的研究认为，工作岗位上的积极性主要来自两个方面。一方面是工作上拥有自主权。当你工作时，你希望老板完全相信你，而不是密切监视你。另一方面是你在公司里有良师益友，他或她重视你，时常给你忠告。遗憾的是，我们大部分人并没有足够的动机。这在我们做新年计划时非常明显。许多人做了计划，但却没有几个人能够完成。如果你做了某项计划，并且持之以恒，那么你将会鹤立鸡群。然而，调查统计显示，我们正在打一场失败的战争，因为大多数人最终还是未能坚持住。

如果你正遭受缺乏动力的痛苦，请不要绝望，这并不是世界的末日。以下有几条建议能激发你的动机。首先，吃好并适当加以锻炼。满身肥肉和过量的咖啡会使你精神萎靡。其次，写下你真正的想法，此乃明智之举。第三，与乐观自信的人交朋友。如果和你经常相处的人总是抱怨生活，我想你该重新择友了。如果你正在做令你讨厌的事情，那么每当你取得一点点成绩，你都应引以为豪。此外，你得保证良好的睡眠并不时地休息，定期休假。即便是你非常喜欢的工作，你也应该放下工作，好好休息一会儿。假若你能把这些想法付诸实施，你肯定会动力十足并会拥有更高品质的生活，而成功也将指日可待。

UNIT 12

Culture Notes

Christmas

December 25, the celebration of the birth of Jesus Christ. The celebration often begins on Christmas Eve, December 24. On that day, you may enjoy attending a candlelight church service, for example a service of "Lessons and Carols", where you will hear the best known Christmas carols. That night, children hang up large stockings at the fireplace, where in the morning they find presents left by Santa Claus.

Language Points

Lesson 1

1. **wise up**

   to realize the unpleasant truth about a situation

   e.g. Wise up. He is cheating us.

2. **at sb's disposal**

   available for someone to use

   e.g. Tanner has a considerable amount of cash at his proposal.

3. **stop (dead) in your track**

   to suddenly stop, especially because something has frightened or surprised you

   e.g. Fay stopped in her tracks and pointed at the house.

4. **pay attention to**

   to be careful about sth or sb

   e.g. The teacher got angry with me when I didn't pay attention to.

5. **hang on**

   to hold something tightly

e.g. We all hung on as the bus swung around a sharp bend.

6. **go to any lengths**

   to willing to use any methods to achieve something that you are very determined to achieve

   e.g. Gorge is prepared to go to any lengths to get his daughter back.

7. **talk sb into**

   to persuade sb to do sth

   e.g. She didn't want to come, but I talked her into it.

8. **continue doing sth**

   go on doing sth

   e.g. They continued talking after meals.

Translation of the Text

Lesson 1

Presentation

天生购物狂

现在应该是我们清醒谨慎的时候了。店主们正用尽一切欺诈手段来掏空你辛辛苦苦赚来的钱，在你进入商店之前，这场"战争"就打响了。

1、第一印象非常重要，因此，能令人驻足的、引人注目的橱窗陈列品确实显得很有必要。橱窗里那色彩光鲜的衣服魅力实在太大了，人们禁不住总想要试试。那么你就不得不走进去…你穿上是不是有点不伦不类？也许这与当前那些穿着流行式样的时装模特们身上的饰针与夹子有关系…

2、对消费者行为模式的研究显示：处理好顾客与店员之间的相互关系非常重要，它实际上能促进销售。因此，店员会特别地关注你，他们会尽量使你在店里多停留一会儿，多购买物品。

3、你可曾注意到超市停车场里总是散发着面包的清香，一些商店弥漫着肉桂香的味道？或者是大部分商店，特别是童装店，播放着声音很大却又吸引人的音乐？所有这一切是店主们用来激发顾客消费意识以鼓励顾客花钱的明智之举。

4、刚一进店，你发现有半数商品可买，因此你很高兴。但随后你发现可供选择的商品非常有限，以至于无论价格多低，你都不愿掏钱。当然，如果你看下去的话，你可能会发现有些商品还是值得去买。

5、当你在更衣间试衣时，你突然注意到自己比过去更瘦了，而且脸上显出一种明亮的光彩。这可能是微斜的镜子以及低功率的灯泡的作用吧…？没错，亲爱的，商家们在暗暗地使用一些招数使你看上去更漂亮些。

6、你做出了选择，正准备掏钱付款，这时另一家商店的店员试图说服你选取他们的购物卡。可要小心哟！取得卡后就意味着你要支付更多的钱，而你又得不到任何好处。再重复一遍：没有任何好处。我们建议你为所购买的东西马上付款，拿上收据，随后离开。

Lesson 2

Reading

怎样做神秘顾客

一些人认为购物绝对令人烦心，另一些人认为购物是在一个使人无精打采的周六下午消磨时光的极好方式，还有些人认为购物是一项工作。没错，信不信由你，一些幸运儿确实通过购物获得报酬，这些人被称为神秘顾客，他们的工作就是假扮成顾客以获取商店、公司或服务部门的商业秘密。神秘顾客在购物时尽可能多地收集商品信息，然后提交报告给他们所受雇的公司。这些公司要么是著名的连锁店，要么是小公司。他们利用神秘顾客的服务以获得产品与其雇员的一些反馈信息。

不过打听商品行情不是一项专职工作，神秘顾客被视为是自由职业者，他们可以随意选择任务，工作时间也比较灵活。几乎任何人都可以做这项工作，包括老年人、大学生以及那些想赚外快的家庭主妇与家庭主夫，再者他们也可以走出家门透透空气。对于那些带着小孩又想做点兼职工作的父母来说，做这项工作是理想的选择，因为在收集商品信息时，小孩（指那些听话有礼貌的小孩）可以带着一块走。

做神秘顾客可能有那么一两点要求，但你不必有任何经验。你应当知道的是怎样使用因特网，以便能搜寻任务并通过电子邮件与你的代理公司取得联系。交际能力也很重要，你应当能与你所调查的商店员工进行交谈。敏锐的观察能力与诚信也是很重要的。以前的任何零售经验、为顾客服务的经验或者市场研究都对你有好处，但并不是极其重要。

神秘购物是赚取外快的极好方式，但你得记住你每月的收入并不一样，因为你并非受雇于人。赚钱的多少取决于你所在地区对神秘顾客的要求以及你所投入的时间。如果你是生活在小城镇，你根本就用不着为找工作而担心，有时在小城镇比在大城市更容易找工作，因为小城镇的神秘顾客更少。除了一笔还过得去的固定收入，神秘顾客通常还能额外得到价格昂贵的免费商品。

那么，你究竟是怎样获取任务的呢？直接向众多的公司申请是不明智的。大部分公司都有人们所熟知的"独立决策者"，这些公司通常是一些小公司，他们招聘神秘顾客来执行各种各样的任务。这些决策者不定期地在网上、报纸和其他媒体上提供招聘信息。在弄清楚你有效的邮箱地址后，公司会口授邮递信息，这样做的目的是尽可能使这项工作专业化。

对工作全身心地投入很重要。如果你因某方面的原因不能完成布置给你的任务，你应当让决策者知道这一情况。神秘顾客也应当确保所提交的报告格式正确，没有拼写和语法错误。记住神秘购物是一种市场研究形式，作为一名神秘顾客，你应当帮助公司达到目的。如果你干得出色，公司会日益兴旺，你将来找到工作的机遇也就越大。这是一种多么快乐的购物方式！

Revision 10-12

萨尔瓦多·达利

如果你问谁是20世纪最有名最成功的画家，答案几乎如出一辙：保罗·毕加索。如果你再进一步问谁是20世纪仅次于毕加索的艺术家，通常你会听到这样的回答：毕加索的同乡——萨尔瓦多·达利。

达利，即萨尔瓦多·达利，1904年5月11日出生于比利牛斯山脚下一个叫菲格尔的小镇，此镇距法国边界只有16英里。他家境殷实，除在菲格尔的房产外，在卡达克渔村也有避暑别墅。达利夫妇在这幢别墅里创建了他第一个工作室。

达利的艺术天才还在小时候就已崭露头角，10岁时已开始上绘画课。达利年轻时代求学于马德里市的圣·费尔南多艺术学院。在学院中，他的天才立刻为众人所公认。21岁时就已在巴塞罗那举办了个人画展。仅仅过了7年，也即1928年，他有三幅作品参加了在匹兹堡举行的第三届卡内基国际展览会，顿时他在国际画坛上名声大噪。那是达利艺术生涯的真正开端。

匹兹堡展览会后不久，达利就移居巴黎，在那里，他开始以当时流行的超现实主义作为自己的绘画风格。超现实主义理论以著名的精神分析学家西格蒙德·弗洛伊德的理论为基础，弗洛伊德主张以释梦来研究一切。超现实主义艺术家通常画人们想像不到的物体，其目的是使观众感到意外甚至震惊。因此，达利的绘画作品既再现了长颈鹿的发怒的情绪，也透过其目光展现了长颈鹿温柔如水的一面。他的作品如此逼真，几乎可以称得上是真正的超现实主义作品。

1929年达利遇到并爱上了加纳·艾吕雅。她成了他的经纪人，并为他的许多杰作提供了创作灵感。1934年完婚后，他们首次到美国旅游，在那里他们住了很长时间，其中包括整个第二次世界大战这一段时间。1982年加纳辞世，达利一直未能从丧偶之痛中自拔，因此，许多人认为没有加纳就没有达利今天的艺术成就。

人如其画，达利的个性以豪放和不拘一格著称。很长一段时间，他曾是美国上流社会的宠儿，为好莱坞巨头杰克·沃纳和化妆皇后海伦娜·鲁宾斯坦画过肖像，为书本画过插图，为珠宝和纺织品作过设计，甚至还制作了好几部电影。1974年达利在他的家乡菲格尔创立了艺术博物馆，在那里他度过了他生命的最后日子，直到1989年1月23日逝世。作为20世纪真正的伟人之一，萨尔瓦多·达利将永远为人们所铭记。

Workbook
(Teacher's Edition)

01 Been around the world?

Lesson One

A Match the sentence halves 1-5 with a-e and fill each space with a suitable verb from the box. Use either the Present Simple or the Present Progressive.

become	want	seem	increase	misplace	need	remind	see	say	love

1. The government _____needs_____ to take stricter measures c
2. I just _____love_____ this lake d
3. The number of Internet users _____is increasing_____ a
4. Though John _____seems_____ to be an organised person, e
5. I _____want_____ you to listen carefully to what I'm about to say Miss Perkins; b

a. as more and more people _____see_____ its potential benefits.
b. not a single person in this courtroom believes a word you _____are saying_____.
c. as the problem of pollution _____is becoming_____ more and more serious.
d. because it _____reminds_____ me of all the good times we had here as children.
e. he often _____misplaces_____ things.

B Read the text below and decide which answer A, B, C or D best fits each space.

Not long ago, cafés were **(1)** ___considered___ to be places you visited for a cup of coffee and a quick bite. These days, cafés offer much more: they are a meeting place, a place where you can relax and listen to some good music, or a place where you can socialise. Cafés in Edinburgh, in particular, are especially distinctive. In fact, the first thing you **(2)** ___notice___ in the Scottish capital is the number of beautiful cafés, which really add to the the city's charm. If you spend some time at the cafés, you'll find that these places can be a real **(3)** ___treat___. Walk around the streets of Edinburgh in the summer and you'll **(4)** ___discover___ a number of bustling little street cafés with a diverse clientele. From university students to businesspeople, everybody likes to **(5)** ___hang out___ at the cafés and **(6)** ___escape___ their tight schedules for a while. And if you think the locals stay indoors when the temperature falls, you're **(7)** ___in for___ a surprise! So, don't **(8)** ___let___ the bad weather spoil your night out ... a steaming hot mug of coffee at a(n) **(9)** ___cosy___ Edinburgh café, will certainly **(10)** ___do___ the trick on a cold winter's night! If you ever find yourself in Edinburgh and are **(11)** ___looking for___ something to do in your free time, visit a café and **(12)** ___see___ for yourself.

1. **A** considered	**B** looked	**C** noticed	**D** told
2. **A** look	**B** watch	**C** notice	**D** detect
3. **A** gift	**B** award	**C** treat	**D** prize
4. **A** invent	**B** meet	**C** introduce	**D** discover
5. **A** hang out	**B** find out	**C** take out	**D** move out
6. **A** prevent	**B** avoid	**C** escape	**D** manage
7. **A** expecting	**B** in for	**C** after	**D** looking forward to
8. **A** allow	**B** make	**C** give	**D** let
9. **A** uncomfortable	**B** hot	**C** cosy	**D** convenient
10. **A** do	**B** throw	**C** play	**D** make
11. **A** looking into	**B** looking at	**C** looking for	**D** looking up
12. **A** criticise	**B** comment	**C** see	**D** state

Lesson Two

A You are going to read an article about game show hosts. Five sentences have been removed from the article. Choose the most suitable sentence from the list A-F for each part (1-5) of the article. There is one extra sentence which you do not need to use.

A These are optional, but one would assume that most game show hosts do have at least some of them in their possession.

B Charm, of course, is vital; in fact, it is the host's charm that helps the proceedings run smoothly.

C Besides, it is considered an asset to be loud and opinionated.

D And a great deal more thought goes into it than you would imagine.

E It should be short, catchy and original.

F Believe it or not, they are even more popular than the game itself, most of the time.

B Find words and expressions in the text and match them with the meanings given.

a. giving all your attention to something _____glued to_____

b. not appreciated enough _____underestimated_____

c. very important _____vital_____

d. various _____miscellaneous_____

C Put the verbs in brackets in the correct form.

1. I'm afraid I won't be in tomorrow morning because I _am seeing_ (see) my lawyer at 10 o'clock.

2. My dad _never misses_ (never / miss) the 8 o'clock news.

3. I _am used to waking up_ (be used to / wake up) early every day.

4. I _am thinking_ (think) of buying a new car.

5. The only thing he _____owns_____ (own) is a second-hand car.

6. Mmm! Something _____smells_____ (smell) great! What's for dinner?

7. You _are always leaving_ (always / leave) your CDs on the floor! It's high time you tidied up your room!

8. Of course I _____mind_____ (mind) you playing loud music in here!

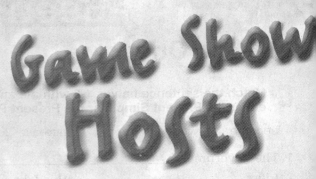

Game Show Hosts

Game shows have become increasingly popular in the last few years, and although game concepts have changed, the basic formula remains the same. Nervous contestants, enthusiastic audiences and witty game show hosts are the essential ingredients that keep us glued to our screens. In many cases, though, the success of the game show depends not only on the originality of the concept, but on the personal magnetism of the game show host. **1** F

To become a game show host, one needs to keep certain criteria in mind. Hosts are usually male, reasonably attractive, and permanently cheerful. In fact, one can't help but get the feeling that game show hosts rehearse *the smile* as often as they rehearse the questions! **2** B In fact, both TV critics and hosts themselves admit that it is a quality that should not be underestimated.

Of course, every game show host needs a 'catchphrase', a truly memorable phrase or sentence that distinguishes them from other game show hosts. **3** E In addition, it should sum up the spirit of the show and be the sort of phrase that could find its way into people's everyday vocabulary. If this happens, the popularity of the host and the show are pretty much guaranteed.

Wardrobe selection is also a vital aspect of the game show host's success. **4** D

Traditionally, hosts wear well-cut suits, plain shirts and colourful ties. A quick analysis of this 'uniform' reveals two things: firstly, the suit makes the host look like something of an authority figure. Secondly, the bright tie creates the impression of a fun-loving guy, a friendly 'fella' that the TV audience can easily identify with.

There are, of course, a number of miscellaneous items that fall under the heading of *Game Show Host Paraphernalia*. These include a sunbed for that year-round tan, a golf club membership (to make the right contacts), and a personalised number plate. **5** A Nice work if you can get it!

D Read the text below. Use the words given in capitals at the end of each line to form a word that fits in the space in the same line.

MORE THAN LEARNING

Nowadays, the university experience offers young people a great deal more than just a good **(1)** education EDUCATE
or the promise of a successful career. To begin with, university gives students the opportunity to behave like adults and be more independent,
(2) especially if it's their first time SPECIAL
away from home.
It's **(3)** doubtful that every single DOUBT
university student has a clear idea of which path to follow **(4)** professionally PROFESSION
. That's why studying also gives youngsters time to think about their careers.
(5) Needless to say, university is the perfect place for students to meet new people and NEED
make new friends as well. Of course, there are also the **(6)** useful perks of being a USE
university student, like travel discounts and cheaper cinema tickets.
(7) Additionally , young people learn how to motivate themselves to do their absolute best, ADDITION
and in this way, they prepare themselves for the very competitive work environment.

Lesson Three

A Complete the following sentences with the words/phrases in the box.

| run out of | it's no wonder | catch on | grab a bite to eat | catch a movie | |
| out of the ordinary | isolation | at a low cost | affectionate | facilities | disrespectful |

1. Keen to experience something that's a little ___out of the ordinary___ ? Try bungee jumping!
2. We've ___run out of___ sugar. I'll go get some from Mrs Greenwood next door.
3. Scientists claim that electric cars will soon ___catch on___ as they offer an effective solution to the problem of pollution.
4. ___It's no wonder___ you failed the test! You didn't study at all.
5. Why don't we ___catch a movie___ at that new cinema complex and then ___grab a bite to eat___ ?
6. He chose to live in total ___isolation___ after his wife's death.
7. I'm new in town and I want some information about sports ___facilities___ in the area.
8. Nowadays, most people can buy mobile phones ___at a low cost___ compared to the prices a few years ago.
9. Mr Douglas is very ___affectionate___ towards his children.
10. Laura's a very ___disrespectful___ girl; she was quite rude to the poor old lady who asked her for some assistance.

B Read the text below and think of the word which best fits each space. Use only one word in each space.

Have you (1) ___ever___ wondered how a new word makes its way into (2) ___a___ dictionary? You might (3) ___be___ in for a surprise when you find out! To begin with, there is a reading team, which consists of about fifty members, and it's their job to read as much written material (4) ___as___ possible, so that they can enter any new words they find into (5) ___a/the___ massive electronic database. The project is ongoing and the team is required to read just about everything, (6) ___from___ magazines and TV scripts to song lyrics. It may sound like they (7) ___have___ a ball at work, but the 'readers' are specially trained and are expected to read through a (8) ___piece___ of literature every day. Once the words have been entered into the database, the database is analysed (9) ___and___ words that appear more than once are investigated further. The readers must bear (10) ___in___ mind the fact that there are lots of words that remain popular for only a (11) ___very___ short time so the criteria for selection are strict. Basically, a word has to appear (12) ___at___ least five times in five different sources over a period of five years before it is included in the dictionary. The team is so thorough (13) ___that___ they not only record the number of times the word pops up, but they also analyse the variety of sources in which the word appears. This means that (14) ___some___ words may be left out because they are used only in rap songs, (15) ___for___ example. It's also worth noting that the context in which the word appears is always taken into consideration, as this can drastically change the meaning of the word. Bet you didn't know all that!

C Read the text below and look carefully at each line. Some of the lines are correct, and some have a word which should not be there. If a line is correct, put a tick (√) in the space provided. If a line has a word which should not be there, write the word in the space provided.

WHAT A WEEK!

1.	Do you believe in lucky days? Well, planning your weekly schedule	✓
2.	will be quite a challenge from now and on if you take this advice. For many	and
3.	people, Monday is the first day of the week and it's no wonder that it's	✓
4.	also the unluckiest day for to sign a contract or spend money. The	for
5.	French also they believe that people who marry on this day will go insane!	they
6.	However, if you are being planning to get married, do so on a Tuesday – it's	being
7.	also a good day for doing business deals. It is not advisable to wear	✓
8.	gloves on a Wednesday, but if it is a good idea to visit the doctor on this day.	if
9.	Thursday it is a good day to see your lawyer, but if you're thinking of	it
10.	grabbing a bite to eat, avoid chicken! Some of people believe that Friday	of
11.	can to be a bad day for making clothes, moving house or laughing! Saturday	to
12.	is not considered a good day for working and the Scottish believe that anyone	✓
13.	born on this day will be able to see ghosts. Don't make your bed, cut hair,	✓
14.	or sew anything on a very Sunday. Also, if you've been singing in a	very
15.	choir, it's likely that you'll find your lunch burnt when you get to home!	to

D Rewrite each sentence, using one of the verbs from the list and making any necessary changes.

think	see	be	smell	taste

1. I think you are behaving very rudely.

   I think you are being very rude.

2. Robert is considering working abroad.

   Robert is thinking about working abroad.

3. I have an appointment with my lawyer tonight.

   I am seeing my lawyer tonight.

4. This perfume has a sweet scent.

   This perfume smells sweet.

5. She's trying the soup to see if it needs more lemon.

   She is tasting the soup to see if it needs more lemon.

E **Read the letter below. The sentences in each paragraph are jumbled. Put them in the correct order and then identify the type of letter.**

Dear Sarah,

Sorry, I haven't written in a while but I've been busy getting ready for an important event – my graduation! I hope you're doing well. In fact, that's why I'm writing – to invite you to come.

It's going to be quite an event as it coincides with the university's 100th anniversary. The graduation ceremony is going to take place after that and the Dean is going to hand out the diplomas. A famous singer, whose son is graduating with us, will also be attending the ceremony. The graduation ceremony is taking place on 2nd July at 10:00 in the Assembly Hall. Rumour has it that there might be a gig afterwards! The Minister of Education has been invited to deliver a speech on the university's long history and tradition. So, make sure you come.

Please, give me a ring to let me know if you're coming. Don't miss out on all the fun! Looking forward to seeing you.

Bye for now,
Emma

Suggested answer

Dear Sarah,

I hope you're doing well. Sorry I haven't written in a while but I've been busy getting ready for an important event – my graduation! In fact, that's why I'm writing – to invite you to come.

The graduation ceremony is taking place on 2nd July at 10:00 in the Assembly Hall. It's going to be quite an event as it coincides with the university's 100th anniversary. The Minister of Education has been invited to deliver a speech on the university's long history and tradition. A famous singer, whose son is graduating with us, will also be attending the ceremony. Rumour has it that there might be a gig afterwards! So, make sure you come.

Don't miss out on all the fun! Please, give me a ring to let me know if you're coming. Looking forward to seeing you.

Bye for now,
Emma

F **Read the phrases below and put them in the correct category.**

Of course I'll come to ...	I'm afraid I can't come because ...
I've already planned something so ...	How could I say no?
I wouldn't miss it for the world!	Sorry, but I can't make it to ...

Declining an invitation	Accepting an invitation
I've already planned something so ...	Of course I'll come to ...
I'm afraid I can't come because ...	I wouldn't miss it for the world!
Sorry, but I can't make it to ...	How could I say no?

G **Write a letter of reply to Emma using the phrases above. Your letter must be between 120 and 180 words. Do not write any addresses.**

02 Eureka!

Lesson One

A Complete the sentences below with an appropriate word. The first letter of the word has been given.

1. A weekend in Paris? What a m<u>arvellous</u> idea! Of course I'll come with you!
2. John is the funniest boy in the class. He does a wonderful i<u>mitation</u> of our science teacher.
3. When I realised that the mixer I had just bought was broken, I went back to the shop and asked for a full r<u>efund</u> .
4. 'I need a hammer to fix the door.'
   'Well, all the t<u>ools</u> are in the garage. Help yourself!'
5. We have to pay the final i<u>nstalment</u> on the car next month.
6. Dr Schwartz is busy carrying out an e<u>xperiment</u> in his lab.
7. Joanne is always busy; she has a very demanding s<u>chedule</u> .
8. I didn't invest any money in Joe's scheme because I knew it would <u>fail</u> .
9. They are trying to come up with the most effective s<u>olution</u> to the problem.
10. Do you think you'll get the o<u>pportunity</u> to travel to the Bahamas for free again?

B Choose the best word a, b, c or d to complete the sentences below.

1. If you don't come to the party, you'll _____ <u>miss</u> out on all the fun.
   a. go   b. take   c.)miss   d. set
2. The bank teller was taken _____ <u>in</u> by the good manners of one of the customers, who turned out to be a notorious bank robber!
   a.)in   b. out   c. up   d. to
3. The little boy got lost because he _____ <u>wandered</u> away from his parents at the fair.
   a. left   b.)wandered   c. was   d. started
4. Mary promised she'd go on holiday with me and now she says she can't make it. That's the third time she's let me _____ <u>down</u> .
   a. up   b. away   c.)down   d. behind
5. Alison keeps _____ <u>putting</u> off going to the doctor and her headaches are getting worse and worse.
   a. taking   b.)putting   c. setting   d. laying
6. When I bought my new car, the dealer _____ <u>threw</u> in a CD player as part of the deal.
   a.)threw   b. placed   c. took   d. got
7. Mrs Connelly managed to squeeze everything _____ <u>into</u> a single suitcase.
   a. on   b. inside   c. at   d.)into
8. No matter how tired Helen is, she makes an effort to work _____ <u>out</u> every day.
   a. on   b.)out   c. in   d. up
9. Please pick _____ <u>up</u> your books off the floor.
   a. out   b.)up   c. at   d. on

C Complete the text with the Present Simple, the Present Progressive, the Present Perfect Simple or the Present Perfect Progressive of the verbs in brackets.

My family and I **(1)** <u>have been living</u> (live) in South Africa for many years. My husband, my three daughters and I **(2)** <u>love</u> (love) living here and cannot imagine living anywhere else.

My husband, Cory, **(3)** <u>has worked/has been working</u> (work) at the Kruger National Park for fourteen years and during this time we **(4)** <u>have learned/learnt</u> (learn) to love and appreciate wild animals. So, when Cory came home one day and said, 'I found a lion cub which has been abandoned by its mother ...', I immediately told him to bring it home.

Every time I hold Leo – that's what we called him – it **(5)** <u>feels</u> (feel) like I **(6)** <u>am holding</u> (hold) a baby! My favourite time of the day is when I **(7)** <u>feed</u> (feed) him with a bottle. Our lives **(8)** <u>have changed</u> (change) a lot since Leo became a part of our family. But, sooner or later, we will have to return Leo to his natural habitat.

Lesson Two

A You are going to read an article about the history of shoes. Choose from the list A-G the sentence which best summarises each part (1-6) of the article. There is one extra sentence which you do not need to use.

A Soft shoes, sandals and boots were worn at the time.

B Sandals were both comfortable and practical.

C Shoes became an option for a greater number of people during the 1800s.

D Shoes, in their present form, are the result of many different influences.

E Class and status determined the appearance of shoes.

F This innovative shoe design had the potential to alter one's appearance.

G Shoes are designed to satisfy a number of tastes and requirements.

If the shoe fits, wear it!

1   **D**

It's unlikely that you consider them to be anything more than a fashion statement, but, believe it or not, those shiny pairs of shoes you keep in your wardrobe are the product of years of evolution. Shoes have developed from animal skins tied around the ankles to modern-day footwear because of a number of factors including climate, availability of materials and even status ... And you thought they were just nice to wear!

2   **A**

In ancient Egypt, it was customary to wear sandals with flat soles made of papyrus or leather. In ancient Greece, laced sandals with thick soles were all the rage. Shoes that were made of soft materials and reached the ankles were popular with Greek women and boots were traditionally worn in times of war and for hunting. The footwear worn by the Romans included light sandals and laced boots, which were open at the front.

3   **E**

During the Middle Ages in Europe, peasants wrapped skins around their feet while nobles and churchmen wore laced shoes of soft cloth or leather. During the 12th century, pointed shoes became the stylish option for noblemen; the points of these shoes were sometimes as long as 60 cm! The common folk, however, wore shoes with points that extended no longer than 15 cm.

4   **F**

High heels, a vital part of most women's wardrobes, were invented in about the late 16th century and became exceedingly popular with both men and women in the 17th century. The French king, Louis XIV, was a particularly big fan of high heels and saw them as the perfect way to boost his height. The high heels of the day were square-toed and fastened with buckles or bows.

5   **C**

Mass production of shoes began in the mid-19th century and they became available to the general public. Ankle boots with laces were popular with men, and women wore high-heeled, ankle-length shoes that were either laced or buttoned. One of the biggest shoe innovations at the time was the running shoe, which was made of canvas and used for sporting activities.

6   G

These days, we have a mind-boggling variety of shoes to choose from and a selection of styles to suit just about every purpose and occasion. Generally, the emphasis is on comfort and informality, especially where male footwear is concerned. Women's shoes, on the other hand, range from more practical options, like sandals, to far less practical platform shoes and spiky high heels. Virtually anything goes nowadays, and fashion rather than the need to protect our feet dictates the trend.

B Match the words and expressions in the text with the meanings given.

1. customary (para. 2)   b   a. extremely
2. common folk (para. 3)   c   b. usual
3. exceedingly (para. 4)   a   c. ordinary people
4. mind-boggling (para. 6)   e   d. almost
5. virtually (para. 6)   d   e. very difficult to imagine

C Complete the following sentences using the Past Simple, the Past Perfect Simple or the Past Perfect Progressive.

1. Jenny ___had waited/ had been waiting___ (wait) in the queue for almost two hours, before she ___managed___ (manage) to buy a ticket for the concert.

2. Harold ___announced___ (announce) that he was going to resign.

3. Mrs Peters ___waited___ (wait) until the plumber ___finished/had finished___ (finish) fixing the leaky tap before she ___started___ (start) cleaning up.

4. By the time Charlotte ___arrived___ (arrive) at the party, most of the guests ___had already left___ (already/leave).

5. Josh ___had been standing___ (stand) outside the restaurant for more than half an hour when he ___saw___ (see) Isabella walking up the road.

6. Kirsten ___had just picked up___ (just/pick up) the receiver to call her best mate when her mum ___told___ (tell) her that she should finish her homework first.

7. Casey, who is a big Westlife fan, ___went___ (go) wild as soon as the group ___walked___ (walk) on stage. She ___had been waiting___ (wait) for that concert for weeks!

8. When I ___moved___ (move) to America, my cousin, Sam, ___took___ (take) me to a hockey game. I ___had never seen___ (never/see) anything like it before!

9. Susan ___had just finished___ (just/finish) her history project when Alex ___called___ (call) to ask her if she ___wanted___ (want) to go to the cinema.

10. Two weeks ago I ___bumped___ (bump) into an old friend who I ___had not seen___ (not seen) for ten years.

D Circle the correct answer.

1. 'Ladies and gentlemen, I would like to thank you all for joining me on this **historic** / historical day.'
2. It is more **economical** / economic to do the week's shopping at the supermarket rather than at the local grocery store.
3. This shirt is too big. I need a smaller form / **size**.
4. I don't think you got your money's value / **worth**, considering how much you paid for it.
5. Janet has finally started to show the first **signs** / marks of recovery.
6. The documents will be **circulated** / issued to everybody before the meeting starts.
7. What's the local cash / **currency**?

Lesson Three

A Read the text below. Some of the lines are correct, and some have a word which should not be there.
If a line is correct, put a tick (√) in the space provided. If a line has a word which should not be there,
write the word in the space provided.

STAR PROBLEMS

1. I had never really been imagined how difficult it is to be a famous person	been
2. until I recently read an article about Vin Diesel, the young actor	√
3. who starred in the blockbuster *The Fast and the Furious*. Vin he believes	he
4. that the biggest disadvantage of it being a Hollywood star is the	it
5. lack of privacy. For example, the other day he went to shopping	to
6. with some of his own mates. The shopping centre was crowded, as usual,	own
7. and Vin was wearing his dark sunglasses to avoid being recognised.	√
8. All it took was one girl to scream out of his name and that was it!	of
9. Within a quite few seconds, there was a group of fans surrounding him	quite
10. asking for his autograph! It's pretty amazing how a relaxing day	√
11. can turn into a nightmare when you are also a celebrity!	also

B Read the text below and think of the word which best fits each space. Use only one word in each space.

ANIMAL E.R.

When you take a look around, it's just like any other
emergency room. There are doctors, nurses and all
(1) _____the_____ latest medical equipment.
Everything seems perfectly normal, except
(2) _____for_____ the patients, who all belong to the
animal kingdom! Sick cats, dogs and even birds are rushed
to the Eric & Joanne Tucker Hospital for Small Animals,
(3) _____where_____ they receive expert treatment.
    According (4) _____to_____ the chief surgeon, Eric
Tucker, the doctors (5) _____are_____ specialists in their fields and are able to treat a variety of
illnesses. The vets in the hospital come (6) _____across_____ different cases each day. He adds: 'When
we see our animal friends happy and healthy again, it is the (7) _____most_____ rewarding feeling in
the world. Unfortunately, we can't save (8) _____all_____ the animals. The truth is that no matter
(9) _____how_____ long we've been doing this job, (10) _____there_____ are still certain things we
can't get used to.'

C Complete the second sentence so that it has a similar meaning to the first sentence, using the word given. Do not change the word given. You must use between two and five words, including the word given.

1. The last time I saw Mike was five months ago.   **have**

   I _____have not/haven't seen Mike for_____ five months.

2. Jim started working on his project three hours ago.   **been**

   Jim _____has been working on_____ his project for three hours.

3. The old lady was deceived by the young man.   **in**

   The old lady _____was taken in by_____ the young man.

4. We had to postpone our trip because of bad weather.   **put**

   We _____had to put off_____ our trip because of bad weather.

5. After jogging for an hour, Bob became out of breath.   **had**

   Bob _____had been jogging for_____ an hour when he became out of breath.

6. John decided to buy the house despite his wife's objection.   **even**

   John decided to buy the house _____even though his wife_____ objected to it.

7. We couldn't continue our journey because of the snowstorm.   **result**

   As _____a result of the snowstorm_____ we couldn't continue our journey.

8. The film started before we arrived at the cinema.   **already**

   The film _____had already started_____ when we arrived at the cinema.

9. If you invest in this deal with me, we'll both become rich in no time.   **rolling**

   If you invest in this deal with me, we'll _____both be rolling in money_____ in no time.

10. I've never read such an interesting book before.   **most**

    This is the _____most interesting book_____ I've ever read.

D Read the text below. Use the word given in capitals at the end of each line to form a word that fits in the space in the same line.

CAREER PLANS

When I was young, I wanted to become a **(1)** _____scientist_____ . I dreamt of   **SCIENCE**

making breakthrough **(2)** _____discoveries_____ , which would be beneficial to the world.   **DISCOVER**

At first I thought of becoming a doctor, but not being able to stand the

(3) _____sight_____ of blood, I gave up that idea.   **SEE**

Next, I decided to become a great **(4)** _____inventor_____ . I started working on   **INVENT**

a machine which would **(5)** _____revolutionise_____ the art of making cakes. I entered **REVOLUTION**

a **(6)** _____competition_____ for young inventors at school, but my science teacher   **COMPETE**

didn't think that my chocolate cake machine was very original. That's

when I became interested in history. I **(7)** _____memorised_____ the names of all the   **MEMORY**

(8) _____historical_____ figures we studied at school and dreamt of performing   **HISTORY**

(9) _____heroic_____ deeds like they had. You'll never guess what I ended up   **HERO**

becoming. A librarian! It's a great job. You're surrounded by books you don't have

to pay to read, which is also very **(10)** _____economical_____ . What a bonus!   **ECONOMY**

E Below is the main part of an essay. Complete the blanks with the appropriate linking word or expression in the box.

| In addition | First of all | However | Furthermore | On the other hand |

(1) _____First of all_____ , DVDs have improved the quality of the
picture and the sound of films that people watch at home. Watching a film
on DVD means that you can rewind it, pause it and restart it as often as
you want without ruining it. You can also select the scenes you want to
see without having to rewind or forward it. (2) __Furthermore / In addition__ ,
DVDs include other features, such as interviews with the actors and the director. (3) __In addition / Furthermore__ ,
it is not necessary to have a DVD player or even a TV set for that matter in order to watch a DVD!
Simply watch it on your computer.
(4) ____On the other hand____ , there has been a great deal of concern among film-makers about people
not going to the cinema any more, as the quality of films on DVDs is exceptionally good.
(5) _____However_____ , new films are always released in cinemas first, and cinemagoing is still
popular. Although it is true that it is often hard to find older films on DVD, this will not be a problem
when DVDs become more available.

F Write the introduction and conclusion of the essay. You may use the words and expressions in the
box as well as your own.

| to sum up | nowadays | technological development | imagine | revolutionise | replace | video |

Introduction   Suggested answer

When DVDs first hit the shop shelves, they were considered to be the greatest invention ever! They have

just about replaced video cassettes and made watching films at home better and more entertaining.

DVDs offer superior sound and picture quality and have added a new dimension to home entertainment.

_____

_____

Conclusion   Suggested answer

To sum up, DVDs have managed, in a way, to bring the cinema into our homes. Nowadays, more and

more people are enjoying their favourite films on DVD as if they were actually at the cinema. As

technology advances every day, we can only imagine what greater inventions the future holds.

_____

_____

G Write an essay on the following topic: Technology has improved our lives in the past 50 years. Your
essay must be between 120 and 180 words.

03 Fast forward

Lesson One

A Match the expressions in the box with the appropriate preposition *in* or *out of* and complete the sentences.

| breath | favour | the long run | charge | order | sight |

1. He carried on waving goodbye until the car was completely ___out of sight___.

2. I asked Tom why he was ___out of breath___, and he told me he had been jogging for an hour.

3. When Mr Peterson went on a business trip, he left his son ___in charge___ of the company.

4. They invested a lot of money in the company as they believed that ___in the long run___ it would make a huge profit.

5. As a result of the heavy rain, the telephones were ___out of order___ for several hours.

6. Everyone was ___in favour___ of postponing the meeting for the following week.

B Match the expressions in the box with the correct form of the verbs *set* or *put*.

| the blame on | a task | eyes on | foot in | a strain on | an end to |

1. He's so moody lately; losing his job has ___put a strain on___ him.

2. Mark refused to ___set foot in___ Linda's house again.

3. What upset Paula was that they ___put the blame on___ her without investigating the matter.

4. The professor ___set a task___ for the students to complete and then left the room.

5. She knew it was Joey's brother the moment she ___set eyes on___ him.

6. A fight broke out at the restaurant, but the police quickly ___put an end to___ it.

C Read the text below and decide which answer A, B or C best fits each space.

In July the Astro cinema (1) ___will be holding___ its annual two-day science fiction marathon. The tickets (2) ___will be priced___ at £10 each. (3) ___Furthermore___, sci-fi enthusiasts can watch as many films as they like with one ticket! Now that's (4) ___value___ for money! In order to ensure that the event is (5) ___carried out___ successfully, a number of volunteers will work shifts so that the cinema remains operational for 48 hours straight. So, if you enjoy watching action-packed films, you (6) ___will love___ the sci-fi marathon! Film critic Burt Taylor will give a short talk on the history of science fiction films before the viewing sessions begin. He will also explain why sci-fi films have gained (7) ___worldwide___ popularity in recent years. It's certainly an event that shouldn't be missed!

1. **A** will have been holding	**B** will be holding	**C** will have held
2. **A** will be priced	**B** will have priced	**C** will be pricing
3. **A** Even though	**B** Although	**C** Furthermore
4. **A** price	**B** amount	**C** value
5. **A** carried out	**B** found out	**C** come out
6. **A** will be loving	**B** will love	**C** will have loved
7. **A** favourable	**B** popular	**C** worldwide

Lesson Two

A You are going to read six reviews of some of the worst science fiction films ever made. For Questions 1-7, choose from films (A-F). Some of the films may be chosen more than once. When more than one answer is required, these may be given in any order.

Which film(s):

1. is about the preservation of a human life? `C`

2. features an experiment that went wrong? `F`

3. features a future world? `B`

4. is about a threat to humanity? `D`

5. became a model for later films? `D`

6. features a man performing unusual mental tasks? `E`

7. are about a chase? `B` `F`

B Find words and expressions in the text and match them with the meanings given.

1. used in the home _domestic_

2. escape _run off_

3. the cinema _the big screen_

4. inexpensive, not costing much _low budget_

5. poor performance _pathetic acting_

6. short, light sleep _snooze_

7. catches _gets hold of_

Sci-fi flops!

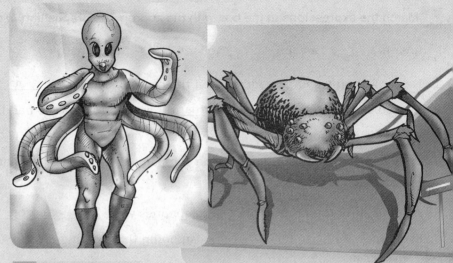

A HEARTBEEPS

Made in 1981, this film tells the ridiculous tale of two domestic robots, Valcom-17485 (played by Andy Kaufman) and Aquacom-89045 (played by Bernadette Peters) who fall in love. Valcom is meant to be a sort of robotic butler and Aquacom's duty is to help out at poolside parties. The two decide to abandon their, uh..., promising careers, in order to run off and explore the world. Absolute nonsense!

B SLIPSTREAM

After starring in the sci-fi smash hit *Star Wars*, actor Mark Hamill appeared in *Slipstream,* which turned out to be a total disaster! The film is set in the near future, at a time when the Earth has been destroyed by pollution. Hamill plays a lawman pursuing Bob Peck, a humanoid on the run. The plot is complicated and the dialogue is embarrassingly bad. No surprise, then, that this film didn't even make it to the big screen. Get it on video, if you dare!

C FANTASTIC VOYAGE

Following an assassination attempt on his life, an important scientist is left with a blood clot in his brain. A futuristic mini-submarine with a team of medical workers inside it is shrunk to microscopic size and injected into his body in order to save his life. Raquel Welch leads the team on a truly bizarre adventure. Very low budget special effects and some pretty pathetic acting guarantee the film is a complete failure.

D METEOR

Meteor tells the story of a team of Russian and American scientists who unite in a desperate attempt to prevent an asteroid from hitting the Earth. To be honest, the only good thing about this film was that it probably provided the inspiration for the somewhat better asteroid disaster films *Armageddon* and *Deep Impact*. And even though big names like Sean Connery and Natalie Wood star, the film is a snooze from beginning to end.

E JOHNNY MNEMONIC

Based on a story by William Gibson, *Johnny Mnemonic* is about a courier (Keanu Reeves), who 'downloads' and stores vital information in his brain (much like a computer) in order to transport it safely to its destination. In his final assignment, Reeves has to transport data from Beijing to Newark within 48 hours, before a futuristic samurai warrior gets hold of it. While the story itself is interesting, the effects are over the top and Reeves's performance is truly awful. The end result is a huge disappointment.

F TARANTULA

If you thought *Eight-Legged Freaks* – the recent science fiction film starring overgrown spiders – was freakishly bad, then you probably shouldn't see *Tarantula*. Made in 1955, *Tarantula* is about a massive spider (the result of a laboratory accident) that roams the Arizona desert in search of its next meal. A group of scientists are in hot pursuit of this spider which creates unbelievable chaos and destroys everything in its way. Predictably, the spider isn't very convincing and the acting is less so.

C Complete the sentences with the words in the box.

cheap	pleased	badge	destination	priceless
miserable	concept	decoder	undesirable	wristwatch

1. He dropped his ____wristwatch____ in the pool but nothing happened to it because it was waterproof.

2. It would be highly ____undesirable____ to increase the number of children in each class.

3. Amy was ____pleased____ when she found out that she had passed her final test.

4. A(n) ____priceless____ ancient statue was stolen from the museum last night.

5. Some children cannot grasp the ____concept____ of equality.

6. I can't stand Linda! All she does is complain. She is such a(n) ____miserable____ person.

7. I bought three beautiful pairs of shoes when I was in Italy and they were really ____cheap____.

8. The police needed a suitable ____decoder____ to figure out what information the secret message contained.

9. Hurry up! If we don't leave soon, we'll never reach our ____destination____ on time!

10. The old lady asked the policeman to show her his ____badge____ before she opened the door.

D Read the text below. Some of the lines are correct, and some have a word which should not be there. If a line is correct, put a tick (√) in the space provided. If a line has a word which should not be there, write the word in the space provided.

SURVIVING IN THE FOREST

1. Before setting out on a trek in the forest, you need to be _____√_____

2. absolutely prepared just in the case something happens. _____the_____

3. There are a number of things you should be include in your _____be_____

4. backpack, like a box of waterproof matches sealed in a _____√_____

5. plastic bag and that a lighter to help you start a fire. _____that_____

6. Furthermore, be sure to pack enough of food and water. _____of_____

7. Snacks like peanuts and chocolates are very great for a quick _____very_____

8. energy boost. It's also so advisable to take a mobile phone _____so_____

9. with you, in case you get lost. Of course, there are also other _____√_____

10. ways in which you can call for help from if you are _____from_____

11. in danger. A whistle, for an example, is vital. _____an_____

12. You can also use a mirror to reflect the sunlight. _____√_____

13. Finally, brightly coloured clothing can easily be detected _____√_____

14. from by the air, thereby indicating your position. In this way, _____by_____

15. it will be more easier for a rescue helicopter to find you. _____more_____

Lesson Three

A Complete the second sentence so that it has a similar meaning to the first sentence, using the word given. Do not change the word given. You must use between two and five words, including the word given.

1. We all agreed to redecorate the house.   **favour**
   We were all _____ in favour of redecorating _____ the house.

2. You can borrow my jacket provided that you don't stain it.   **long**
   You can borrow my jacket _____ as long as you _____ don't stain it.

3. Don't ever go to that place again.   **foot**
   Don't ever _____ set foot in _____ that place again.

4. She said that John was responsible for what had happened.   **blame**
   She _____ put the blame on _____ John for what had happened.

5. 'Make fun of me again and you'll regret it!' said Julie.   **if**
   'You _____ will regret it if you _____ make fun of me again!' said Julie.

6. We can't carry on like this; something's got to change!   **go**
   We can't _____ go on _____ like this; something's got to change!

7. Is he attending the meeting as well?   **attend**
   Is _____ he going to attend _____ the meeting as well?

8. No, I don't need the car tonight.   **needing**
   No, _____ I will not be needing _____ the car tonight.

9. Her latest CD will certainly top the charts.   **bound**
   Her latest CD _____ is bound to _____ top the charts.

10. I tried everything but I couldn't make him understand what I meant.   **message**
    I tried everything but I couldn't _____ get my message across _____ to him.

B Read the text below and decide which answer *A*, *B*, *C*, or *D* best fits each space.

FIT OR FAT?

It's 7 am, and you are heading for the bus stop when you see the bus moving off into the distance. You have to act quickly! You start running, hoping that you'll manage to catch it. But after just a few steps, you are already out of **(1)** _____ breath _____. And the bus ... it's out of **(2)** _____ sight _____! Look at yourself! When was the last time you **(3)** _____ set _____ foot in a gym? You probably can't think that far back! So, it's about time you took some action and **(4)** _____ put _____ an end to this terrible situation. According **(5)** _____ to _____ Garry Whitmore, a 34-year-old personal trainer, the key to good health is balance.

To begin **(6)** _____ with _____, you need to change your eating habits. You should **(7)** _____ include _____ plenty of fruit and vegetables in your diet. Fatty foods and sweets are completely out of the **(8)** _____ question _____. Furthermore, you should start exercising on a **(9)** _____ regular _____ basis. If, **(10)** _____ however _____, you are too busy to squeeze a gym workout into your daily **(11)** _____ schedule _____, remember that it is possible to get in shape in the comfort of your own **(12)** _____ home _____! **(13)** _____ Cheer _____ up, there's still hope! After all, your health is the most **(14)** _____ valuable _____ thing in the world. So, next time you see that bus coming, make sure you are ready for it! You'll be so **(15)** _____ pleased _____ with yourself once you're on it!

1.	**A** air	**B** breath	**C** power	**D** strength
2.	**A** picture	**B** place	**C** view	**D** sight
3.	**A** set	**B** place	**C** put	**D** lay
4.	**A** gave	**B** put	**C** made	**D** showed
5.	**A** with	**B** for	**C** to	**D** about
6.	**A** from	**B** in	**C** out	**D** with
7.	**A** include	**B** involve	**C** contain	**D** enclose
8.	**A** topic	**B** interest	**C** question	**D** issue
9.	**A** usual	**B** regular	**C** common	**D** normal
10.	**A** although	**B** despite	**C** however	**D** but
11.	**A** timetable	**B** arrangement	**C** organisation	**D** schedule
12.	**A** house	**B** room	**C** home	**D** place
13.	**A** Smile	**B** Cheer	**C** Speak	**D** Talk
14.	**A** valuable	**B** valueless	**C** priceless	**D** overpriced
15.	**A** miserable	**B** enjoyable	**C** pleased	**D** sad

C Read the text below and think of the word that best fits each space. Use only one word in each space.

JUST A DREAM

Most of us know what it's **(1)** ___like___ to wake up abruptly after having had a bad dream. Almost everybody has nightmares every now and again and children are no exception. **(2)** ___In___ fact, research suggests that up to 80% of children aged **(3)** ___between___ three and ten have nightmares. When children have had a nightmare, they usually **(4)** ___wake___ up screaming or crying. In **(5)** ___some___ cases they immediately start telling their parents **(6)** ___what___ happened in the dream. When parents hear their children cry out at night, they should **(7)** ___take___ action at once. They should go to their children immediately because the longer the children are left alone, the more frightened they become. **(8)** ___As___ a result, children take much longer to get back to sleep afterwards. Parents need to **(9)** ___make___ an effort to comfort their children, discuss their dream with them, and stay with them until they are ready to go back to sleep. Research has shown that such nightmares **(10)** ___are___ often caused by frightening films or books and seem to be **(11)** ___more/quite/rather___ frequent when the children are overtired. Another reason **(12)** ___for___ this could be anxiety or stress. So, **(13)** ___if/when___ a child has frequent nightmares, parents should consider the possibility **(14)** ___that___ the child is finding some aspect of their life too difficult to cope with. Parents must encourage their children to talk about any situations that could be putting a strain **(15)** ___on___ them. This might help prevent future nightmares.

D Match the essay beginnings with the endings below. Then decide which of the topics A-C is appropriate for each one of them.

Beginnings

1   We often hear people complaining that they do not have any time for themselves, and that when they do they are often too tired to do anything but watch TV. Although television can inform and entertain viewers, people should look for other alternatives as how to spend their free time.

B

2   Electricity has undoubtedly made our everyday lives a lot easier and simpler and it is really hard to imagine a day without it. Today, we take electricity so much for granted that a power cut can temporarily turn our lives upside down.

C

3   Nowadays, computers have been introduced in schools and pupils become familiar with them at a very early age. With the help of computers, teachers can do their job more effectively and students can learn more easily. This has led many people to believe that computers will eventually replace both teachers and books. In my opinion, this is highly unlikely for a number of reasons.

A

Endings

A   To sum up, it is true that computers are becoming more and more popular as the years go by. However, no matter how important they become, I do not think that they will ever be able to provide pupils with the things that books and teachers can offer.

B   All in all, I believe that people should put a limit on the time they waste watching TV and try to spend their free time in a more creative way. This will help them relax and recharge their batteries after a hard day's work.

C   As already stated, electricity has definitely improved the quality of our lives. Without it, things would change dramatically and life as we know it today would be very different.

A. In the future, computers will eventually replace teachers and books.   3

B. Nowadays, people waste their free time watching TV.   1

C. Electricity has dramatically changed our everyday lives.   2

E Now choose one of the topics above and write the main part of the essay.

Lesson One

A Read the following situations and decide what you would say in each of them. Use *must, have to, need, may, could*. There may be more than one answer.

1. A friend of yours wants to go into a building where entrance is forbidden unless you have special permission.

   You mustn't go into that building. You need special permission.

2. According to school regulations, it is compulsory to wear a school uniform.

   You have to wear a school uniform.

3. It is possible that I dropped my keys in the parking lot.

   I could/may have dropped my keys in the parking lot.

4. It really wasn't necessary for you to order so much food.

   You needn't have ordered so much food.

5. It's possible that I'll see Sue at the meeting tonight.

   I may see Sue at the meeting tonight.

B Choose the best word/phrase a, b or c for each blank.

1. Donna had an accident and she had to _____put_____ her wedding _____off_____ until March.
   (a.) put...off   b. go...on   c. move...on

2. The police are still not sure what time the victim _____met_____ his death.
   a. had   (b.) met   c. found

3. Phyllis stood _____gazing_____ at the painting for some time.
   a. observing   b. glancing   (c.) gazing

4. The lecturer _____paused_____ for a moment to refer to his notes.
   a. researched   b. examined   (c.) paused

5. Claire leaned over and _____whispered_____ something in my ear.
   (a.) whispered   b. uttered   c. murmured

6. That waiter was so rude he actually _____snatched_____ the money out of my hands!
   (a.) snatched   b. held   c. got

C Complete the blanks with a suitable preposition.

Recent research carried **(1)** ___out·___ by the Department of Transport revealed that parents are more worried than ever **(2)** ___about___ their children's safety on the roads. According **(3)** ___to___ research findings, the reason **(4)** ___for___ this anxiety is the increasing number of accidents involving young children. Children are taught road safety rules at school, but most young children seem to misunderstand some of the rules, as their brains are still unable **(5)** ___to___ process complex instructions. Researchers have therefore decided to pilot a special programme to put road safety rules **(6)** ___into___ practice. They have also issued a questionnaire to determine **(7)** ___which___ areas have the highest rate of traffic accidents, as they will be given priority when the programme is piloted. More effective teaching methods should help reduce the number of accidents **(8)** ___in___ the long run.

Lesson Two

A You are going to read an article about a hike along the Great Wall of China. Choose the most suitable heading from the list A-H for each part (1-7) of the article. There is one extra heading you do not need to use.

A Prepared for anything

B The final stretch

C Kind-hearted companions

D The chance of a lifetime

E Refreshments for all

F Getting fit and ready

G From one extreme to another

H Mixed feelings of anxiety and excitement

B Find words and expressions in the text and match them with the meanings given.

1. unbearably hot
   sweltering

2. huge
   massive

3. manage, deal with
   handle

4. very strong
   overwhelming

5. travelled with
   accompanied

6. regain one's strength
   get a second wind

Keep on Trekking

1   D

Being middle-aged with my stable job at the bank and my cosy life in the suburbs, I was sure that adventure was a thing of the past for me. So, you can imagine my surprise when a colleague of mine asked me if I was interested in spending a week hiking along the Great Wall of China. I was thrilled and I gratefully accepted the invitation.

2   F

As you can imagine I was not in the best physical condition, but luckily I had two months to prepare before the trip. I started going to the gym three times a week and spent my weekends taking long walks in the hills outside of town. I also bought myself a good pair of hiking boots.

3   H

The big day finally arrived and after a ten-hour plane trip my hiking companions and I landed in a sweltering Beijing. We were about to experience in real life what we had only seen in books, like the massive Tiananmen Square, the mysterious Forbidden City, the beautiful temples and parks. We spent the next few days sightseeing and resting to prepare ourselves for the hike. We were all looking forward to it, but we were concerned about how we were going to handle the overwhelming heat.

4   A

When we finally arrived at the village where we were to begin our trek, we found that everything had been organised for us. We were given excellent guides and there were even a couple of doctors there in case anything went wrong. We then got started on our 80 km walk along the wall. Although I had been told what to expect and I believed that I was reasonably fit, it was still a bit of a shock when I saw the steep stairs and narrow paths we would have to climb.

5   G

When we set out, it was very early in the morning and still very chilly. I was wearing a heavy fleece jacket, a sweatshirt and a T-shirt. A few hours later, however, I was down to just my T-shirt. The heat was unbelievable and the journey along the wall very challenging as in some places the stairs were incredibly steep. Despite the difficulties, I enjoyed every moment of the trek. The view was spectacular and the scenery simply reathtaking.

6	C

However, we wouldn't have made it without the help of the locals. They quickly befriended us and even served us refreshing jasmine tea. We found out that they made their living as guides and souvenir sellers. Some of them even accompanied us part of the way and helped us tackle the most difficult slopes as they knew the best way to approach them. I became particularly friendly with a young man called Ming; we chatted in English

and he told me that he had been studying the language for a number of years. He stayed with us till the very end, even though he was a long way from his village.

7	B

The last part of the trek was the most difficult as, in some places, the ascent was almost vertical and many of the steps were knee high. But I seemed to get a second wind because the finishing line was in sight. Believe it or not, we walked up about 25 000 steps. Of course, I had my camera with me and I went back home with rolls and rolls of film. My trip taught me that it is never too late to have an adventure!

C Rewrite the following sentences starting with the words given.

1. Perhaps he'll be able to help you with your project.

   He _may be able to help you with your project._

2. It's not necessary to turn the air conditioner on now.

   You _don't need to/needn't/don't have to turn the air conditioner on now._

3. It's likely that she told me about it, but I don't remember.

   She _may/could/might have told me about it, but I don't remember._

4. Is it really necessary to pick Auntie Mary up from the station?

   Do we _really need to/have to pick Auntie Mary up from the station?_

D Complete the text below with the words in the box. You may need to change the form of the verbs.

inspire	precautions	take no notice	thrilled
feel at home	turn down	hesitate	tremendous

When Claudie Andre-Deshays was told that she was going into space, she was **(1)** _thrilled_ ! She was the only woman in a group of seven astronauts to be selected for the mission. "I immediately felt a **(2)** _tremendous_ responsibility towards the French people and I just couldn't **(3)** _turn down_ the proposal. I didn't **(4)** _hesitate_ even for a moment", says Claudie.

She also says that the first time she felt the urge to travel outside this world was when she saw the first moon landing. She says, "I was just seven years old but the whole picture was what **(5)** _inspired_ me. From that moment on I knew I just had to go".

Claudie remembers that the preparations for the trip were exhausting. "We had to take all the necessary **(6)** _precautions_ to ensure a safe mission. Fortunately, all my colleagues and I worked very well together."

"Being out in space was a most extraordinary experience. Strangely enough, I **(7)** _felt at home_ ; I even took my make-up kit with me! The press had a field day with that when I got back. However, I chose to **(8)** _take no notice_ of what they said. I was over the moon already!"

Lesson Three

A Read the text below and look carefully at each line. Some of the lines are correct, and some have a word which should not be there. If a line is correct, put a tick (√) in the space provided. If a line has a word which should not be there, write the word in the space provided.

ANTI-CELEB MUMMIES

1.	When we think of mummies, we tend to think of kings,	√
2.	queens and noblemen, who were buried with them their precious	them
3.	belongings. However, despite archaeologists in Ain Labakha,	despite
4.	in southern Egypt, found that some mummies they were,	they
5.	in fact, peasants. After thorough tests and X-rays were being	being
6.	carried out, scientists made some important discoveries	√
7.	with regard to the peasants' own living conditions, jobs	own
8.	and nutrition. Tests also revealed that there too was a high	too
9.	rate of infant mortality and that people sometimes starved	√
10.	to death. The people of Ain Labakha believed that they	√
11.	would have come back to life again, so they were buried	have
12.	with the belongings which these they would need in their	these
13.	next life. Unlike also their royal masters, their wish to	also
14.	have be left in peace was respected and they were returned	have
15.	to their tombs instead of being exhibited in museums.	√

B Read the text below and think of the word which best fits each space. Use only one word in each space.

THE UNKNOWN MOCHE

Although we are all aware of the ancient Inca civilisation, few people know about their ancestors, the Moche. Max Uhle, **(1)** ___a/the___ German archaeologist, found proof of their existence in 1900. The Moche lived **(2)** ___in___ Peru in around 200-600 AD. They founded a civilisation that **(3)** ___was___ as advanced as that of the ancient Greeks. They were powerful and wealthy, and they also had tremendous technological know-how. Their cities **(4)** ___and___ life spread around two Huacas, the platforms of the Sun and the Moon, **(5)** ___which___ consisted of two huge pyramid-like structures. They had rooms, temples and yards, built one **(6)** ___on___ top of the other over the centuries. Their religious system was **(7)** ___extremely/ quite___ (very/) strict and ceremonies were a part of their everyday lives. The Moche were also **(8)** ___able___ to develop arts and crafts. Magnificent items have been discovered at the excavation sites **(9)** ___in/during___ recent years. Ceramics, gold artefacts and wall paintings that were found in tombs, as well as the Huacas are all evidence of **(10)** ___their/this___ advanced civilisation. However, there are **(11)** ___still___ many things that have to be investigated. It's not known **(12)** ___where___ their knowledge came from, how they lived, **(13)** ___what___ their rituals were, or **(14)** ___how/why___ they disappeared. Hopefully, archaeologists will eventually be able to find the answers **(15)** ___to___ some of these questions.

C Read the text below and complete the blanks with words from the box. You may need to change the form of the verbs and you will not need to use all the words.

utter	constant	unbearable	tremendous	inexplicable	tranquillity precaution used
approach	response	notice	optional	introductory	roar suffer

Close your eyes and listen. Are you surrounded by peace and quiet or is your **(1)** ___tranquillity___ constantly being interrupted by phones ringing, the TV blaring or an aeroplane engine **(2)** ___roaring___ overhead? Research carried out by the World Health Organisation has revealed that most Europeans live in a noisy environment, which besides being annoying, can be a(n) **(3)** ___tremendous___ threat to our health. People who work in a noisy environment might initially find that their hearing recovers overnight, but after a while the damage becomes permanent. In addition, when somebody is exposed to **(4)** ___constant___ noise, they may end up feeling tense and angry. Surveys found that the most **(5)** ___unbearable___ noises include loud stereos and barking dogs. In some extreme cases, people have been forced to move because of the noise their neighbours made.

According to medical experts, when somebody **(6)** ___suffers___ from lack of sleep or stress as a result of constantly being exposed to a particular noise, it is wrong to assume that they will get **(7)** ___used___ to it and won't take any **(8)** ___notice___ of it eventually. Studies have shown that noise can affect mental performance and even cause high blood pressure and heart disease. So, taking **(9)** ___precautions___ is not **(10)** ___optional___. It is a must for sufferers to invest in double glazed windows to reduce noise from outside and plan as many quiet times throughout the day as possible.

D Complete the second sentence so that it has a similar meaning to the first sentence, using the word given. Do not change the word given. You must use between two and five words, including the word given.

1. There is a possiblity that she got lost on her way to Sally's house. **might**
   She ___might have got lost___ on her way to Sally's house.

2. Visitors are not allowed to touch the exhibits. **must**
   Visitors ___must not touch___ the exhibits.

3. Susan wasn't feeling well so she decided to stay at home. **weather**
   Susan ___was feeling under the weather___ so she decided to stay at home.

4. You should think carefully about the dangers involved before you make a decision. **take**
   You should ___take into account___ all the dangers involved before you make a decision.

5. It wasn't necessary for you to go to all this trouble. **gone**
   You ___needn't have gone___ to all this trouble.

6. You'd better see a specialist as soon as possible. **ought**
   You ___ought to see___ a specialist as soon as possible.

7. They set off early in the morning in order to avoid heavy traffic. **dawn**
   They set off ___at the crack of dawn___ in order to avoid heavy traffic.

8. Visitors are obliged to wear name tags in the building. **have**
   Visitors ___have to wear___ name tags in the building.

9. Perhaps you've left it on the bus. **could**
   You ___could have left it___ on the bus.

10. The board of directors rejected Joanne's proposal. **down**
    The board of directors ___turned down___ Joanne's proposal.

E Read the advertisement and the notes that you have made. Then read the letter and decide what is wrong with it.

Cruising around the Mediterranean

AT Travel is offering you a unique opportunity to discover the magic of the Mediterranean. Book with us now and enjoy a (ten-day) cruise around the Mediterranean (calling at) Spain, Italy, Greece and Cyprus. (Five-star luxury liners) will add a new dimension to your travelling experience. All for (less) than you'd expect - special offers for families with young (children) and groups.

For more information, please contact Ms Lawrence. 42 Avon Way, Colchester, CO2 9NX, Essex

fixed dates?/ can we choose when to go?

time to shop at every port?

what kind of facilities?

how much?

twin girls, aged 5

Dear Ms Lawrence,

I'm fed up with spending my summer holidays in the same place year after year. So, when I saw your advertisement, I thought I'd drop you a line and ask you about the cruise holiday around the Mediterranean Sea.

It isn't clear in your ad when the cruise is scheduled to begin. Are there fixed dates during the summer or can we choose when we want to go? You see, my wife, Pamela, and I would rather go at the end of August. As we also like shopping, do you think we'll have time to go shopping at every port? Some friends of ours went to Spain last year and they found some real bargains! You also mention that we'll be travelling on a luxury liner. Since we've never travelled on a cruise ship before, will we have lots of things to do on board? I suppose there will be a fully equipped gym with a sauna or a jacuzzi at least!

However, I'm mostly interested in finding out how much this is going to cost. Will I have to put my hand real deep in my pocket? You say that there are special offers, especially for families with children. We're taking our twin daughters, Emily and Julie, aged 5, with us so I'm really anxious to find out the total cost as soon as possible.

I'm looking forward to your reply.

Best regards,
Simon Adams

Suggested answer

The letter:
- has inappropriate layout (blocked paragraphs/signing off)
- irrelevant information (We're taking our twin daughters, Emily and Julie, aged 5 with...)
- informal structures (I'm fed up, it isn't clear)
- style / too informal (asking too many questions)

F Now rewrite the letter above in an appropriate style including only the relevant information.

Lesson One

A Read the text below. Use the word given in capitals at the end of each line to form a word that fits in the space in the same line.

OOPS! THAT'S WHAT I CALL HIGH!

Acrophobia or, to put it more **(1)** _____simply_____ , the fear of heights, is a very   **SIMPLE**

common fear. People suffering from acrophobia feel **(2)** _____terrified_____ when   **TERRIFY**

they do simple things like using a lift or walking out on to a balcony.

A lot of research has been done on this subject in an attempt to provide

(3) _____explanations_____ as to why certain people get these panic attacks. According   **EXPLAIN**

to the research findings, an individual's tendency to be acrophobic is

(4) _____dependent_____ on their ability to balance themselves. In actual fact,   **DEPEND**

this balancing act involves the co-ordination of many muscles and organs.

One's balance is affected by many different things. For example, sitting at a

computer all day long will **(5)** _____certainly_____ cause dizziness, sweating,   **CERTAIN**

numbness and a fast heartbeat. **(6)** _____Scientists_____ have worked hard to   **SCIENCE**

find different ways to treat individual patients. Some **(7)** _____suggestions_____   **SUGGEST**

include keeping fit by doing simple things such as playing hopscotch!

Still, boosting your **(8)** _____confidence_____ is probably the most effective way to   **CONFIDENT**

combat acrophobia.

B Complete the text below with the full infinitive, the bare infinitive or the -ing form of the verbs in brackets.

WHO'S AFRAID OF THE BIG BAD WOLF?

If you are one of those folks who believe that wild animals like
bears are cute and cuddly creatures, then perhaps you should
(1) _____think_____ (think) again. Bears, wolves and even hippos
are considered **(2)** _____to be_____ (be) among the most dangerous
carnivorous animals, given the right circumstances.

Many tourists have died because they felt like **(3)** _____taking_____
(take) pictures of animals in their natural habitat and refused to listen
to their guides' warnings **(4)** _____not to go_____ (not go) near them.
Unfortunately, no detailed records of these incidents have been kept
and many go unreported.

What is it that makes these animals **(5)** _____kill_____ (kill)? The reason they become so
hostile varies depending on the species. Wolves, for instance, kill when they want **(6)** _____to protect_____
(protect) their cubs, food or pregnant females. Polar bears attack humans when there's no other source
of food and people seem **(7)** _____to be_____ (be) the easiest targets. You must also **(8)** _____beware_____
(beware) of lions; old lions tend to attack people as they're easier **(9)** _____to catch_____ (catch) than their
regular prey.

So, what can man do? Start **(10)** _____killing_____ (kill) wild animals threatened with extinction? Of
course not! Next time you go on a safari, we recommend **(11)** _____listening_____ (listen) to your guide and
(12) _____taking_____ (take) his warnings seriously.

Lesson Two

A You are going to read a magazine article about animals that live in deserts. Four paragraphs have been removed from the article. Choose the most suitable paragraph from the list A-E for each part (1-4) of the article. There is one extra paragraph which you do not need to use.

A Did you know that these 'desert limousines' are capable of drinking up to twenty gallons of water in ten minutes and can survive for days without a single drop? They also tend to huddle together when the sun is at its hottest in order to keep cool. The reason for this is that there is less surface area for the sun to heat.

B Larger mammals, however, don't have the luxury of being able to hide underground. The main way these animals keep cool is by absorbing the heat more slowly.

C The head-standing beetle in particular, has come up with a very creative way to deal with the problem of living in an extremely dry environment. This tiny creature stands facing the wind and then drops its head to allow moisture to collect on its body.

D In fact, the male can carry up to twenty times its own weight in water. Other small animals such as mice and rabbits get their water supply from plants like the cactus and other vegetation.

E Every day is a battle for survival for these animals. They live a somewhat nomadic life, moving from place to place on a regular basis – usually when the seasons change.

B Find words and expressions in the text that match the definitions below.

a. inhabitants   _dwellers_
b. cruel   _harsh_
c. hold, save   _retain_
d. go somewhere despite
knowing that it is
dangerous   _venture_
e. gradual development
of a species   _evolution_

Desert Life

When you hear the word "desert", you probably imagine a barren landscape with very little life. But, believe it or not, a number of creatures actually make their home there. The remarkable thing about these desert dwellers is the way in which they have adapted in order to survive in such a harsh environment.

Reptiles, insects and birds, for example, have developed physical characteristics which allow them to live in the desert. Lizards have scales on their bodies and the insects there have waterproof shells, which help them to retain moisture.

1   C

The sidewinding adder lives in the Namib desert and barely touches the hot sand as it moves across it. Then, there's also the chameleon, which is able to change colour so that it either absorbs heat or reflects it when necessary.

Desert birds have feathers that protect them from the heat during the day and from the cold at night. Some birds which live in deserts where there are watering holes, use this water as a means of survival.

One example of this type of animal is the sandgrouse, which soaks itself in water in order to absorb as much of it as possible and then carries its load back to its nest.

2   D

Life is not so easy, however, for warm-blooded animals. They usually stay underground during the day and only venture out at night. Some of the smaller ones, like the ground squirrel that lives in the American and Asian deserts and the Australian kangaroo mouse hibernate all summer.

| 3 | B |

Perhaps the animal that is best suited to life in the desert is the camel. Contrary to what is commonly believed, a camel's hump is not filled with water but with fat, which supplies it with energy if it has to go without water for a long period of time.

| 4 | A |

Deserts are an excellent example of Mother Nature taking care of her own. Years of evolution, together with a very strong instinct for survival, have resulted in a bustling desert community. And you thought it was just a lot of sand and hot air ...

C Complete the blanks with the words in the box changing the form of the verbs where necessary. You will not need to use all the words.

| impending | famine | insignificant | stand out | confident |
| debris | bring about | unreasonable | eruption | wipe out |

1. Some animal species have been _____ wiped out _____ as a result of man's greed.
2. David was hit by bits of flying _____ debris _____ after the explosion.
3. Eric is so tall, he really _____ stands out _____ in a crowd.
4. The minister's statement _____ brought about _____ a negative reaction from the public.
5. Not surprisingly, a number of developing countries are still dealing with the problem of _____ famine _____.
6. He had very mixed feelings about his _____ impending _____ retirement.
7. Jessica was not very _____ confident _____ that she'd pass when she took the exam, but ended up doing very well.

D Complete the sentences by using the -ing form or the full infinitive.

1. Ladies and gentlemen, I regret _____ to inform _____ (inform) you that the show has been cancelled because of technical difficulties.
2. Although their time was up, some students carried on _____ writing _____ (write) the test.
3. Paula stopped _____ to get _____ (get) some groceries from the supermarket on her way home.
4. I can't help _____ wondering _____ (wonder) what the outcome will be.
5. Kate will never forget _____ going _____ (go) to the opera for the first time.
6. It was very kind of them _____ to lend _____ (lend) us their car.
7. Passengers are advised _____ to return _____ (return) to their seats and fasten their seat belts.
8. She stopped _____ working _____ (work) for that company six months ago.
9. I forgot _____ to set _____ (set) my alarm clock yesterday and I was late for work.
10. _____ Surfing _____ (surf) the Internet is very time-consuming.

Lesson Three

A Read the text below and think of a word which best fits each space. Use only one word in each space.

MARY CELESTE: THE MYTH

In November, 1872, a cargo ship loaded with industrial alcohol left New York **(1)** ___for___ Genoa, Italy. There were ten people on board, the captain with his wife and daughter, as **(2)** ___well___ as seven crew members. **(3)** ___However___ , they did not even make it half way to their destination: a month later the ship was found abandoned with all its provisions and cargo untouched. The people on board, along with the sole lifeboat, **(4)** ___had___ completely disappeared.

Investigations began immediately in an attempt **(5)** ___to___ shed some light on the mystery. The main suspect was Captain David Moorhouse, **(6)** ___whose___ ship was the first to approach the Mary Celeste, 600 miles west of the Azores. He was accused **(7)** ___of___ having hijacked the Mary Celeste believing that it had valuable cargo on board. However, **(8)** ___there___ was no concrete proof to support this allegation. Another theory suggested that perhaps the crew **(9)** ___had___ become alarmed by the amount of water the ship had taken in during a storm and jumped into the lifeboat to save **(10)** ___themselves___ but drowned. Still, the evidence to support this assumption was inadequate so four months later, the investigation was closed. That was **(11)** ___when___ the myth of Mary Celeste was born.

The case appeared again as a newspaper highlight in about 1929 when somebody came forward and claimed to **(12)** ___be___ the sole survivor of the ship. Although his name was not even on the official crew register, he was **(13)** ___able___ to convince the officials to take him seriously. Still, as the ship had been destroyed **(14)** ___by___ a fire 12 years after its crew disappeared, there was nothing left for further analysis. So, the Mary Celeste remains **(15)** ___one___ of the greatest naval myths in maritime history.

B Read the text and look carefully at each line. Some of the lines are correct, and some have a word which should not be there. If a line is correct, put a tick (√) in the space provided. If a line has a word that should not be there, write the word in the space provided.

THE SAHARA DESERT

1. Once you've been seen one desert, you'll probably think you	been
2. have seen them all, based on the assumption that all deserts	√
3. are exactly the same. In fact, deserts cover one seventh of the world's	√
4. surface but we really don't know enough about them neither.	neither
5. If you asked somebody to imagine a typical desert scene, like	like
6. they'd probably describe a palm tree oasis, surrounded	√
7. by sand dunes with a couple of the camels nearby.	the
8. This doesn't apply to the Sahara Desert even though. The Sahara	even
9. is the hottest, driest, largest desert in all the world. But there	all
10. is plenty of its life in the Sahara Desert. Reptiles, insects,	its
11. camels and birds have successfully adapted to such desert life.	such
12. It's a different story where humans are concerned, however. These	these
13. people have to drink gallons of water to stay alive in the desert	√
14. and even if then they dehydrate at a rate of about five per cent	if
15. per one day. So, take care if you're planning a trip to the desert!	one

Read the text below and decide which answer A, B, C or D best fits each space.

NAUGHTY MOTHER NATURE

Since the beginning of time, natural disasters have caused widespread destruction and tremendous

(1) _____loss_____ of life. Perhaps the most frightening thing about them is that they

(2) _____take_____ place randomly and often without warning. In Pompeii, for example, an entire

civilisation was **(3)** _____wiped_____ out in a matter of minutes when Mount Vesuvius erupted.

Scientists have attempted to make sense of all this chaos by coming up **(4)** _____with_____ a number

of ways to predict when natural disasters will strike. They spend an enormous **(5)** _____amount_____

of time studying certain signs and signals so that they'll be able to warn people to evacuate potentially

dangerous areas. For example, a series of earthquakes in the area surrounding a volcano usually means

that an eruption is **(6)** _____likely_____. By also monitoring water levels over a specific time period,

scientists are able to tell, with accuracy, when a flood is about to hit. Fortunately, scientists' predictions

are quite reliable and, it's worth **(7)** _____noting_____ that the natural disaster death

(8) _____toll_____ has decreased in recent years. But, nature isn't always very co-operative and

(9) _____unusual_____ weather conditions have been known to occur without any warning. Floods, for

instance, that occur as a result of out-of-season rainfall have caused **(10)** _____massive_____ problems

and **(11)** _____claimed_____ many lives, particularly in underdeveloped countries. Throughout history,

it was commonly believed that it was the anger of the gods that brought **(12)** _____about_____ natural

disasters. Of course, this is not the case, but there are certain factors that make the catastrophic

(13) _____effect_____ of natural disasters much worse. In poverty-stricken countries, for

example, people often build homes in the direct path of monsoons and typhoons, resulting in a

(14) _____huge_____ number of deaths each year. The good news is that scientists have

(15) _____assured_____ us that technological advancements are going to make it much easier

to predict the coming of a natural disaster, thus helping us to prepare for nature's unpredictability.

1.	**A** loss	**B** end	**C** take	**D** finish
2.	**A** bring	**B** make	**C** give	**D** take
3.	**A** disappeared	**B** wiped	**C** pulled	**D** washed
4.	**A** with	**B** about	**C** in	**D** out
5.	**A** load	**B** weight	**C** amount	**D** number
6.	**A** expecting	**B** likely	**C** soon	**D** possibly
7.	**A** noting	**B** accounting	**C** thinking	**D** believing
8.	**A** number	**B** figure	**C** age	**D** toll
9.	**A** interesting	**B** particular	**C** unusual	**D** painful
10.	**A** massive	**B** small	**C** insignificant	**D** confusing
11.	**A** borrowed	**B** stopped	**C** killed	**D** claimed
12.	**A** over	**B** about	**C** around	**D** out
13.	**A** affect	**B** result	**C** effect	**D** influence
14.	**A** huge	**B** tiny	**C** strange	**D** bizarre
15.	**A** lied	**B** said	**C** assured	**D** warned

D The following is an extract from a travel guide about Cairo, Egypt. Read the information and write the opening paragraph of an article describing Cairo.

CAIRO:
a dream come true

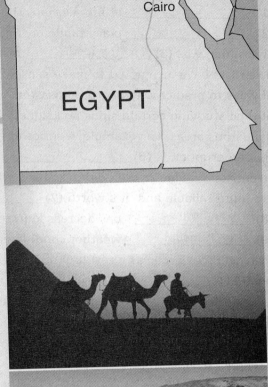

EGYPT

Cairo

Where is it?
· located on the River Nile at the base of the Delta in northern Egypt
· the capital of the country and the largest city in Africa, has a number of institutions, commercial establishments, governmental offices, universities and tourist hotels

Where to stay
· choose from a wide variety of 4 and 5-star hotels

Where to eat
· dine on a Nile sailing boat on a hot summer's evening

Where to go
· experience the magic of the Pyramids and the mystery of the Sphinx in Giza
· the Egyptian Museum of Antiquities which houses treasures from the time of King Tutankhamun
· the famous Khan al Khalili Bazaar selling almost everything from jewellery to antiques and carpets

Don't miss
· the sunrise over the Pyramids
· riding through the desert on a camel
· sailing down the Nile on a *felluca*, a traditional Egyptian boat

Suggested answer

If you like adventure and history then Cairo is the place for you. Sailing down the Nile in a traditional sailing boat, experiencing the magic of the Pyramids and exploring the treasures of ancient Egypt are just some of the things you can do.

E Now copy your introduction from the exercise above and write the rest of the article.

06 Let the fun begin!

Lesson One

A **Read the text below and decide which answer A, B, C or D best fits each space.**

WHO WANTS TO BE A STAR?

Film stars seem to have it all, right? A glamorous lifestyle, constant travel, millions of fans ... Sounds too good to be **(1)** _____true_____? Well, that's because it is. Being **(2)** _____famous_____ is not what you think it is; it's a privilege that comes with a huge responsibility. Unfortunately, most actors, blinded **(3)** _____by_____ the glare of flashing cameras, aren't able to handle the demands of stardom. Of course, fame has its advantages, like the financial rewards and adoring film **(4)** _____audiences_____ but you have to pay a price for it. Film stars have particularly hectic **(5)** _____schedules_____ and are rarely in one place for very long. This is, **(6)** _without a doubt_, the number one reason why they find it difficult to balance their careers with their personal lives. Then, there is the problem of the paparazzi, the photographers who follow stars day and night **(7)** _____in the hope_____ of capturing their most private moments on film. This is, of course, a major invasion **(8)** _____of_____ privacy and many celebrities have, understandably, lost their tempers with **(9)** _____members_____ of the paparazzi. Bear in mind that the pressure of living your life under a microscope is sometimes enormous. So, next time you're sitting in a darkened cinema wishing you were as rich and **(10)** _____popular_____ as your favourite star, remember: fame is not all it seems to be!

1. **A** true	**B** real	**C** believe	**D** exist
2. **A** favourite	**B** dear	**C** beloved	**D** famous
3. **A** in	**B** by	**C** for	**D** on
4. **A** viewers	**B** spectators	**C** audiences	**D** customers
5. **A** hours	**B** times	**C** programmes	**D** schedules
6. **A** without a doubt	**B** with respect to	**C** with regard to	**D** without delay
7. **A** in fear	**B** in case	**C** in the hope	**D** in addition to
8. **A** in	**B** out	**C** on	**D** of
9. **A** crowds	**B** members	**C** people	**D** parts
10. **A** loving	**B** special	**C** favourite	**D** popular

B **Use the Passive Voice to complete the sentences with the correct form of the verbs in the box.**

lock	repair	publish	keep	send	describe

1. Medicine must _____be kept_____ out of the reach of young children.
2. That book _____was published_____ years ago, when the writer was still very young.
3. I plan to go on a long trip once my car _is repaired/has been repaired_.
4. Her joy at winning the award could not _____be described_____.
5. Julie _____was sent_____ an e-mail with all the latest gossip yesterday.
6. When my parents _____were locked_____ out of the house, they had to wait two hours for the locksmith to arrive.

Lesson Two

A You are going to read a magazine article about Thanksgiving. For Questions 1-6, choose the correct answer A, B, C or D.

1. Why was the winter of 1621 difficult for the settlers?
   A because it was very cold and there was a lot of snow
   B because they had just arrived in America
   C because they had no food
   D because they had to deal with the Indians

2. Why did the Indians participate in the Thanksgiving feast?
   A because the Pilgrims owed them money
   B because the Indians had given assistance in hard times
   C because the Pilgrims had been invited to a similar Indian feast
   D because the Indians needed food

3. Who or what does 'them' in line 16 refer to?
   A Indians
   B Pilgrims
   C crops
   D food

4. Which of the following statements is true?
   A Thanksgiving became a holiday throughout America in the 19th century.
   B Thanksgiving is celebrated on the fourth Thursday of every month.
   C Canada and the USA celebrate Thanksgiving at the same time.
   D The Day of Thanks became an official holiday in 1863.

5. In the Thanksgiving Day,
   A the food is sweeter.
   B there is plenty of exotic food.
   C there is lots of sugar.
   D there is a better variety of food and desserts.

6. On Thanksgiving Day people celebrate
   A the life and times of the Pilgrims.
   B the Pilgrims and Indians living in harmony.
   C the 400 years of Thanksgiving.
   D their many blessings in life.

THANKSGIVING

With the coming of November, in countries like Canada and the United States people get ready to celebrate one of their favourite holidays: Thanksgiving. Most people know that Thanksgiving is simply a day of 'thanks' but very few people know exactly how and why it all started.

The early settlers arrived in America in 1621 in the hope of a better life. Their first winter there, however, was one of starvation and despair. But the following year's harvest was one of plenty, so the Governor at the time, William Bradford, declared a day of Thanksgiving. It was a 'thank you' for such a fruitful harvest! The happy event was to be celebrated with a great feast! The first settlers, or Pilgrims as they were called, decided to share the feast with the Native Americans because they owed them a lot for their survival. It was the Native Americans who showed them how to plant crops and hunt. Without their help the settlers may not have survived the harsh winter.

Slowly this yearly event became a custom and then an annual holiday in the northeastern part of the United States. By the middle of the 19th century, Thanksgiving Day had been adopted by many other states. In 1863, Abraham Lincoln, the president at the time, issued a proclamation stating that the fourth Thursday of every November would be known as Thanksgiving Day. In Canada, it has been an official holiday since 1957 and is celebrated on the second Monday in October.

There are many Thanksgiving events for all ages. Just a few days before, schools organise plays and parades. In the plays the students are dressed up as Pilgrims and Indians and act out the events that led to the first Thanksgiving feast. Many cities also hold major parades for the whole family to attend. But the major event is the preparation of the Thanksgiving dinner. According to tradition, which is still practised today, Thanksgiving meals included autumn fruits and vegetables like potatoes, apples and corn. Of course, the feast would not be complete without the roasted turkey, cranberry sauce and mashed potatoes. In the past, desserts were very different to what they are today. Back then, delicious pumpkin, apple and pecan pie did not exist, as they do in our times, because sugar was scarce. But people managed without it and dinner was still very tasty.

Thanksgiving though, is not just about food. It is a day when family and friends get together to celebrate their good fortune, as well as relax and enjoy each other's company, during this event which is almost 400 years old.

B Circle the correct answer.

1. She is such a good speaker that time always **flies**/ **drags** when she gives a presentation.
2. He says he's always **short of time** / **time to kill** and he can't speak to anyone.
3. Maria was made redundant, so now she has quite a lot of time **in** /**on** her hands.
4. I really think it's **high**/ **great** time we had a talk about your behaviour.
5. He had plenty of **short of time / time to kill** before his departure, so he bought a magazine and sat at the café.

C Complete the sentences with the phrasal verbs/expressions in the box. You may need to change the form of the verbs.

| make one's mark | come upon | dress up | get one's hands on | speak one's mind |

1. John's habit of always ___speaking his mind___ has made him quite unpopular with many people.
2. As I was looking through my drawers, I ___came upon___ some old photographs of a school trip.
3. My sister loves ___dressing up___ when she goes out. She usually spends hours in front of the mirror.
4. Ambitious people are usually quite determined to ___make their mark___ on the world.
5. I'm a huge fan of that band. I can't wait to ___get my hands on___ their latest CD.

D Complete the following sentences using the correct form of the verbs in brackets in the Active or Passive Voice.

1. It ___is said___ (say) that only children ___are___ (be) often quite mature.
2. Nobody really ___knows___ (know) how he made his money, but he ___is believed___ (believe) to ___have obtained___ (obtain) it illegally.
3. Picasso ___is considered___ (consider) ___to be___ (be) the father of Cubism.
4. It ___is widely believed___ (widely/believe) that eating fruit and vegetables regularly can help us lead a long active life.
5. English ___is spoken___ (speak) all over the world and ___is___ (be) the language of international communication.
6. Passengers on flight BA 326 to London ___are kindly requested___ (kindly/request) to proceed to gate B12.
7. 'Everybody should ___be given___ (give) a second chance,' said Sandra to her teacher.
8. They ___played___ (play) an important match against Manchester United on Sunday.
9. He ___is regarded___ (regard) as one of Britain's most promising writers.
10. I ___was taken in___ (take in) by her innocent appearance and ___let___ (let) her into my house.

Lesson Three

A Complete the second sentence so that is has a similar meaning to the first sentence, using the word given. Do not change the word given. You must use between two and five words, including the word given.

1. Nobody told me that the meeting was cancelled.

    I __wasn't informed that__ the meeting was cancelled. **informed**

2. I suddenly realised that a suspicious-looking man was watching me.

    I suddenly realised that I __was being watched__ by a suspicious-looking man. **being**

3. You need to start studying for your exams soon.

    It's __high time you started studying__ for your exams. **high**

4. A lot of people think that Robert is arrogant and self-centred.

    Robert __is considered to be__ arrogant and self-centred. **be**

5. Jane left the house in a hurry and forgot to take her keys with her.

    Jane left the house in a hurry __without taking__ her keys. **without**

6. My mother has cooked a big lunch for us.

    A big lunch __has been cooked for us__ by my mother. **been**

7. We haven't painted our house since we moved in last year.

    The house __hasn't been painted__ since we moved in last year. **been**

8. Paul gave Kimberly a ring for her birthday.

    Kimberly __was given a ring__ for her birthday by Paul. **was**

B Read the text below and think of the word which best fits each space. Use only one word in each space.

CLASS REUNION

A few weeks ago, my best friend Sophie, whom I've known **(1)** __since__ we were at school together, decided to have **(2)** __a__ party to celebrate her 28th birthday. She decided to gowild and turn her birthday party into a class reunion.

First, she made a list **(3)** __of__ all our old classmates. **(4)** __Then__, she started making calls to try **(5)** __to/and__ locate them. **(6)** __It__ was not an easy task. Many of them had moved away or got married and she ended up making dozens of calls to find them. It **(7)** __must__ have been her lucky week, because, not only did she locate everyone, but they all agreed to **(8)** __come__ as well. Even those who had moved away were delighted by the idea and promised to make the trip back home **(9)** __so__ as not to miss out on the event.

When the big day came, my friend's house **(10)** __was__ beautifully decorated. **(11)** __There__ was lots of delicious food and everyone was thrilled to see their old friends again. Some of us **(12)** __had__ not seen each other in over ten years. Everyone was talking about what they had achieved in the last few years. Some of them had already had children, others were about to get married. The greatest surprise, **(13)** __however__, was when the bell rang and three of our favourite teachers walked in! We set the night **(14)** __on__ fire! We danced for hours and it felt like we were at a school dance. Everything was different, yet nothing seemed **(15)** __to__ have changed. At the end of the party, we promised to meet the following year and not let another ten years go by before we see each other again.

C Read the text below. Use the word given in capitals at the end of each line to form a word that fits in the space in the same line.

EVERLASTING LOVE

Every year we have a party to celebrate my grandparents' wedding

anniversary. It's become a **(1)** ___traditional___ family event. **TRADITION**

Their 50th anniversary was last month, so we **(2)** ___decided___ to organise **DECISION**

a **(3)** ___celebration___ that they would never forget. We told all our relatives **CELEBRATE**

and friends that it was an important event, and asked them to dress

(4) ___formally___. The house was full of balloons and beautiful **FORMAL**

(5) ___decorations___ on the day of the party and every room looked lovely. I felt **DECORATE**

great in my **(6)** ___favourite___ blue dress but it was my **FAVOUR**

grandmother who looked fantastic! She wore a beautiful dress and a

(7) ___fashionable___ hat. She was so happy! Once all the guests had arrived, **FASHION**

the party began. The living room was so **(8)** ___crowded___ we had to go out **CROWD**

into the garden. The best moment was when my dad brought out the cake. It

was so big it looked like a **(9)** ___wedding___ cake! We all gathered around **WED**

my grandparents and my grandfather gave my grandmother a beautiful

diamond ring!

It was **(10)** ___certainly___ a party to remember! **CERTAIN**

D Read the text below. Some of the lines are correct, and some have a word which should not be there. If a line is correct, put a tick (√) in the space provided. If a line has a word which should not be there, write the word in the space provided.

CHILD'S PLAY

1. 'Playing is fundamental to a child's development and	√
2. should to be taken seriously,' says psychologist Elizabeth	to
3. Whilston, who specialises in all child psychology. You don't have to teach	all
4. children to play – it comes naturally. Take smiling for an example.	an
5. Nobody teaches the babies to smile. For them, smiling is an instinctive	the
6. reaction and an early form of playing. In the early years, through play,	√
7. babies start developing their skills and their senses. They will	√
8. not use the toys they are given as well as anything else they can get	not
9. their hands on to learn how to hold things with, and to explore their	with
10. world by smelling, touching and listening. Playing provides	√
11. children with what they need; in fact, it is of the most important activity	of
12. up until the age of five. Parents should provide a safe and caring	√
13. environment in which for their child can explore, experiment and learn.	for
14. As Dr Whilston points out, 'Parents should only watch, listen and	only
15. join in. Most of us have been forgotten how to play – and children can	been
be great teachers.'	

E **Read the task below. Then read the introduction to the story below and rewrite it so that it sounds more interesting.**

A student magazine has asked its readers to send stories that end with the following words: 'I was really proud of myself!' Your story must be between 120 and 180 words.

I was going home after a hard day at school and the wind was blowing. I couldn't walk because of the strong wind. There was nothing I could think about except being in my warm home.

<u>Suggested answer</u>

I was on my way home after a hard day at school. The sky was dark and it was still raining hard. There was a cold wind blowing so I pulled my coat tightly around me. The only thing I could think about was sitting in front of the telly in my warm home.

Below are the second and the third paragraphs that form the main part of the story. The sentences of the second paragraph are jumbled up. Put them in the correct order by numbering them. Then expand on the notes in paragraph 3 and make full sentences.

Paragraph 2

4   After I got over the initial shock, I approached the car and looked inside.

2   I ran down the road –it was an overturned car.

6   He was alive!

1   Suddenly, something at the end of the road caught my attention.

5   I heard a man whisper: 'Please, help me!'.

7   I froze and didn't know what to do!

3   There was not a living soul around!

Paragraph 3

With all the courage I had left, manage / open the door / overturned vehicle / pull out / man.

He / in great pain. Luckily / have / mobile phone. Call an ambulance / arrive in no time.

Taken to hospital / treated for minor injuries / released a couple of days later.

<u>Suggested answer</u>

With all the courage I had left, I managed to open the door of the overturned vehicle and pull the man out. He was in great pain. Luckily, I had my mobile phone with me. I called for an ambulance and it arrived in no time. The man was taken to hospital where he was treated for minor injuries. He was released a couple of days later.

Now write an appropriate concluding paragraph for the story.

Some days later, I received a phone call. It was the man I had pulled out of the car.

He had called to thank me for saving his life and told me I was a hero. Can you imagine, me, a hero?

I was really proud of myself!

07 Dig in!

Lesson One

A Read the recipe below and circle the correct word.

SPAGHETTI Delight!

Ingredients: 1 packet of your favourite pasta
2 cartons of cream
2 cans of whole mushrooms
2 teaspoons cornflour
salt, pepper, olive oil
cheese (optional)
parsley

Preparation:
(Boil)/ roast the pasta in salted water, adding some oil so that it doesn't stick together. Preparation time is approximately 10 minutes, depending on your **kitchen /**(cooker) and on whether you like your pasta al dente or not. Drain the pasta and add some olive oil or butter. While the pasta is cooking,(chop)/ slice the parsley and **swallow /**(slice) the mushrooms. Pour the cream into a saucepan, season with salt and pepper. Stir 250 mls of water into the cornflour and add it to the cream. Stir over a moderate heat until it starts **steaming /**(boiling) Add the mushrooms. Serve the pasta while it's still hot.(Grate)/ slice some cheese and sprinkle it on top if you wish. Finally, decorate with parsley. Spaghetti Delight makes an excellent main **cuisine /**(dish) Bon appetit!

B Fill in the questions using *who* or *what*.

1. _____Who_____ hit the dog with the ball? <u>John</u> did.
2. _____What_____ is the food like there? <u>Delicious!</u>
3. _____Who_____ left a message on the answering machine? <u>Kim</u> did.
4. _____What_____ did Samantha do? <u>Nothing</u> at all.
5. _____What_____ are you making? <u>Nothing</u> special, just some French fries.
6. _____Who_____ is that? It's <u>Pamela</u> when she was 12 years old.
7. _____What_____ started the fire? A <u>candle</u>.
8. _____Who_____ does your husband work for? <u>Mr Peterson</u>.
9. _____Who_____ is at the door? It's just <u>Simon</u>.

C Complete the following sentences with the appropriate question tag.

1. It's cold in here, _____isn't it_____?
2. Mark doesn't have time to see anyone today, _____does he_____?
3. Mary can't speak Spanish, _____can she_____?
4. You are coming with us, _____aren't you_____?
5. You have an extra suitcase, _____don't you_____?
6. I'm not late, _____am I_____?
7. Pete usually works late, _____doesn't he_____?
8. John gave you a birthday gift, _____didn't he_____?
9. The boys are playing football tonight, _____aren't they_____?
10. You had breakfast this morning, _____didn't you_____?

Lesson Two

A You are going to read a magazine article about ice cream. Choose the most suitable heading from the list A-G for each part (1-6) of the article. There is one extra heading which you do not need to use.

A Processing techniques improve

B Something for everyone

C The joy of eating

D For young and old alike

E Unclear origin

F The modern approach

G A significant breakthrough

B Find words and expressions in the text and match them with the meanings given.

a. to say firmly that something is true — insist

b. add one substance to others — mix with

c. the ability to predict what is likely to happen — foresight

d. were following very closely — were hot on one's heels

e. profitable — big business

f. delivered — distributed

g. buy something you will enjoy — treat yourself

Let's all scream for ice cream

1	B

So, how many scoops will you have? One vanilla and one chocolate? How about a scoop of lemon, caramel or pistachio? What would you like on it? Cherry syrup or chocolate sprinkles? Would you like it in a cone with wafers or in a tub? Whichever way you like it, you have to admit that ice cream is nearly everybody's favourite, particularly on a hot summer's day.

2	E

Have you ever wondered who came up with such a brilliant idea? Well, the answer is that no one is really sure. There are some who say that it was the Chinese as long ago as 2000 B.C. Others insist, however, that it was the invention of a French chef employed by King Charles I of England. Then, there is the story of the Roman Emperor Nero who is said to have sent slaves into the mountains to collect snow and ice to mix with the fruit drinks he loved so much.

3	G

What we do know, however, is that up until the mid-nineteenth century ice cream was made by hand. In 1846 an American woman named Nancy Johnson invented a hand-cranked freezer. The ice cream mix was shaken in a bed of salt and ice inside this freezer until frozen. Unfortunately, Johnson lacked the foresight to patent her invention, and received nothing for her efforts. A little unfair, perhaps, when you think about the billions of people who have been enjoying ice cream since.

4 **A**

However, there were other inventors hot on Mrs Johnson's heels. Between 1847 and 1887, more than 70 different ice cream churns were patented. In 1851 the first ice cream factory opened and soon ice cream became really big business.

5 **F**

Nowadays, ice cream is a multi-million euro industry. In modern plants the ice cream process is as follows: the basic ingredients are poured into a tank where they are mixed and pasteurised. The mixture is then homogenised in order to

break up the particles of butterfat in it. After that, the mixture is cooled, and then piped to a tank for freezing. There it is beaten until it becomes smooth. Finally, the partially frozen ice cream is packed into containers and distributed.

6 **D**

These days there are literally hundreds of flavours to choose from and ice cream is not just popular with children. According to statistics, almost half of all ice cream novelties are consumed by adults. So, whatever the reason, do yourself a favour and treat yourself to one of life's little pleasures. Go on, have some ice cream!

C Complete the second sentence so that it has a similar meaning to the first sentence, using the word given. Do not change the word given. You must use between two and five words, including the word given.

1. The show started with a wonderful dance performance.   **kicked**
   The _____ show kicked off with _____ a wonderful dance performance.

2. Mary managed to extinguish the small fire she started in the kitchen.   **out**
   Mary managed _____ to put out the _____ small fire she started in the kitchen.

3. I had a strong urge for chocolate when I saw Mike buying a bar.   **mouth**
   My _____ mouth watered _____ when I saw Mike buying a bar of chocolate.

4. Elizabeth thought the math exercises were very easy.   **cake**
   'These math exercises are _____ a piece of cake _____,' thought Elizabeth.

5. His new CD is selling very well in Britain.   **cakes**
   His new CD is selling _____ like hot cakes _____ in Britain.

6. He quickly ate his lunch before the meeting started.   **gobbled**
   He _____ gobbled down his lunch _____ before the meeting started.

7. Paul was happy to finish his book but its publication was the best thing for him.   **icing**
   Paul was happy to finish his bok but its publication was _____ the icing on the cake _____ for him.

8. The supervisor was very clear about what Jim's responsibilities were.   **record**
   The supervisor _____ set the record straight _____ about what Jim's responsibilities were.

D Complete the following sentences using *whoever, whatever, whichever, whenever, wherever.*

1. You can say _____ whatever _____ you want, but I won't change my mind.
2. I make new friends _____ wherever _____ I go.
3. Judy's always there for me _____ whenever _____ I need her.
4. _____ Whoever _____ gave you this blouse certainly appreciates quality!
5. Choose _____ whichever _____ one you want. I don't mind, I like both of them.
6. I always got _____ whatever _____ I wanted when I was a child.
7. _____ Whenever _____ we get together, we go out for dinner and chat for hours.
8. _____ Whatever _____ you decide to wear to the party, you'll look great.
9. _____ Whoever _____ it is, take a message. I'm too busy to chat on the phone.
10. _____ Whatever _____ Jack does at weekends, he always has a great time.

Lesson Three

A Read the text below. Use the word given in capitals at the end of each line to form a word that fits in the space in the same line.

HEALTHY JUNK FOOD!

We all know that junk food is (1) _____unhealthy_____ and   **HEALTH**
(2) _____fattening_____. However, if you prepare your own 'junk food'   **FAT**
at home, it can be delicious and (3) _____nutritious_____. For instance, you can   **NUTRITION**
enjoy home-made hamburgers as often as you like and an added bonus is
that they're much (4) _____cheaper_____ when you make them yourself. 'Healthy'   **CHEAP**
junk food is a great way to avoid a (5) _____monotonous_____ diet and is also a wise   **MONOTONY**
(6) _____choice_____ for those who are watching their weight. You might be   **CHOOSE**
tempted by the (7) _____convenience_____ of buying junk food when you're short of time,   **CONVENIENT**
but keep in mind that eating healthily is both (8) _____advisable_____ and   **ADVISE**
(9) _____fashionable_____. If you can balance a sensible eating plan with regular   **FASHION**
exercise, you'll soon be able to feel the (10) _____difference_____. Now that's something   **DIFFERENT**
worth striving for, isn't it?

B Complete the blanks by using the expressions in the box below.

| high in fibre | healthy meals | workouts | | stay in shape | balanced diet |
| high in protein | keep fit | measure your body fat | | burn calories | source of vitamins |

Tired of diets and exhausting (1) _____workouts_____? Sick of
almost starving yourself to death just to lose a couple of kilos, only to gain them
back a few weeks later? If you really want to (2) _____keep fit / stay in shape_____,
there are some basic guidelines you should follow. First, eat
(3) _____healthy meals_____ that include meat and fish as they are
both (4) _____high in protein_____. Fruit, of course, is an excellent
(5) _____source of vitamins_____ A, B and C, so it's an important part of
any (6) _____balanced diet_____. Starchy carbohydrates are
(7) _____high in fibre_____, but low in fat, which makes them
filling, but not fattening. Of course, going to a dietician is also a good idea, as they
can (8) _____measure your body fat_____ and determine exactly what food
you should eat. Finally, some form of exercise is necessary. But don't overdo it!
Half an hour of brisk walking every day is enough to help you (9) _____burn calories_____
and (10) _____stay in shape / keep fit_____.

C Read the text below and decide which answer A, B, C or D best fits each space.

A SPANISH DISH

What would you do if your friends suddenly dropped (1) _____in_____ for dinner? What would you offer them? Well, a (2) _____dish_____ they'll definitely gobble (3) _____down_____ is ... paella! Here's your (4) _____chance_____ to show your knowledge as well as your abilities in the (5) _____kitchen_____ . (6) _____Kick_____ off your food history lesson by saying that paella originally came (7) _____from_____ Valencia, a city that is closely associated (8) _____with_____ rice dishes that are made from the short grain Arbodio rice which grows there. Then invite your mates into the kitchen to observe your culinary skills. Make sure you have all the (9) _____ingredients_____ before you start (10) _____boiling_____ the water. Then, (11) _____cut_____ the chicken breast into small chunks, (12) _____chop_____ the onions, garlic and peppers into small pieces and soon the smell will be making your friends' (13) _____mouths_____ water. Follow the recipe carefully and your paella will be ready in no time! In the meantime, ask your mates to help you (14) _____set_____ the table. Once everyone's eaten and praised your cooking, tell them that for a great chef like you, it's a (15) _____piece_____ of cake!

1. **(A)** in	**B** off	**C** at	**D** to
2. **A** kitchen	**B** cuisine	**(C)** dish	**D** plate
3. **A** over	**(B)** down	**C** in	**D** to
4. **A** ability	**B** fact	**C** hope	**(D)** chance
5. **A** cook	**B** cooker	**(C)** kitchen	**D** cuisine
6. **(A)** Kick	**B** Hit	**C** Take	**D** Give
7. **A** to	**(B)** from	**C** at	**D** across
8. **A** at	**B** in	**C** to	**(D)** with
9. **(A)** ingredients	**B** recipe	**C** barbecue	**D** microwaves
10. **A** roasting	**B** grilling	**(C)** boiling	**D** frying
11. **A** slice	**B** spread	**C** peel	**(D)** cut
12. **A** slice	**B** make	**(C)** chop	**D** grate
13. **(A)** mouths	**B** eyes	**C** faces	**D** hands
14. **A** place	**(B)** set	**C** make	**D** fix
15. **A** part	**(B)** piece	**C** slice	**D** chop

D Read the text below and think of the word which best fits each space. Use only one word in each space.

GO ON, HAVE A BITE!

Are you the sort of person (1) _____who/that_____ goes out to dinner vowing not to order a starter or a dessert, only to end up ordering both? Or are you (2) _____one_____ of the fortunate few who (3) _____can_____ have a box of chocolates just sitting in their house for a whole week or accept a second helping of food without feeling guilty?

Unfortunately, most of us seem to fall into the first category. However, there is no need to despair. All you have to do is re-learn your eating habits. According (4) _____to_____ experts, it's a myth that naturally slim people have high metabolic rates (5) _____which / that_____ magically burn calories. It is true, however, that genetic differences play a role and some people (6) _____are_____ blessed with smaller appetites than others.

However, social, educational and psychological influences are also very important and mustn't (7) _____be_____ overlooked. The way you were taught to eat (8) _____as_____ a child can affect your eating habits. Your general approach to life affects your attitude to food, too. Stop thinking of food (9) _____every_____ minute of the day and don't categorise it as being either good or bad. This kind of behaviour is destructive and can ruin your chances (10) _____of_____ staying slim. It's all right to eat crisps and chocolate as (11) _____long_____ as you don't overeat. Don't confuse hunger with appetite; they are not (12) _____the_____ same thing. Most of us tend to eat when our appetites are stimulated by external stimuli (13) _____such_____ as the aroma of food, seeing a bar of chocolate or simply feeling bored. The way to find (14) _____out_____ if you are really hungry or not is to wait 20 minutes. If you still feel hungry after that, then go ahead and eat. If you don't, then you weren't hungry (15) _____in_____ the first place.

E Read the task below and complete the letter using the words and phrases in the box.

turn left/right	go past	pedestrian crossing	go around the roundabout
on your left/right	go up/down	traffic lights	opposite

You are studying in England and a friend of yours, who is also studying in England but in another town, is visiting you for the first time. You won't be able to meet her/him at the station. Look at the map below and write a letter (120-180 words) to your friend giving her/him directions as to how she/he can get to your house on foot.

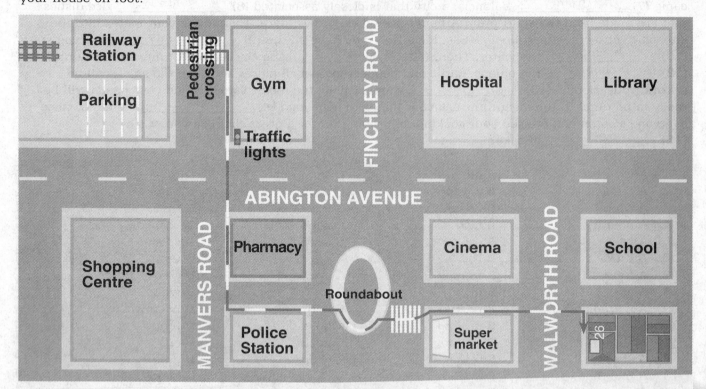

Suggested answer

Dear Shelley ,

How's it going? Hope you're doing fine! Unfortunately, I have some bad news. You see, something came up and I won't be able to meet you at the train station as we had planned. I'm really sorry!

However, don't let this get to you! Since my house is quite close to the station, I don't think you'll have a problem finding it if you follow my directions. This is how you can get here from the railway station.

Walk out of the station and cross Manvers Road at the pedestrian crossing. Then turn right and go straight ahead. Cross Abington Avenue and carry on straight. Go past the pharmacy and turn left at the police station. Go around the roundabout and continue going straight past the supermarket on your right. My house is just opposite the supermarket, at 26 Walworth Road. You can't miss it!

Once again, I do apologise! I'm really looking forward to seeing you.

Your friend,
Laura

08 Our four-legged friends

Lesson One

A Complete the dialogue with the correct form of the phrases in the box below.

fight like cat and dog	let the cat out of the bag	crocodile tears
no room to swing a cat	like a bear with a sore head	when the cat's away the mice will play
a wolf in sheep's clothing		

Bob   Hi Mike! What's wrong? You look upset.

Mike   Well, my parents went away last weekend and I decided to have a little get-together.

Bob   Oh, I see! **(1)** _When the cat's away the mice will play_ !

Mike   I just wanted to invite a few friends over. Unfortunately, I invited John, as well.

Bob   And?

Mike   Well, John **(2)** _let the cat out of the bag_ and told all his friends about it!

Bob   Wow! Then what happened?

Mike   There were so many people, we couldn't even move! Believe me, there was **(3)** _no room to swing a cat_ !

Bob   Oh, no! Did you have any trouble?

Mike   Everyone was making a lot of noise and the neighbours called the police, who then notified my parents. They cut their trip short and came back early.

Bob   What a mess! What did they say?

Mike   My dad was **(4)** _like a bear with a sore head_ ! He grounded me for 3 weeks. To make matters worse, we had an argument this morning. We **(5)** _fought like cat and dog_ !

Bob   And John?

Mike   He told his parents he had nothing to do with it and accused me of lying.

Bob   No way! He definitely is **(6)** _a wolf in sheep's clothing_ !

Mike   His father called and said that John was so upset that he cried all night.

Bob   Cried? I'm sure he cried **(7)** _crocodile tears_ ! He just didn't want his dad to punish him.

Mike   Hey, do you want to come over on Saturday? I'm not allowed to go out and I could use some company. We can even…

Bob   Sorry, I've been invited to a party… at John's house!

B Complete the second sentence so that it has a similar meaning to the first sentence, using the word given. Do not change the word given. You must use between two and five words, including the word given.

1. 'Go to your room,' said my mother.   **go**
   My mother told _me to go to my_ room.

2. 'Tom is arriving tomorrow night at 9 o'clock,' said Paul.   **was**
   Paul told us that _Tom was arriving the following_ night at 9 o'clock.

3. 'I went to the bookshop on Monday,' said Kim.   **gone**
   Kim said _(that) she had gone to_ the bookstore on Monday.

4. 'Who took my keys?' asked Mike.   **had**
   Mike wanted to know _who had taken his_ keys.

5. 'They left yesterday,' said Linda.   **had**
   Linda said that _they had left the day_ before.

6. 'I won't do it again,' Ben said to his father.   **do**
   Ben told his father _(that) he would not do_ that again.

7. He told us not to open that door.   **open**
   'Do _not open this_ door,' he said.

Lesson Two

A You are going to read a magazine article about sloths. Choose the most suitable heading from the list A-G for each part (1-6) of the article. There is one extra heading which you do not need to use.

A A limited diet

B Wrong side up

C Not as bad as the name suggests

D When the stars come out

E Now you see me, now you don't

F Two's a crowd

G Good-looking or what?

B Find phrasal verbs and words in the text and match them with the meanings given.

a. having fun	gadding about
b. because of	due to
c. to some extent, but not very much	fairly
d. the way in which an animal's colour matches its surroundings	camouflage
e. see, notice	detect
f. not have	go without
g. correct, true	justified

Life's a drag!

1   B

Who wouldn't like to spend all day sleeping and all night gadding about? Well, believe it or not, that is the life of a sloth. These strange creatures, which are mammals, spend most of their lives hanging upside down from the highest branches of trees. They eat, sleep and even give birth to their young upside down in the trees. In fact, the only time they ever come down to the ground is to go to the toilet and that only happens about every seventh or eighth day due to their very slow metabolic rate.

2   G

The average sloth is about the same size as a fairly large cat although much less attractive. It looks like it's permanently smiling and has big eyes, a short nose and tiny ears that look like they've been cut off. Most sloths don't have tails, but when they do, they're usually very short. Their legs are fairly long and end in strong curved claws, which they use to hang from the branches of trees. They are covered in a thick brown fur with a greenish tint, which acts as camouflage. This makes them almost impossible to detect from ground level.

3   A

Sloths are herbivores, which means that they do not eat meat, they feed only on leaves, fruit and plants. Their body temperature is very low and as a result they have a very slow metabolic rate. This means that they can go without food and water for long periods of time. When they do eat, it takes them days to digest. Therefore, they don't need to eat every day, hence the saying 'hang around doing nothing'.

| 4 | D |

Sloths are nocturnal creatures, which means they spend all day asleep and are active at night. In fact, they sleep for as long as 18 hours in any given twenty-four-hour period and they do this hanging upside down. They frequently change trees and can move quite long distances in the course of a night despite being the slowest moving mammals on earth.

| 5 | C |

The fact that they move so slowly has earned

them their reputation for being lazy, which is not entirely justified. It's true that sloths don't walk unless it's absolutely necessary and most of the time they make their way through the jungle upside down. However, on the rare occasions that they are on the ground, they actually walk upright. Another little known fact about sloths is that they are excellent swimmers.

| 6 | F |

Sloths aren't very social creatures, not even with their own kind. This is especially true of the males who are by nature very quiet and solitary creatures. The females are a little more sociable and might occasionally get together. Of course, like everything else they do, this would be at night somewhere in the treetops in the tropical forests of Central or South America.

C **Choose the reporting verb that best completes each sentence.**

1. Tony **denied** / **refused** breaking the window.
2. Jenny **refused** / **apologised** for forgetting her best friend's birthday.
3. She **threatened** / **told** to reveal my secret.
4. Maggie **suggested** / **begged** her mother to let her go to the party.
5. He **refused** / **threatened** to tidy his room, although it was an absolute mess.
6. My mother **suggested** / **said** going shopping on Saturday.
7. He **said** / **admitted** his mistake and promised to make up for the trouble he had caused.

D **Complete the sentences with a phrasal verb or an expression in the box making any necessary changes.**

| be in the dark | cast light on | get along with | put one's finger on | pick up on | close the door on |

1. Mark and Peter don't _____ get along with _____ each other; they're always fighting.
2. 'There are some files missing from the university library, Professor. We were hoping you could _____ cast light on _____ the matter!'
3. My accountant informed me that my business associate was stealing money from me. I _____ had been in the dark _____ up until then.
4. When Eric walked into the room, he quickly _____ picked up on _____ the fact that Sarah was upset.
5. There's something wrong with this text but I can't _____ put my finger on _____ it.
6. It's time to _____ close the door on _____ this chapter of your life and make a fresh start somewhere else.

Lesson Three

A Read the text below and think of the word which best fits each space. Use only one word in each space.

BLACK PEARLS

White pearls are considered, by most women, to **(1)** ___be___ an absolutely essential accessory. They add a touch **(2)** ___of___ class to just about any outfit and their prices range from relatively inexpensive to very expensive.

Black pearls, on the other hand, **(3)** ___which___ are to be found in French Polynesia, are bigger, shinier and far **(4)** ___more___ rare. The oysters that produce black pearls are four times the size of Japanese oysters, which are the source of most of the world's pearls.

Black pearl oysters also come in a variety

(5) ___of___ colours, including black, silver-grey and grey. White pearl oysters are often artificially hatched, whereas black pearl farmers wait **(6)** ___for___ the oysters to hatch in their own time, at temperatures of about 20⁰ C in the crystal-clear waters of the Polynesian lagoons.

It **(7)** ___takes___ a very long time for the pearls to form and pearl farmers have to be very patient.

(8) ___When/Once/After___ the oysters have hatched, (usually after about two years), they are returned to the lagoon. After that, the pearls need another three years to develop before the oysters are harvested again, and the pearls are removed. Finally, the pearls are sorted out and graded. They are then ready to

(9) ___be___ sold in different countries all **(10)** ___over___ the world.

B Circle the correct word to complete the sentences.

1. Martin works for an animal training school that (teaches)/ learns dogs obedience.
2. This lion has been calm /(tamed,) he won't attack you!
3. The koala bear is considered to be an (endangered)/ dangered species.
4. Firemen have dogs that assist them on help /(rescue) missions.
5. Animal rights groups claim that wild animals in slavery /(captivity) suffer and are mistreated.
6. When my cat, Kitty, got sick I took her to the doctor /(vet.)
7. Bill (trained)/ educated his parrot to say 'Hello' and 'Thank you'.
8. It's time for the (zookeeper)/ animal researcher to feed the animals and clean their cages.
9. The (owner)/ companion of the shop accused some youngsters of shoplifting.
10. Our partnership /(friendship) goes back several years, ever since we were kids.

C Read the text below and look carefully at each line. Some of the lines are correct, and some have a word which should not be there. If a line is correct, put a tick (√) in the space provided. If a line has a word which should not be there, write the word in the space provided.

MOVING ABROAD

1. Last summer, while I was on holidays, I met a plenty of people,   _a_
2. most of whom live abroad. After I chatted to them, I   _√_
3. realised it was just high time I did something different with   _just_
4. my life and not something like about changing jobs or   _about_
5. redecorating my house. It had to be special and a bit risky.   _√_
6. So, after giving it a lot of thought, I decided to try living on abroad.   _on_
7. I already had friends living in the Australia and I knew they would help me.   _the_
8. So I started to packing my bags. It was something totally radical.   _to_
9. When I first arrived in Sydney, I had to deal with looking for a flat, unpacking   _√_
10. and getting to also know the area. I was lucky as my friends had found me   _also_
11. a great job as a sales executive. However, I soon realised that my own   _own_
12. new life was different from the life I had in Essex.   _√_
13. I was also missed my family. Luckily, this feeling didn't last long.   _was_
14. I made a lot of new friends and my social life quickly improved.   _√_
15. Now, I can't imagine living anywhere else but for Sydney.   _for_

D Read the text below. Use the word given in capitals at the end of each line to form a word that fits in the space in the same line.

NOT JUST SUGAR AND SPICE!

Up until a few decades ago, women in the

(1) _____working_____ world were usually teachers,   **WORK**

nurses or nannies. Although some women were happy with those

stereotypical jobs, others were (2) _____dissatisfied_____   **SATISFY**

and decided to work in professions that were once

(3) _____exclusively_____ for men. With hard work and   **EXCLUSIVE**

determination they became very (4) _____successful_____.   **SUCCESS**

So, today it is not (5) _____surprising_____ to see a female doctor,   **SURPRISE**

lawyer or judge. But women have even ventured into other, more

(6) _____dangerous_____ fields. They've become fighter pilots, and have reached high   **DANGER**

ranks in the military. Furthermore, women have shown their (7) _____ability/abilities_____ in   **ABLE**

(8) _____leadership_____ and have had successful careers as politicians and even Prime   **LEADER**

Ministers. Women have become astronauts and (9) _____scientists_____ and have   **SCIENCE**

proven that they can do a (10) _____better_____ job than many of their male   **GOOD**

counterparts!

E The City Council is thinking of opening a video arcade in your town. They have asked residents to send reports on the proposed construction. Read the report a resident has written and rewrite the main part of the report adding a heading to each paragraph.

To: The City Council
From: Daniel Brand
Subject: The opening of the video arcade

Introduction

This report refers to the residents' reactions to the local committee's decision to build a video arcade in the area. The members of the local committee hope there will not be any serious objections to the idea. However, many residents have expressed their concern regarding this matter and are urging the committee to reconsider its decision.

Some residents think it's a good idea. The video arcade will bring money to the area. Many people can work there. Youngsters won't be able to enter. It's 20 minutes away from the city centre, so there won't be any noise. More visitors will come and local shops will make a lot of money. Part of the profits from the video arcade will go back to the town. Opening time is 9 am and closing time is 9 pm; at weekends closing time is 11 pm. A private security firm will supervise the arcade. It's a cheap form of entertainment. The latest video games will be available. However, others don't like it. The construction will destroy the environment and the people won't be able to enjoy the local park any more. Youngsters will find ways to enter. They might play truant, not do their homework and spend all their money there. It's bad for their health and their eyes in particular.

Suggested answer

Overall benefits

Some residents think that it is a good idea as the video arcade will bring financial benefits to the area. First of all, it will offer job opportunities to many people. Young children under seventeen years old will not be allowed to enter at all. The video arcade will not bring any disturbance to the community as it is 20 minutes away from the city. Furthermore, it will attract more visitors and local shops will profit. Part of these profits will go towards the improvement of the town. It will be open to the public from 9 am to 9 pm on weekdays but it will close at 11 pm at weekends. Furthermore, a private security firm will supervise the arcade. It must be noted that the video arcade is an inexpensive form of entertainment, and will offer the latest games to the public.

Drawbacks

However, some do not approve of the idea. They feel the construction will have a negative effect on the environment and the locals will be deprived of their beautiful park. Young children will be tempted to enter and will find ways to succeed in doing so. They might even play truant, stop doing their homework and spend all their pocket money there. It could also be hazardous for their health and their eyes in particular.

Conclusion

On the whole, I believe that the video arcade will bring more benefits to the town than disadvantages. However, it must be under close observation so that problems do not occur.

09 Where the heart is

Lesson One

A **Read the text below and decide which answer A, B, C or D best fits each space.**

When the luxury liner, The World of Residensea, first set sail from Oslo in March 2002, it was really something to write home **(1)** _____about_____. The floating apartment block has **(2)** _____everything_____ you could possibly hope for — from shops to leisure facilities. The only problem is that with apartments costing as **(3)** _____much_____ as £5 million, very **(4)** _____few_____ people can afford to live there. Living on a boat, **(5)** _____however_____, is not a new idea. There are **(6)** _____about_____ 15 000 people living on the rivers and canals of the UK today. Research suggests that nowadays, a **(7)** _____lot_____ of people are attracted to life on water for a number of reasons including **(8)** _____economic_____ concerns, the desire to get closer to nature or to escape the pressures of life on land. Compared **(9)** _____to_____ buying a home on dry land, **(10)** _____houseboats_____ are less expensive. You can buy a brand new, fully equipped 58-foot boat that makes an ideal permanent residence for around £65,000. There is also a second-hand boat market, and **(11)** _____a lot_____ of boats are advertised in boating magazines, newspapers, and on the Internet. It's common for boat interiors to look exactly like a **(12)** _____home_____ from home. Showers and bathrooms on board offer all the **(13)** _____comforts_____ of home, even if space is limited. You can have a fully equipped kitchen to cook **(14)** _____home-made_____ meals, as well as carpeting, curtains and furniture to create a **(15)** _____cosy_____ atmosphere. Still thinking about it?

1. **A** of	**B** about	**C** to	**D** of
2. **A** little	**B** every	**C** everything	**D** much
3. **A** many	**B** few	**C** little	**D** much
4. **A** little	**B** a little	**C** few	**D** a few
5. **A** although	**B** however	**C** even though	**D** despite
6. **A** about	**B** hardly any	**C** tons of	**D** many
7. **A** lot	**B** lots	**C** much	**D** plenty
8. **A** economical	**B** economic	**C** economy	**D** economically
9. **A** on	**B** at	**C** to	**D** for
10. **A** households	**B** homemakers	**C** houseboats	**D** homeboats
11. **A** lot	**B** many	**C** much	**D** a lot
12. **A** house	**B** home	**C** boat	**D** place
13. **A** convenient	**B** comforts	**C** accommodation	**D** luxury
14. **A** home-made	**B** housekeeping	**C** homesick	**D** homework
15. **A** home town	**B** cosy	**C** hot	**D** theme

B **Complete the sentences with the words in the box.**

carving	homesick	home town	dip	household
cosy	contrary	wonders	homework	house guest

1. 'I think you should relax and take a _____dip_____ in the pool.'
2. _____Contrary_____ to what most people think, he's actually a kind and helpful person.
3. The Pyramids are one of the seven _____wonders_____ of the ancient world.
4. He spends his time _____carving_____ wooden figures which he then sells.
5. My _____home town_____ has changed a lot since I left.
6. My son finished his _____homework_____ quickly, so I took him to the cinema.
7. The best thing about this café is its _____cosy_____ atmosphere.
8. Being away from home for a long time can make one feel _____homesick_____.
9. Jim is our _____house guest_____, he's staying with us for a few days.
10. James hates doing _____household_____ chores.

Lesson Two

A You are going to read an article about the Chinese art of feng shui. Six sentences have been removed from the article. Choose from the sentences A-G the one which fits each gap (1-6) of the article. There is one extra sentence which you do not need to use.

A It's best to choose round or oval frames and make sure you do not hang them too high as this could make people feel a little uncomfortable.

B Western doctors seem to be warming to the idea that some ailments can be blamed on bad chi.

C In fact, it's become so popular that even international companies and financial institutions are designing their buildings in accordance with the principles of feng shui.

D One suggestion might be as simple as applying a fresh coat of paint.

E Having too many unnecessary things lying about can even cause you to feel like you lack energy.

F Any home that overlooks a river, a lake or even the ocean is likely to bring wealth to its owner.

G It includes family, wealth, career, knowledge, fame, marriage, children and helpful people.

B Find words in the text that match the definitions below.

1. fortune   luck
2. possibly   potentially
3. adviser   consultant
4. making less   lowering
5. very important   significant
6. produce   radiate

Go with the flow...

Is it really possible to change your luck, improve your financial situation and even solve a health problem simply by moving about a few pieces of furniture? According to the principles of the ancient Chinese art of feng shui, it certainly is. Feng shui is based on the idea that 'chi', which means energy in Chinese, should be allowed to move freely through the environment in order to achieve greater happiness and success. **1** C

The application of feng shui principles in the home has also become quite fashionable. A feng shui consultant will draw a plan of your home and then place a map called the 'Bagua' on top of the plan. The Bagua consists of eight sections. **2** G Each of these sections corresponds to different areas in the home; if an area is missing, or a room is badly organised, this could have potentially negative consequences for that particular aspect of your life.

Once the problem area has been identified, the consultant will offer a number of different solutions to 'unblock' the energy. **3** D Colour can influence people's moods quite dramatically – yellow, for example, creates an optimistic atmosphere and is ideal for kitchens. Be sure not to select a shade that's too bright, though. Don't overuse white; while it does symbolise cleanliness, it gives an unwelcoming impression. Blue is perfect for relaxation and green represents balance and healing.

Aside from colour changes, there are several basic rules of feng shui that should be followed. Firstly, all clutter should be removed. **4** E Similarly, make sure that all doors open easily and are not blocked in any way – a blocked door could lead to career problems. Everything in the house has to be operational; either fix anything that's broken or throw it away. Otherwise, you run the risk of lowering your energy levels. To encourage the positive flow of energy, hang a few mirrors in strategic places. **5** A Don't position mirrors too low either as this could cause headaches. Another way to circulate energy is by hanging up crystals, especially if you have several doors in a straight line.

Of course, it's not just the interior of your home that's significant; location and structure play equally important roles. Your consultant will tell you that it's better to build a house that faces south, as this is the most favourable point on the compass. One of the principles of feng shui is water which has a positive effect on people. **6** **F** And sharp, angular corners should be avoided as they are said to trap bad energy and radiate negative chi.

While some of the basic ideas of feng shui may seem quite appealing and reasonably easy to put into practice, it's important to keep in mind the fact that feng shui alone won't do the trick. If you'd like to see an improvement in some areas of your life, it's best to combine a positive attitude with decisive action.

C **Complete the sentences with the words in the box. You may need to change the form of the verbs.**

| growl | interrupt | request | mutter | encourage |
| nod | convince | whisper | meddle | instruct |

1. During the test, Jerry _____whispered_____ the answers to Mark when the teacher wasn't looking.

2. When his boss told him he had to work at the weekend, he _____muttered_____ something to himself and returned to his office.

3. Oh no! Here comes Betty Barker. She's always _____meddling_____ in other people's affairs, she's so annoying.

4. I hate James' dog. He starts _____growling_____ every time somebody knocks on the door.

5. When I asked her if she liked the idea, she simply _____nodded_____ in agreement.

6. You are kindly _____requested_____ not to smoke inside the building.

7. We tried hard, but we couldn't _____convince_____ him not to go bungee jumping.

8. We should _____encourage_____ children to eat healthy food.

9. Our supervisor _____instructed_____ us to keep quiet.

10. You keep _____interrupting_____ me and that's very rude.

D **Complete the following sentences with the comparative or superlative form of the adjectives in brackets and the word *than* whenever necessary.**

1. That's ___the most impressive___ birthday cake I've ever seen. (impressive)

2. The _____more_____ you travel, the _____wiser_____ you become. (much / wise)

3. Ben works _____harder than_____ George so he got the promotion. (hard)

4. Today must be the _____the coldest_____ day of the year so far. (cold)

5. Mary is _____the cleverest_____ student in the school. (clever)

6. Pete Jones is considered to be _____the best_____ football player ever. (good)

7. This is the group's _____most successful_____ album so far. (successful)

8. The _____faster_____ you work, the _____quicker_____ you'll finish the job. (fast / quick)

9. Since Kathy got married, she looks _____happier_____ than ever. (happy)

10. The film I saw last week was boring, but the one I saw yesterday was _____worse_____ . (bad)

Lesson Three

A Read the text below and look carefully at each line. Some of the lines are correct and some have a word, which should not be there. If a line is correct, put a tick (√) in the space provided. If a line has a word which should not be there, write the word in the space provided.

KITCHEN FRIENDLY

1. Re-decorating your kitchen can be very easier and cheaper than ___very___
2. you think. Whatever your budget, with a few smart steps you can ___√___
3. turn to your kitchen into a colourful and cheerful place! ___to___
4. A new coat of paint is the best way to start. The very most ___very___
5. appealing colour to choose is the bright yellow. Yellow ___the___
6. undoubtedly adds light and warmth to any room, and can make ___√___
7. you feel happy. However, if you are decide on a white kitchen, ___are___
8. you can brighten it up with colourful accessories. ___√___
9. Accessories and kitchen utensils also play a very too important ___too___
10. role. You can make many colourful combinations using ___√___
11. them bottles and jars and look out for decorative knives ___them___
12. and forks. You can also too brighten your day by putting up ___too___
13. colourful curtains in your kitchen. There are many fabrics to ___√___
14. choose from and it doesn't have to cost you also an arm and ___also___
15. a leg. With some minor changes your own kitchen will look ___own___
   great! Don't you think?

B Complete the sentences with the words in the box.

ideal	convenient	double room	nursery school	extension	rent
hesitate	suitable	landlord	peace and quiet	facilities	assistance

1. I don't think that a house with two bedrooms is ___suitable___ for a family with four children. We should look for something bigger.
2. When we bought the property, my father built a(n) ___extension___ which he uses as an office.
3. 'Good morning, Madam. Could I be of any ___assistance___ ?' asked the manager.
4. If you ever need any help, don't ___hesitate___ to ask me!
5. I drop the kids off at the ___nursery school___ every morning before going to work.
6. I shop online. I think it's more ___convenient___ .
7. Dogs make ___ideal___ pets.
8. Our school has a number of sports ___facilities___ including a basketball court and a swimming pool.
9. They didn't have a ___double room___ , so we took two singles.
10. I decided to move to another flat, because the ___landlord___ wouldn't allow us to have any pets.
11. Pam enjoys the ___peace and quiet___ in the house when the kids are asleep.
12. I pay the ___rent___ on the first of each month.

C Read the text below and decide which answer A, B, C or D best fits each space.

STUCK IN TRAFFIC

It's happened to all of us **(1)** _____plenty_____ of times. You're running late anyway and you're stuck in traffic. Sounds familiar? Well the experts' advice is that if you are **(2)** _____sick_____ and tired of similar situations, you should leave your car at home and walk, take the bus or cycle to work. You may well wonder if you'll be able to manage without your car, but you need to **(3)** _____look_____ at the problem of traffic jams objectively. There are currently 20 million cars being driven up and **(4)** _____down_____ the roads of the world and it is estimated that another 25 million will be on the roads by the year 2025.

Since the traffic is getting worse, **(5)** _____sooner_____ or later more and more people will turn to public transport and that is the reason why public transport must be improved. However, at the moment public transport is considered to be expensive and dirty and it is definitely not **(6)** _____convenient_____ for people who live in rural areas. However, if public transport improved, moving around the city would be a breeze. With **(7)** _____hardly_____ any cars in the city centre, there'll be more **(8)** _____space_____ for people to walk and even the air will be cleaner. So, next time you want to drive to work, consider taking the bus. You'll get to work safe and **(9)** _____sound_____ and **(10)** _____on_____ time, for a change!

1. **A** lot	**B** all	**C** plenty	**D** many
2. **A** sick	**B** ill	**C** exhausted	**D** diseased
3. **A** face	**B** look	**C** observe	**D** notice
4. **A** down	**B** around	**C** out	**D** over
5. **A** late	**B** sooner	**C** faster	**D** quicker
6. **A** comfort	**B** suitable	**C** cosy	**D** convenient
7. **A** a little	**B** little	**C** hardly	**D** lots of
8. **A** home	**B** area	**C** space	**D** place
9. **A** sound	**B** quiet	**C** later	**D** peace
10. **A** on	**B** for	**C** at	**D** about

D Complete the second sentence so that it has a similar meaning to the first sentence, using the word given. Do not change the word given. You must use between two and five words, including the word given.

1. 'Sit down, relax and have some coffee.' **home**
   'Sit down, _____make yourself at home_____ and have some coffee.'

2. There are just two biscuits in the jar. **any**
   There _____are hardly any biscuits left_____ in the jar.

3. 'Don't worry, I've bought lots of food for the party.' **plenty**
   'Don't worry, there will _____be plenty of food_____ at the party.'

4. Judy has travelled a lot and believes that her home is the best place. **there**
   Judy has travelled a lot and believes _____there is no place like_____ home.

5. 'If you start working early, you'll finish more tasks.' **the**
   'The earlier _____you start working, the more_____ tasks you'll finish.'

6. There were two bedrooms in our old house and there are four in the new one. **than**
   Our new house is _____bigger than our_____ old one.

E Read part of the letter your friend has sent you and the notes you have made. Then write back, giving all the information required. The ending has been given. Your letter must be between 120-180 words.

MAIN CAMPUS BUILDING

MONDAYS — WEDNESDAYS — FRIDAYS

10-12 am

Since you already have the schedule, I need you to tell me which days we have classes and at what time they meet. Furthermore, I want you to tell me, which building I should go to and what the number of the room is. Apart from that, I must know which books and extra material, if any, I'll need for the course. Finally, do you think you can photocopy the notes that you took in the classes I missed?

107

Thanks in advance for all your help.

Love,
Pat

HAVE ALREADY
PHOTOCOPIED THEM

'INTRODUCTION TO
LITERATURE'

EXTRA MATERIAL
PROVIDED BY PROFESSOR

Suggested answer

Dear Pat,

How are you? I'm writing to give you the information you asked for about our classes.

First of all, we have classes on Mondays, Wednesdays and Fridays from 10 am to 12 am. The lectures take place in room 107 which is on the first floor of the main campus building.

You should also know that you won't spend a fortune buying books for the course. The only book that you need is called "Introduction to Literature". Any extra material will be given to us by the Professor, which is great!

Finally, we started classes last Monday so we don't have a lot of homework but I have the notes from all the classes you missed and have already photocopied them for you. So you don't need to worry about that! I'll give them to you when I see you.

So, relax. Everything's under control. See you in class!

Your friend,
Brad

10 Art works

Lesson One

A **Read the text below and decide which answer A, B, C or D best fits each space.**

My father is an excellent **(1)** _____artist_____. Although he's a(n) **(2)** _____architect_____ and designs houses and other structures, his hobby is **(3)** _____pottery_____. He likes to experiment with clay and enjoys making different things. He began by making simple objects and now he makes sculptures of people. He usually works in the garage and listens to music for inspiration. **(4)** _____When_____ he enters the garage, he often forgets to come out! My mother usually shouts at him to take a break till she's **(5)** _____blue_____ in the face, but he refuses. My mother wonders why dad doesn't like reading or writing **(6)** _____poetry_____, which are things she likes to do and they could do them together.

Then one day, out of the **(7)** _____blue_____, my father decided to have a little exhibition in the garden. Just like that! We were all surprised, but mum gave him **(8)** _the green light_ to have a party. On the day of the **(9)** _____event_____ my father exhibited his best works. I must admit everyone was impressed and I was extremely proud. All our friends praised my dad who was **(10)** _tickled pink_ and had a silly grin on his face all day.

1. (A) artist	**B** art	**C** artistic	**D** artistically
2. **A** painter	**B** poet	(C) architect	**D** musician
3. **A** pot	(B) pottery	**C** paint	**D** painter
4. (A) When	**B** Since	**C** However	**D** Although
5. **A** green	(B) blue	**C** pink	**D** white
6. **A** art	**B** painting	**C** sculptures	(D) poetry
7. (A) blue	**B** green	**C** pink	**D** dark
8. **A** in black and white	**B** in black boots	(C) the green light	**D** green with envy
9. **A** display	(B) event	**C** ceremony	**D** incident
10. **A** seeing red	**B** in black boots	**C** green with envy	(D) tickled pink

B **Join the sentences below using a relative pronoun or a participle clause where possible.**

1. These are home-grown vegetables. I planted them in the summer.
   These are home-grown vegetables (which/that) I planted in the summer   .

2. Mary often stays at the hotel. I stayed there for a week.
   Mary often stays at the hotel where I stayed for a week/Mary often stays at the hotel (which/that) I stayed at for a week
   .

3. Georgia's father made an important discovery. He's a scientist.
   Georgia's father, who is a scientist, made an important discovery   .

4. That man is my brother. He's presenting a TV programme on extreme sports.
   The man (who/that is) presenting a TV programme on extreme sports is my brother   .

5. She went to the cinema with some friends. They are her classmates.
   She went to the cinema with some friends who/that are her classmates   .

6. That baby is my teacher's son. He's trying to walk.
   The baby (who/that is) trying to walk is my teacher's son   .

7. Keith's car broke down. He bought it last month.
   Keith's car, which he bought last month, broke down   .

8. Mrs Nosey knows everything about the tenants in the building. She's our neighbour.
   Mrs Nosey, who is our neighbour, knows everything about the tenants in the building   .

Lesson Two

A You are going to read an article about Riverdance. Four paragraphs have been removed from the article. Choose the most suitable paragraph from the list A-E for each part (1-4) of the article. There is one extra paragraph which you do not need to use.

A On another level, Riverdance is the story of mankind's creative exploration of nature through the arts. The show features not only Irish dance but also Spanish, Russian and African-American dance. This reinforces the river comparison, because the music and the dances come from different sources, like the streams of a river, which all eventually flow into one mighty river.

B Upon arrival in the new world, these people were also exposed to other cultures, which is illustrated by the American tap dances and Russian dervish dances in the show. Then the show brings us to the present time when descendants of the immigrants have returned to Ireland and feel very much at home despite never having been there before.

C This was not the case, however, when Ireland hosted the concert in the early 1990s, because it was the fill-in that actually stole the show. The reaction to this mixture of traditional music, song and dance was so strong and positive that it was developed further and became Riverdance – The Show. But what story does Riverdance tell?

D Once again, the immigrants have come from the sea, but this time to a new land. However, the streets were not paved with gold. The immigrants had to struggle for survival against the local people who were suspicious of them. This was a feeling they shared with other immigrants and minorities. As a result, they all joined together in a cry for freedom.

E It culminates in 'Cloudsong', which underlines the theme of the connection and includes a chorus singing the Gaelic words for water and life in the background. This is followed by 'Riverdance' itself, where music and dance come together in a magnificent celebration of life.

Riverdance - The Show

It's traditional to have an interval halfway through the Eurovision song contest. It takes place after the last song has been sung, and before the voting commences. The interval features a fill-in act of some kind that is usually instantly forgettable.

1   C

At its most basic, Riverdance is an exciting display of music, dancing and singing. Another way of looking at it is that it is the story of Ireland and its people. The country is like a river that is fed by many streams and then runs into the ocean. People came to Ireland from many different places and then, centuries later, flowed out of Ireland into other parts of the world.

2   A

As far as the presentation of the show itself is concerned, Act One is set thousands of years ago and opens with the number "Reel around the Sun", which highlights the earliest civilisations, who believed that the sun had mystical powers. It is followed by the "Heart's Cry", which explores the emotional connection between people and nature and then focuses on different aspects of Irish culture.

3   E

The beginning of the second act is set in Ireland in the middle of the nineteenth century at a time when famine was widespread. As a result of that, thousands of people left for America. The first number is "American Wake" and is about the families that said "goodbye" to loved ones who were leaving and who they would probably never see again. There is also an element of celebration as the immigrants were taking their culture, which was a gift from their ancestors, with them.

4   B

The show culminates in the "International Riverdance", a spectacular finale which involves all the performers from all the different cultures dancing together. This represents the river of the human race's creativity that is fed by many sources.

Riverdance has played all over the world and has received more praise than any other musical ever. A truly stunning achievement.

B Match the words in the box below with their definitions.

commence	stunning	famine	culminate	interval	praise

1. brilliant   _stunning_
2. to begin   _commence_
3. admiration   _praise_
4. a period of time between events   _interval_
5. a shortage of food   _famine_
6. to reach the highest point   _culminate_

C Complete the sentences with the correct form of the phrasal verbs and expressions in the box below.

a standing joke	schools of thought	put out	point out	rumour has it	pick out

1. _Rumour has it_ that he's a very wealthy man, but no one knows for sure.
2. Kim usually finds it difficult to _pick out_ an outfit for a party.
3. Although it's _a standing joke_ , some people don't find it amusing.
4. There are various _schools of thought_ about how the universe was created.
5. Tom was _put out_ when he found out that his hotel reservation had been cancelled.
6. During her speech, the doctor _pointed out_ the importance of a healthy diet.

D Complete the second sentence so that it has a similar meaning to the first sentence, using the word given. Do not change the word given. You must use between two and five words, including the word given.

1. I can't speak and I can't eat because I've got a sore throat.   **neither**
   I can _neither speak nor eat_ because I've got a sore throat.
2. At 8 o'clock my mother leaves for work and my father leaves for work then, too.   **both**
   At 8 o'clock _both my mother and my father_ leave for work.
3. We can go to the party or we can go to the cinema.   **either**
   We can go _either to the party or_ to the cinema.
4. Did you know that George speaks Japanese and John does too?   **and**
   Did you know that _both George and John_ speak Japanese?
5. After three weeks of auditions, Julie was finally chosen for the part.   **out**
   After three weeks of auditions, Julie _was finally picked out for_ the part.
6. The firemen didn't leave until the fire was completely extinguished.   **put**
   The firemen didn't leave until they _had completely put out_ the fire.
7. The headteacher kept emphasising the importance of studying hard.   **pointing**
   The headteacher _kept pointing out_ the importance of studying hard.

Lesson Three

A Read the text below and look carefully at each line. Some of the lines are correct, and some have a word which should not be there. If a line is correct, put a (√) in the space provided. If a line has a word which should not be there, write the word in the space provided.

NOT JUST A HOTEL

1.	Would you ever stay in a hotel that it looked like	it
2.	the sinking Titanic in its final moments? Well, you believe it	you
3.	or not, if such a hotel exists. It's in Dubai and it costs	if
4.	£3000 a night! At 321 m high, the Jumeirah Beach Tower Hotel,	√
5.	off the coast of Dubai is the very tallest hotel in the world.	very
6.	But it's not just the height of the hotel that's impressive, it's also	√
7.	the dramatic of appearance. Architect, Tom Wills Wright, got his	of
8.	inspiration for the shape of the hotel from the image of the famous	√
9.	ship in its final moments, just before it sank there to the bottom	there
10.	of the ocean! The hotel is being quite luxurious and offers guests a	being
11.	number of facilities including in limousine parking, a private port	in
12.	that accommodates up to 50 yachts and a private helipad,	√
13.	on to which hotel guests can land their helicopters! One of	to
14.	the hotel's restaurants is on the top floor and there is also an	√
15.	underwater restaurant at where you can actually see real sharks!	at
	So, if you can afford it, go for it!	

B Read the text below. Use the word given in capitals at the end of each line to form a word that fits in the space in the same line.

A WEEKEND TO REMEMBER

When I won a competition to attend a **(1)** _____designer_____ fashion show **DESIGN**
I was thrilled! Although it meant spending a weekend away from home,
my parents gave me **(2)** _____permission_____ to go. **PERMIT**
I knew that I would be **(3)** _____impressed_____ by everything, **IMPRESS**
so I took my camera with me to take as many pictures as possible.
The trip was **(4)** _____unbelievable_____! I never imagined that London **BELIEVE**
was that fantastic! But, I did have one problem. There was a mix-up at the
airport and I took someone's suitcase by mistake. **(5)** _____Fortunately_____, **FORTUNE**
I found the man whose suitcase I had taken and the situation was quickly sorted out.
The man, wasn't **(6)** _____amused_____ because he claimed **AMUSE**
he had some very **(7)** _____important_____ things inside it. **IMPORTANCE**
I apologised to him and he said it was all right. He then said he was
a **(8)** _____dancer_____ and invited me to one of his performances. **DANCE**
I went after the fashion show, and Mark - the guy I met - was
excellent and the show was very **(9)** _____successful_____ indeed! **SUCCESS**
It was the most **(10)** _____interesting_____ weekend I've ever had! **INTEREST**

C Choose the words/expressions in the box to complete the sentences.

frightening	box-office hits	desperate	unpredictable	hugely entertaining

1. She was alone and _____desperate_____ in a foreign country and she went to the embassy for help.
2. If you like adventure films, you'll love "Action Arnie". It's impossible to guess what's going to happen next! It's completely _____unpredictable_____.
3. We went to the new comedy club that has just opened and it was _____hugely entertaining_____. We had a great time
4. 'E.T.' was one of the biggest _____box-office hits_____ ever.
5. Looking down from the top of an 80-storey building can be quite _____frightening_____.

D Read the text below and think of the word which best fits each space. Use only one word in each space.

HOTELS

Hotels used to be places where weary travellers could **(1)** _____spend_____ the night. In towns, small hotels or 'inns', as they used to **(2)** _____be_____ called, were used as taverns by the locals, but also provided food and a place to sleep for travellers.

Hotels have come a **(3)** _____long_____ way since then. People staying in hotels are not considered to **(4)** _____be_____ customers, they are referred **(5)** _____to_____ as 'guests'. The reason for this is that people are travelling now more than ever before either **(6)** _____on_____ business or for holidays. People **(7)** _____who / that_____ go on business trips quite often need to feel **(8)** _____as_____ comfortable as they would at home. Hotel staff aim to make their guests' stay as pleasant as **(9)** _____possible_____. Modern hotel rooms **(10)** _____are_____ air conditioned, they have satellite TV, mini-bars full of snacks and refreshments, and they are even equipped with electric kettles for **(11)** _____making_____ hot drinks like coffee or tea. Many hotels also have business centres, spas and gyms. The bigger the hotel, the greater the number of services provided, and the **(12)** _____more_____ comfortable a guest feels.

There are many major hotel chains to choose **(13)** _____from_____ for business trips or holidays. **(14)** _____However_____, you should bear one thing **(15)** _____in_____ mind: there is always a bill at the end of your stay; so, go easy on the room service!

E Complete the second sentence so that it has a similar meaning to the first sentence, using the word given. Do not change the word given. You must use between two and five words, including the word given.

1. You remembered to take the map, didn't you?   **forget**

   You _____didn't forget to take_____ the map, did you?

2. You can buy the markers or maybe you'd like the crayons instead?   **either**

   You can buy _____either the markers or the_____ crayons.

3. The last time I went to the cinema was two months ago.   **since**

   It's _____been two months since_____ I last went to the cinema.

4. Remember to leave your name and number with us before you go.   **without**

   Don't _____go without leaving_____

   your name and number with us.

5. Isn't there a better solution than that?   **the**

   Is _____that the best solution there_____ is?

6. Didn't Tina manage to catch the last train to London?   **able**

   Wasn't _____Tina able to catch_____ the last train to London?

7. If you are careful, I'll let you hold the vase.   **long**

   I'll let you hold the vase _____as long as you are_____ careful.

8. Someone fixed her radio yesterday.   **fixed**

   She _____had her radio fixed_____ yesterday.

F Read the following parts of a film review and match the positive with the negative expressions.

POSITIVE	NEGATIVE
- The film is a box-office hit	- It's a waste of money
- It's worthwhile	- It's poorly directed
- It's a high quality production	- The stunts have no suspense
- It's action-packed	- The plot is weak
- The stunts are breathtaking	- The film is highly disappointing
- It has a surprising end	- The script is badly written
- Exciting	- The ending is predictable
- The plot is clever	- Unappealing

G Now read the conclusion of the following film review which expresses a negative view and write the introduction and the main part, using as many expressions from the exercise above as possible and adding your own ideas.

POLICE ACADEMY III: BACK IN TRAINING

Suggested answer

If you enjoyed the first two Police Academy films, then you might be one of the very few who actually enjoys Police Academy III: Back in Training.

Steve Guttenberg is back as Sgt. Carey Mahoney and he returns together with the rest of the gang to the Academy to train rookies in order to prevent the school from closing. This film isn't very different from the previous two films.

There is really nothing noticeable about the film. The scenery is the same as the previous two films and therefore it's quite unattractive. Due to the badly written script, the plot is very weak and the viewers listen to repetitive jokes with cliché punchlines.

Each scene is so predictable the viewer knows exactly what is going to follow. Police Academy III is poorly directed and gives the impression that the director was either bored or in a hurry to finish the film. The film has almost no stunts and the few adventure scenes have absolutely no suspense. Of course, there are some scenes that can make the viewers laugh but they are so unimportant that nobody really notices them.

All in all, even though there are some funny scenes, the film is, for the most part, an absolute bore. It's definitely not a must-see!

Lesson One

A Read the text and decide which answer A, B, C or D best fits each space.

IT'S A TEENAGER'S LIFE

It's important for teenagers to understand that there is always a way to deal with tricky situations. If you are a teenager who feels **(1)** _____angry_____ because your parents won't let you go to a party, for example, don't worry! There is a solution. Firstly, don't keep your feelings a secret and come **(2)** ____clean____ with them about how you really feel. Tell them that you are **(3)** ____dying to____ go, and promise you won't be out too late. Don't **(4)** _____push_____ your luck, by breaking your promise. The last thing you want is your father hitting the **(5)** _____roof_____ when you don't get home on time.

Having a fight with your best friend can be stressful too. Whatever the problem is, it's best to talk it over. **(6)** _____Tell_____ your mate how you feel and try to solve the problem. Finally, probably one of the most stressful situations that a teenager can face is exams! The very word can send a **(7)** ____chill____ down your spine. Calm down! All you have to do is plan ahead. Draw up a timetable and stick to it. That way you'll **(8)** ____avoid____ potential problems and you won't be shaking in your **(9)** ____shoes____ when it's time to take the test.

You see, it's simple! So next time you find yourself **(10)** ____in____ a difficult situation, you'll know what to do!

1.	**A** angry	**B** co-operative	**C** defensive	**D** eager
2.	**A** clean	**B** dirty	**C** clear	**D** shiny
3.	**A** straining at the leash	**B** dying to	**C** in your element	**D** hit the roof
4.	**A** push	**B** cause	**C** provoke	**D** transport
5.	**A** wall	**B** roof	**C** door	**D** floor
6.	**A** Speak	**B** Tell	**C** Present	**D** Express
7.	**A** cool	**B** cold	**C** chill	**D** feeling
8.	**A** create	**B** conclude	**C** give	**D** avoid
9.	**A** shoes	**B** boots	**C** feet	**D** hands
10.	**A** up	**B** out	**C** in	**D** to

B Complete the second sentence so that it has a similar meaning to the first sentence, using the word given. Do not change the word given. You must use between two and five words, including the word given.

1. The mechanic will service my car before I go on holiday. **have**
   I _____will have my car serviced_____ before I go on holiday.

2. A technician upgraded my computer last month. **had**
   I _____had my computer upgraded_____ last month.

3. Josh's mom asked him to help her with the housework. **had**
   Josh's mom _____had Josh/him help her with_____ the housework.

4. It's high time the plumber fixed that pipe before it bursts. **fixed**
   It's high time we _____had that pipe fixed_____ before it bursts.

5. She decided to change her hairstyle for the party. **have**
   She decided to _____have her hairstyle changed_____ for the party.

6. She asked her husband to paint the house, as they could not afford a professional painter. **paint**
   She _____had her husband paint_____ the house, as they couldn't afford a professional painter.

Lesson Two

A You are going to read a magazine article about happiness. For Questions 1-6, choose the correct answer A, B, C or D.

1. What was true of people forty years ago?
   - **A** They were richer.
   - **Ⓑ** They were generally happier.
   - **C** They had a reasonable amount of material possessions.
   - **D** They were generally less happy.

2. What does the writer find surprising?
   - **Ⓐ** that disabled people are not generally unhappy
   - **B** that people who do not have much of a social life are not happy
   - **C** that people with busy social lives are happy
   - **D** that sick people are unhappy

3. What happens when people discover something bad is about to happen?
   - **A** They feel miserable.
   - **B** They feel like they have been leading meaningless lives up to that point.
   - **Ⓒ** They feel like their previously unbearable lives weren't that bad after all.
   - **D** They feel that their lives could not be any worse than they already are.

4. What happened each time the rat pressed the handle?
   - **A** its appetite disappeared
   - **B** it fell into a trap
   - **C** it ate and drank
   - **Ⓓ** it felt very good

5. According to the writer, what do we need to do to be happy?
   - **A** live without negative feelings
   - **B** make sure that nothing goes wrong
   - **Ⓒ** learn to accept that life is sometimes difficult
   - **D** keep our lives free of bad things

6. How does one achieve the feeling of *flow* (line 43)?
   - **Ⓐ** by doing something one really likes
   - **B** by being pushed beyond one's ability
   - **C** by doing something that will be rewarded
   - **D** by doing things that are really dangerous

Happiness

Everyone wants to be happy, but it seems that not many people can achieve happiness. There are some clues, however, as to what makes us happy. We know, for example, that it is necessary to have a reasonable amount of material possessions, but more than that doesn't make much difference. On average, people in America and Europe are twice as wealthy as they were forty years ago, yet surveys show that they are not as happy. In fact, in many cases they are less so.

It's not surprising that people who have a large circle of friends are usually happier than those who do not have much of a social life, and that healthy people are happier than sick people. What's surprising to most of us is that disabled people have the same possibility for happiness as the rest of us do. Even people who have been seriously injured in an accident describe themselves as happy three weeks afterwards.

The truth is that happiness is a relative state. If you discover that something absolutely awful is going to happen, then the life you had been leading up to that point can seem like absolute bliss, although you probably thought it was miserable while you were living it.

It seems, however, that those of us who are lucky enough to achieve happiness are going to mess it up anyway. Unfortunately, many of the things that give us pleasure are also the things that we can become addicted to. In order to prove this, scientists carried out an experiment. They attached electrodes to a rat's brain and connected them to a handle in the animal's cage so that it could directly stimulate its pleasure centres by pressing the handle. The result was that the rat kept on pressing the handle instead of eating or drinking. Humans are a bit more complicated than that, but research has shown that they, too, can fall into this trap.

One of the reasons we have such a problem with happiness is that we confuse it with a life untouched by negative feelings such as anxiety, rage, doubt or sadness. We have a naive belief that happiness means that nothing ever goes wrong. In order to be happy, we must learn how to live contentedly with the negative elements of life rather than attempting to live a life where nothing bad ever happens.

A professor at the University of Chicago, Mihaly Csikszentmihalyi, has spent a great deal of time researching 'happiness'. He believes that the key to happiness is something he calls *the flow*. *The flow* is the state you are in when you are doing something that completely absorbs you. It comes when you are pushed right up to the limit of your ability, but not beyond it. People can get a feeling of flow from dangerous sports like mountain climbing or driving fast, but it can also come from less strenuous pursuits, like painting or reading a great book. The point is that people do these things because they want to and not because they are looking for some kind of reward.

The really curious thing is that despite the fact that we know what makes us feel good, we still do not do those things very much. For example, a study showed that while playing sport, people have a flow of 35% whereas when they are watching television, they have no flow at all. Yet, they watch TV for ten times as long as they spend playing sport!

A good measuring stick for those of us who are desperately seeking happiness is asking ourselves, 'Is what I am doing today contributing to the things that are most important in my life?' If not, why are you doing it?

B Complete the sentences with the expressions in the box. You may need to change the form of the verbs.

| last but not least   fight a losing battle   sense of achievement   the bottom line   bring to light |

1. When she was made manager of the company, Jill was filled with a great ___sense of achievement___.

2. The two Presidents have been negotiating for two weeks; ___the bottom line___ is that they'll never reach an agreement.

3. '___Last but not least___, always smile at the customers,' said the manager.

4. A great deal of information about prehistoric people was ___brought to light___ as a result of professor Martins' discoveries.

5. 'Jane, you ___are fighting a losing battle___. No matter what you do, you won't be able to convince Paul to buy a new car.'

C Complete the second sentence so that it has a similar meaning to the first sentence, using the word given. You must use between two and five words, including the word given.

1. I was late for work again because there was a demonstration in the city centre. **due**
   I was late for work again ___due to a demonstration___ in the city centre.

2. He changed all the locks when he bought the house. **as**
   He changed all the locks ___as soon as he bought___ the house.

3. Jerry finished the project in time even though he wasn't feeling well. **fact**
   Jerry finished the project in time ___despite the fact that he___ wasn't feeling well.

4. Samantha is a great science fiction fan, but she didn't like 'Robotland' at all. **of**
   In ___spite of being a great___ science fiction fan, Samantha didn't like 'Robotland' at all.

5. Did she go to the hairdresser's to have a haircut? **cut**
   Did she ___have her hair cut___ at the hairdresser's?

Lesson Three

A Find the opposites of the words below. More than one answer may be possible.

1. satisfied   dissatisfied
2. borrow   lend
3. stressed   relaxed/carefree
4. possible   impossible

5. hard-working   lazy
6. confident   uncertain
7. success   failure
8. positive   negative

B Now use some of the above words to fill in the following sentences.

1. He's a very _____ lazy _____ person. He completes half the tasks and he is always behind schedule.

2. Although the working conditions were excellent and I was very _____ satisfied _____, the salary was bad so I quit.

3. _____ Success _____ only comes after hard work and lots of effort.

4. My daughter is really _____ confident _____. She always speaks her mind and is not afraid of criticism.

5. Josh _____ lent _____ money to a friend of his a month ago and is still waiting for him to pay it back.

6. It was _____ impossible _____ to meet the deadline with all that work.

7. He always thinks in a _____ positive _____ way. It helps him reach the right decisions and avoid mistakes.

8. When I'm _____ stressed _____, I get a sharp stomach ache and a pounding headache.

C Read the text below and think of the word which best fits each space. Use only one word in each space.

THE TWO TOWERS

Cinema audiences are sitting down again to enjoy a second helping of Tolkien via the spectacular directing skills of Peter Jackson, who seems to have been **(1)** _____ in _____ his element once again. **(2)** _____ Although _____ some fans of the book have complained that in The Two Towers Jackson has moved away from the original story, there's **(3)** _____ no _____ doubt that everybody will enjoy the film.

The film picks up **(4)** _____ where _____ Part I The Fellowship of the Ring left off, with Frodo and his friend Sam **(5)** _____ on _____ their way to Mount Doom in Mordor to destroy The Ring of Power. Frodo and Sam are fighting a losing **(6)** _____ battle _____, though, as they try to find a way to enter Mordor.

Meanwhile, Aragorn the warrior, Gimli the dwarf and Legolas the elf are in pursuit of the two remaining hobbits, Pippin and Merry, **(7)** _____ who _____ have been captured **(8)** _____ by _____ the Orcs.

(9) _____ If _____ you thought that the special effects in The Fellowship of the Ring were spectacular, you'll be even **(10)** _____ more _____ impressed by The Two Towers. The cast is excellent and the film is well-paced. Look **(11)** _____ out _____ for the creature Gollum, slave to the ring, who was briefly introduced to us in Part I, but here accompanies Frodo and Sam throughout their journey to Mordor.

The digital effects in the scene featuring The Battle of Helm's Deep where Aragorn, Gimli and Legolas join up **(12)** _____ with _____ the Horselords of Rohan to fight the army of the evil wizard Saruman will leave you breathless. All in **(13)** _____ all _____, it's a rollercoaster ride **(14)** _____ from _____ beginning to end. The film is action-packed with not **(15)** _____ much _____ time for some of the lighter scenes that were included in The Fellowship of the Ring.

D Read the text below and look carefully at each line. Some of the lines are correct, and some have a word which should not be there. If a line is correct, put a tick (√) in the space provided. If a line has a word which should not be there, write the word in the space provided.

CHILL OUT

1. Tired of going on holiday to the same place over and over again?   √
2. Looking for some of excitement? Then try the South Pole!   of
3. Actually, getting there is very easier than you might think. In   very
4. fact, all you have to do is read out the newspapers to find a job   out
5. vacancy there! The qualifications required vary, though being able   √
6. to work in a team is essential. The British Antarctic Survey which   √
7. is looking for staff for their own ships, planes and bases, has   own
8. opportunities for everyone. Professionals required include the   the
9. meteorologists, biologists, physicists and pilots, but if there is also   if
10. a need for the support staff like dentists, cooks and even ice-climbers!   the
11. If you were decided to go on a trip to the South Pole on your own,   were
12. it would cost you over £14 000 for an accommodation, supplies and   an
13. flights round the continent. Also, you would have to pay extra for the   √
14. appropriate clothes. Another way of getting to there is by joining the   to
15. few yachts that head south each year. Not all of them get there but it's   √
    free and you'll never forget the moment you set eyes on an iceberg.

E Read the text below. Use the word given in capitals at the end of each line to form a word that fits in the space in the same line.

WHALES

When we think of whales, we tend to think of huge, hostile fish that attack ships and eat people. **(1)** <u>Actually</u>, whales are not like that at all. **ACTUAL**
Firstly, we think they are fish but they aren't. The truth is that whales are mammals and there is a big **(2)** <u>difference</u> between them and fish. **DIFFER**
According to **(3)** <u>scientists</u>, whales used to **SCIENCE**
have legs and hooves and were meat-eaters 50 million years ago! Over a period of 10 million years the legs and hooves **(4)** <u>disappeared</u> **APPEAR**
and slowly these mammals evolved into the whales we know today. Nowadays, there are about 80 species of mammals classified as whales. **(5)** <u>Unfortunately</u>, whales are **FORTUNATE**
hunted because their fat is considered **(6)** <u>valuable</u>, especially in the cosmetics **VALUE**
industry. As a result, these mammals are one of the most **(7)** <u>endangered</u> species on **DANGER**
the planet. In order for these **(8)** <u>beautiful</u> creatures to continue to exist, it is our **BEAUTY**
(9) <u>responsibility</u> to do everything in our powers to save them. Animal rights **RESPONSIBLE**
organisations are working hard on this and truly hope that in a few years they will be **(10)** <u>successful</u> in saving whales. Then, once again, they will be swimming freely **SUCCESS**
in the deep oceans.

F Read the following essay on the advantages and disadvantages of the Internet. Fill in the gaps with the appropriate linkers from the list below.

Adding points:	furthermore, in addition to, besides, what is more, also
Contrast:	on the one hand, on the other hand, however, although, despite, in spite of, whereas
Result:	therefore, so, as a result, as a consequence
Listing points:	firstly, to begin with, secondly, finally

In recent years, the Internet has become a great part of our lives. More and more people have access to it and have discovered many benefits from using it.

_____To begin with_____, the Internet offers us unlimited information and knowledge on just about every topic. Access to the Net is easy and fast, and schoolchildren regularly use the web to research school projects or to browse just for fun. _____Furthermore_____, people can communicate with people all over the world with a system called e-mail. You can _____also_____ start conversations in chat rooms and even see your friends in other parts of the world with the help of a special 'web cam'. You can view products from different countries and use your credit card to do your shopping from the comfort of your own home. _____On the other hand/However_____, surfing the Internet is not the best way of spending all your free time. Too many hours in front of the screen can damage your eyes. Also, studies have shown that people who prefer to spend their evenings in front of their PCs tend to become antisocial. This also applies to children so parents should supervise their children while they are on the Net and limit time spent surfing. _____Finally_____, there are some concerns about security on the Internet as hackers can easily steal valuable personal information such as bank account numbers, etc.

_____Despite_____ all these drawbacks, the Internet has certainly made life easier and, if used properly, it may make our lives better, too.

G Write an essay on the advantages and disadvantages of living on your own. Your essay should be between 120 and 180 words.

Lesson One

A Complete the sentences below with the correct form of the idioms and expressions in the box.

| wise up | at one's disposal | stop one in one's tracks | go to any lengths | clear up | talk into |

1. Sarah will _go to any lengths_ to save her company; she's a very determined woman.
2. Thankfully, little Mickey's rash has finally ___cleared up___. I think he might be allergic to the dog.
3. Marshall tried ___to talk___ his wife ___into___ moving to Spain, but she wouldn't hear of it.
4. 'You should ___wise up___, Bernie. Don't tell Marcus your secrets – he can't keep his mouth shut.'
5. 'The hotel staff is entirely ___at your disposal___, Your Highness. We hope you have a pleasant stay'.
6. Have you seen that new bronze sculpture outside the library? It's so awful, it's bound to ___stop you in your tracks___.

B Complete the second sentence so that it has a similar meaning to the first sentence, using the word given. Do not change the word given. You must use between two and five words, including the word given.

1. Tom won't help you now because he is very busy.
   Tom's ___too busy to___ help you now. | **too**
2. Samantha does nothing but read because of her interest in books.
   Samantha ___is so interested in books___ that she doesn't do anything else but read. | **so**
3. The earring I lost was so small we couldn't find it.
   The earring I lost was ___too small (for us) to___ find. | **too**
4. I had a tiring day and I didn't go out after work.
   I had ___such a tiring day (that)___ I didn't go out after work. | **such**
5. She started crying because she was very upset.
   She was ___so upset that she___ started crying. | **that**

C Read the text below and decide which answer A, B, C, or D best fits each space.

WHAT A SURPRISE!

Last Saturday, my friend Laura and I went shopping. There was a **(1)** ___sale___ on at our favourite shoe shop. They were offering 30%, 40% and even 50% off some of the shoes in the shop! I was pleased that I wouldn't have to **(2)** ___spend___ much money. There was a huge variety of boots, sandals and high heeled shoes for us to choose from. After looking **(3)** ___around___ for a while, I came **(4)** ___across___ a beautiful pair of leather boots. Luckily, they had them in my **(5)** ___size___. Without even looking at the **(6)** ___price___, I just took them and ran to the till to pay. When I got home and tried them **(7)** ___on___, I noticed that one of the zippers was broken! I went back to the shop and showed the shop assistant the boots and the **(8)** ___receipt___, but she said that I couldn't get a **(9)** ___refund___ because of the special price reduction they had.

1. **A** market	**B** sale	**C** cheque	**D** bill
2. **A** spend	**B** spare	**C** waste	**D** get
3. **A** at	**B** into	**C** up	**D** around
4. **A** on	**B** across	**C** into	**D** up
5. **A** number	**B** length	**C** size	**D** measures
6. **A** value	**B** price	**C** cost	**D** payment
7. **A** on	**B** in	**C** up	**D** into
8. **A** account	**B** cheque	**C** bill	**D** receipt
9. **A** refund	**B** cheque	**C** return	**D** deal

Lesson Two

A You are going to read a magazine article about Klever Karts. Choose the most suitable heading from the list A-G for each part (1-6) of the article. There is one extra heading which you do not need to use.

A Upgrading an existing invention

B Always something new

C Well-informed assistants

D Let's wait and see

E Products on sale

F A great help to retailers

G Not all positive

B Find phrasal verbs, words and expressions in the text and match them with the meanings given.

a. have information about something — keep track of
b. near something — close proximity
c. for some time — for a while
d. more than is necessary — over the odds
e. the state of being alone — privacy
f. observe closely — watch over
g. be more important than something else — outweighs

KLEVER KART

1   B

What will they come up with next?! If you got a dollar every time you heard an expression like that, you would probably end up with quite a healthy bank account. In this age of technological advancement, not much time goes by without some trendy invention appearing in our lives. That goes for shopping, too.

2   C

What recently caught my attention was a new addition to some supermarkets in the United States. They call it the *Klever Kart*. The Klever Kart is an electronic device which is attached to a very ordinary shopping trolley and acts as your very own personal shopping guide. Each shopper who uses the Klever Kart is issued a personal identification card. When customers arrive at the supermarket, they swipe their cards through the Klever Kart. The card then accesses the customers' shopping history in that particular shop. The card keeps track of what products people buy, where and when they shop, and generally how much they spend. It also keeps track of which aisles the customers go down, and how long they spend in each department.

3   F

Of course, all this information is stored and used for marketing purposes by the supermarket. Knowing their customers' shopping habits is of great benefit to the shopkeepers. It helps them identify who their best customers are and they can design target advertising and money-off coupons. It also helps them to make stores more convenient for shoppers by placing popular items in close proximity to one another.

4   A

The good thing about the Klever Kart technology is that it makes the customers' shopping experience easier as they are actually being given the information they need. They will be reminded that they have not bought some items for a while and they will also be told about new brands that have just come on the market. In fact, it's not so different from the 'loyalty cards' system that has been operating in many supermarkets for quite some time.

holding customers only. This means that they pay what the product is worth anyway, while the poor cardless folks pay over the odds.

5	G

Some people don't like the idea because they say it is an intrusion into people's privacy and that it gives people the impression that they are saving money when actually they are not. Shops actually charge cardholding customers less than the shelf price for many items. However, critics say that the shops raise the shelf prices first and then give a small discount to card

6	D

One thing is for sure, though; the Klever Kart simplifies things and it's economical. It also opens people up to new things. As time goes by, we will be able to tell whether people's need for privacy outweighs the practical advantages of the Klever Kart or not.

C Read the text below and decide which answer A, B, C or D best fits each space.

Sometimes sitting at home doing nothing can be an absolute **(1)** _____bore_____. You want to do something but you're not exactly sure what. Well, **(2)** _____folks_____, here's some good advice! You might not know it but you could be the extreme type! All you have to do is read this guide and try out **(3)** _____some_____ of these sports!

The **(4)** _____latest_____ craze is base-jumping. This involves jumping off a very high building, bridge etc. If that doesn't sound like a hundred **(5)** _____per_____ cent thrilling, you can give ice-climbing a try. All you need is incredible physical and mental strength, special equipment and ... a lot of ice! If you are in two **(6)** _____minds_____ about what to do, you can always take **(7)** _____up_____ high wiring. It would be a good idea to practice on a wire that is close to the ground, because nine out of ten **(8)** _____times_____ you'll fall before you get it right! And if all these don't get you out of your chair, maybe sky surfing will! People from all **(9)** _____four_____ corners of the globe gather at sky surfing competitions to watch surfers do acrobatics in the sky! So, next time you have nothing to do, check out this sports list and turn your day into a thrill!

1. **A** bore	**B** bother	**C** pain	**D** headache
2. **A** parents	**B** family	**C** folks	**D** relatives
3. **A** much	**B** more	**C** a little	**D** some
4. **A** largest	**B** latest	**C** greatest	**D** highest
5. **A** to	**B** a	**C** per	**D** for
6. **A** eyes	**B** heads	**C** minds	**D** hands
7. **A** on	**B** in	**C** to	**D** up
8. **A** times	**B** turns	**C** rounds	**D** hours
9. **A** three	**B** four	**C** one	**D** two

D Fill in the sentences with the words in the box. You may need to change the form of the verbs.

recruit	fulfil	requirements	evaluate	feedback	freelancers

1. Many journalists work as _____freelancers_____ for magazines and newspapers.
2. The company has _____recruited_____ ten experts to do market research.
3. This team has been assigned the task of _____evaluating_____ the employees' performance.
4. Peter has always worked hard to _____fulfil_____ his ambitions.
5. After we had handed in the first draft of our essays, we waited for the lecturer's _____feedback_____ before we rewrote them.
6. UK universities have specific language _____requirements_____ that foreign students have to meet.

Lesson Three

A Read the text below and look carefully at each line. Some of the lines are correct, and some others have a word which should not be there. If a line is correct, put a tick (v) in the space provided. If a line has a word which should not be there, write the word in the space provided.

POWERFUL BEGINNING

1. Do you really need to have had breakfast in the morning? — had
2. The answer is 'yes'! You need to wake up to the idea of just how — √
3. important breakfast really it is! As well as giving you energy, — it
4. it can improve your concentration and the memory! — the
5. The word 'breakfast' originates from the phrase 'breaking the fast'. — √
6. When you will wake up, it can be as long as 14 hours since — will
7. you last time ate, so you need to get something in your stomach! — time
8. Breakfast options can vary depending on individual likes and dislikes. — √
9. A very great choice would be 'an exotic breakfast' that consists of — very
10. kiwis, mangoes and strawberries. Fruit is full of few vitamins, which — few
11. they help you keep in shape. The 'power breakfast' with cereal, — they
12. fruit (bananas, oranges) and a bagel, is high in vitamin C — √
13. and gives you a lots of energy. Why not try the 'Indulged Breakfast' — a
14. with much smoked salmon and scrambled eggs which — much
15. is rich in those vitamins A, B, D and E. So, tomorrow morning — those
    in order to feel like a king maybe you should eat like one!

B Read the text below. Use the word given in capitals at the end of each line to form a word that fits in the space in the same line.

EVERYBODY ON BOARD

If you like travelling and have good **(1)** ___communication___ skills, **COMMUNICATE**

then you should probably apply for a job as a Port and Shopping Guide.

Our company provides **(2)** ___training___ and **TRAIN**

(3) ___employment___ for Port and Shopping Guides who work on **EMPLOY**

luxurious cruise ships around the world. You will leave our training centre with

enough **(4)** ___knowledge___ to start travelling immediately. **KNOW**

DESCRIBE

The job **(5)** ___description___ for what you will be doing goes as follows:

employees work on board luxury ships, which travel to exotic destinations such as the

Caribbean, Alaska and Hawaii. Your aim will be to promote **(6)** ___sales___ **SELL**

ashore for items, such as jewellery, watches and electronics. Guides regularly meet with

shop representatives and monitor the **(7)** ___effectiveness___ of their strategies. **EFFECTIVE**

If you are **(8)** ___energetic___, like working with people **ENERGY**

and are **(9)** ___experienced___ in sales, this is **EXPERIENCE**

(10) ___certainly___ the job for you! **CERTAIN**

C Read the text below and think of the word which best fits each space. Use only one word in each space.

MUSIC TO MY EARS

What else can music do for us, apart from entertaining us and helping us to relax? Well, according
(1) _____to_____ studies that have been carried **(2)** _____out_____ in the United Kingdom and
Sweden, music **(3)** _____can_____ improve one's health, memory span and even combat stress.

Barbara Young, **(4)** _____who_____ is a musical communication expert, claims that music encourages
the development of a baby's mind. Furthermore, children who take extra music classes do better
(5) _____in_____ maths and science, sometimes as **(6)** _____much_____ as 25% better. What is also
incredible, is that music helps people who have trouble sleeping, sleep better **(7)** _____than_____
before.

Music is an enjoyable experience and it has **(8)** _____even_____ been suggested that listening to songs
can actually protect you **(9)** _____from/against_____ a number of illnesses, ranging from the common cold to
heart disease!

Recently, some very encouraging research that **(10)** _____has_____ been carried out **(11)** _____proved_____
the benefits of using music in the area **(12)** _____of_____ pain management. Some hospitals have
(13) _____already_____ started using music to speed up the patients' recoveries.

So, next **(14)** _____time_____ you listen to your favourite song, bear in mind that it can do a lot more
for you than just put a smile **(15)** _____on_____ your face!

D Complete the second sentence so that it has a similar meaning to the first sentence, using the word given.
Do not change the word given. You must use between two and five words, including the word given.

1. Lying to your parents is wrong.   **should**
   You _____ should not lie to _____ your parents.

2. My mum lets me go to the cinema only on Saturdays.   **allowed**
   I _____ am allowed to go _____ to the cinema only on Saturdays.

3. 'Please, reconsider moving abroad, Debbie,' said Sophie.   **begged**
   Sophie _____ begged Debbie to reconsider _____ moving abroad.

4. 'You should work harder if you want to be promoted,' said my brother.   **advised**
   My brother _____ advised me to work harder _____ if I wanted to be promoted.

5. An interior decorator redecorated my living room recently.   **had**
   I _____ had my living room redecorated _____ recently.

6. George regrets not having bought that car; it was a great bargain.   **wishes**
   George _____ wishes he had bought _____ that car; it was a great bargain.

7. People planted dozens of flowers in the park yesterday.   **planted**
   Dozens of flowers _____ were planted in the _____ park yesterday.

8. Take your coat or you'll catch a cold.   **take**
   Unless _____ you take your coat, you _____ will catch a cold.

E Read the leaflet below and the sample letter. Write what is wrong with the letter and tick the features of the letter.

Burnt

waiter took 40 minutes to take order

Outrageous!

Staff unaware/ paid full-price

'FANCY RESTAURANT'

ENJOY YOUR MEALS

IN A COSY ATMOSPHERE
- Delicious international dishes
- Fast service
- Experienced staff
- Convenient parking
- Reasonable prices
- Special discounts for group bookings

Book in advance
Telephone number: 225-612

Waiter mixed up orders

Car park small and full

Did so/Waited 20 minutes to be seated

Dear Sir/Madam,

Hi! My name is Mark Webster and a few days ago I went to your restaurant with seven friends to celebrate my birthday. Trust me, it was the biggest mistake of my life! Why? Well, firstly I booked a table ten days in advance and we still had to wait 20 minutes to be seated. That was very annoying!

When we finally sat down, we had to wait another 40 minutes for the waiter to serve us. In your advertisement, you said that all your employees are experienced. Well, the waiter didn't know what he was doing and kept mixing up the orders.

Your dishes weren't 'delicious' as you said they'd be. They were tasteless and burnt. When the bill came, we expected a discount as you promised, but the waiter was unaware of the offer and the total amount was unbelievable! Luckily, I had my credit card with me.

Oh! I forgot to tell you that when we left, we had to walk 15 minutes to get to our cars because your 'convenient car park' was small and already full by the time we got there.

So, I think you should give my money back or I'll tell everybody your restaurant is terrible.

I'll be waiting for a prompt answer.

Bye for now,

Mark Webster

Suggested answers

Inappropriate layout (informal letter)

Inappropriate language (hi!/they'd etc.)

Aggressive style/threat

Friendly	√	Enthusiastic	
Apologetic		Dissatisfied	√
Forgiving		Aggressive	√
Offensive	√		

F Rewrite the above letter in the appropriate style, omitting any unnecessary information. Your letter must be between 120 and 180 words.

Key to supplementary exercises

Unit 01

I Vocabulary and Structures

1. arrives   2. amazed   3. is   4. are tying / try   5. drinking   6. originally

II Reading Comprehension

1. F   2. T   3. T   4. T   5. F

III Translation & Writing

NOTICE

We are arranging for a bus tour to Guilin from Oct.2 to Oct.6. The bus will depart from the company at 8:00 am on Oct. 2. We will stay in Guilin for four days and we believe that you are able to spend a happy and unforgettable holiday.

If you would like to join us, please tell Xiao Liu or Xiao Wang at the front desk.

Public Relation Section

Unit 02

I Vocabulary and Structures

1. had joined   2. developing   3. have passed
4. fixed   5. have come   6. have been writing
7. valuable

II Reading Comprehension

1. B   2. C   3. D   4. A

III Translation & Writing

Reservation Office

Groupsales@aston.com

Reservation Office,

I want to book a single room with a bath and three standard rooms with bat from Dec.25 to Dec.27. And I also want to rent a meeting room for business meeting in the afternoon, Dec.26.

Please reply as soon as possible, telling me if the rooms are available, what the price is and if I should pay the deposit. Thank you.

Key to supplementary exercises

Unit 03

I Vocabulary and Structures

Section A

1. B   2. C   3. C   4. A   5. B
6. D   7. C   8. B   9. A   10. D

Section B

11. leaving   12. to be having   13. addition
14. watching   15. valuable   16. informed
17. had been ringing   18. will be held   19. agreement
20. handy

II Reading Comprehension

1. (G)(M)   2. (A)(K)   3. (I)(C)   4. (L)(F)   5. (N)(O)

III Translation

1. C   2. A   3. B   4. D
5. 仿真木PVC彩板门在我国门业市场上一枝独秀。它采用进口高分子PVC复合板，表面采用PVC彩板纹理复合膜，基板通过磷化，具有防潮、防腐功能；韧性好，曲折不裂色，其逼真的实木效果和永不褪色的特色符合国际市场以钢代木的潮流。

Revision 01-03

I Vocabulary and Structures

Section A

1. C   2. C   3. D   4. B   5. A
6. D   7. A   8. B   9. D   10. D

Section B

11. imagination   12. was reading   13. has done
14. had been waiting / had waited   15. Compared   16. left
17. undoubtedly   18. earlier   19. moves
20. are trying

II Reading Comprehension

Task 1   1. D   2. C   3. B   4. C   5. C
Task 2   6. F   7. N   8. V   9. E   10. I
         11. H   12. T   13. K   14. B   15. G
Task 3   16. a bank   17. a statement of purchases
         18. save up   19. too much   20. the credit card

Key to supplementary exercises

III Translation

1. A   2. B   3. A   4. D

5. 丹尼尔公司生产一种杀虫剂已经许多年了。过去的几年中这种杀虫剂一直是这家公司的主要盈利产品。然而，公司一名研究人员的近期研究表明，这种杀虫剂可能引起老鼠患癌症。因此，这名研究人员要求，在进一步的研究得出更确切的结果前，立即停止生产这种杀虫剂。

IV Writing

265 Lushan Road

Fenglin Hotel

Changsha, Hunan

Dec. 9 2010

Mr. Li, Xiaoming

76 Furong Road

Changsha, Hunan

Dear Mr Wang,

Thank you for your letter of Nov. 17 in which you applied for the post of Manager of the Service Department in our hotel.

I'd like to invite you to attend an interview at 8:30 am on Dec. 19 (Monday) at the Personnel Office. Could you please confirm your presence for the interview either in writing or by telephone (0731-83XX076)

I'm looking forward to meeting you.

Yours sincerely,

Yanbing

Unit 04

I Vocabulary and Structures

Section A

1. D   2. C   3. D   4. C   5. C

Section B

6. hesitant   7. advertisement   8. pounding   9. west   10. scary

11. entrance   12. blotting   13. unfamiliar   14. misunderstanding   15. competition

II Reading Comprehension

Task 1   1. B   2. C   3. B   4. B   5. D

Task 2   6. (C) (L)   7. (Q) (I)   8. (A) (R)   9. (N) (J)   10. (F) (K)

III Translation

1. 英语被用来和别国人民交往，通常用来促进贸易发展和科学进步。

2. 阅读水平属于中等的人读一般的书，每天读15分钟，一年可以读20本书。

3. 当前的形势是，世界人口增长的速度超过了食物和可用资源供应的增长速度。

4. 对学校的任何财物不加爱护、随便加以浪费或损坏都是不好的行为。

5. 一个国家的国际收支中最重要的两大项目就是有形贸易与无形贸易，其次便是投资。投资是一国利用别国资金建造工厂，开采矿藏的一种手段，以建立本国的工业基础。

Unit 05

I Vocabulary and Structures

1. jumped at the chance
2. evolution
3. impending
4. wiped out
5. brought about
6. enhance
7. gives me the creeps
8. insignificant
9. nightmarish
10. a real feast for the eye

II Reading Comprehension

1. D   2. B   3. A   4. C   5. C

III Translation

1. The flying birds grouped together in the island — a real feast for the eyes!
2. After the flood all the villages were wiped out.
3. The volcanic eruption brought about great changes to the environment .
4. Suddenly the room was completely blacked out .
5. The scientists are given the opportunity to better understand the far reaches of our universe.

Unit 06

I Vocabulary and Structures

1. poverty-stricken
2. cracked a joke
3. emigrated
4. fell in love with
5. adopted
6. spoken her mind
7. bard

Key to supplementary exercises

8. made his mark
9. banquet
10. keep the wolf from the door

II Reading Comprehension

1. A   2. C   3. D   4. B   5. A

III Translation

1. Today I came upon an old friend in the street.
2. In this field, as a young scientist he made his mark.
3. He made the best use of all the resources he could get his hands on.
4. People should be encouraged to speak their mind.
5. Do you believe that people may fall in love with each other at the first sight?

Revision 04-06

I Vocabulary and Structures

1. A   2. D   3. A   4. A   5. B
6. D   7. B   8. D   9. C   10. C

II Reading Comprehension

Task 1   1. A   2. C   3. A   4. A   5. A
          6. D   7. B   8. B   9. C   10. A

Task 2   11. Making an appointment and declining an appointment.

Task 3   12. The possible benefits of the service offered their members.

          13. It's increasing.

          14. The training of personnel at all levels in management skills and techniques.

          15. No, he isn't.

III Translation

1. 近年来，出现了一种新型的运输方式，它就是陆海、陆空、海空等多种方式联运。中华人民共和国根据平等互利的原则,促进和发展同其他国家和地区的贸易关系。在贸易中我们也成功地开展了上述多种联运业务。

2. Finding your way around is not so easy when you are new in town. The map you have may not be very detailed or it may be outdated. Also, and this is a common problem, the map may be in one language while all the street signs are in another. If this is the case, you'll probably have to ask for directions

Key to supplementary exercises

Unit 07

I Vocabulary and Structures

1. high in protein
2. lust
3. lose weight
4. nutrition
5. made his mouth water
6. moderate
7. ingredients
8. gobbled down
9. peel
10. crave

II Reading Comprehension

1. A   2. C   3. C   4. B   5. A

III Translation

1. The delicious sundae made the children's mouth water.
2. We should set the record straight. It is the earth that moves around the sun, rather than the sun around the earth.
3. They gobbled down their lunch quickly and run away.
4. Let's kick off the first round of the competition.
5. Pandas usually live on bamboo.

Unit 08

I Vocabulary and Structures

1. tapped   2. faithful   3. descendent   4. a hint   5. gifted
6. migrate   7. get along with 8. Primitive   9. were not compatible 10. has fulfilled

II Reading Comprehension

1. visit Switzerland   2. Walking, swimming, riding   3. Listening to music
4. in the afternoon   5. the best place

III Translation

Task 1

在最近几年，许多研究项目已经进行调查人类最好的朋友——狗，是如何赢得这个头衔的。很久以前据研究者报告，所有的狗，从微型的奇瓦瓦狗到大型的大麦狗都是被驯养的狼的后代。可是，科学家

Key to supplementary exercises

仍然不知道究竟从什么时候开始狗不再是嗜血的野生动物而开始和人类和睦相处的，甚至还赢得人类最好朋友的称号。

Task 2

1. Extensive tests have been carried out on the patient.
2. They made no attempt to escape/at escaping.
3. I can't quit put my finger on the flaw in her argument.
4. In spite of these insults, she managed not to get angry.
5. I put her success down to her hard work and initiative.

Unit 09

I Vocabulary and Structures

1. have been instructed 2. still 3. has not taken to 4. rent 5. are requested
6. rushed 7. contacted with 8. leapt 9. mumbled 10. offended

II Reading Comprehension

1. B 2. B 3. C 4. D 5. A

III Translation

Task 1

"见鬼！到底是怎么回事？"当希斯克历夫先生返回时问到。

"是啊，真是见鬼！"我咕噜着。"您倒不如把我丢给一群老虎的好！"

"对于不碰它们的人，它们不会多事的。"他说，"狗是应该警觉的。喝杯水吗？"

"不，谢谢您。"我说到。

"没给咬着吧？"

"是的，没有。"

Task 2

1. I took to her the moment I met her.
2. It annoys me when people forget to say thank you.
3. I soon got accustomed to his strange ways.
4. I told the boys off for making so much noise.
5. Inflation has got out of control.

Revision 07–09

I Vocabulary and Structures

Section A

1. A 2. C 3. B 4. D 5. A

Section B

6. reading   7. to tell   8. known   9. is said   10. erupting

II Reading Comprehension

Task 1   1. contrast two cultures / some single dimension
2. focus on this ideological difference
3. assign a positive value to one group / a negative value
4. regeneralize this process to the entire group

Task 2   5. D K   6. F N   7. O B   8. M H   9. A J

Task 3   10. piquant flavors and aromas
11. with a sensitive stomach
12. local agriculture and husbandry
13. paprika and garlic

Unit 10

I Vocabulary and Structures

1. acquire   2. appeals   3. miserable   4. will be going / will go
5. Having worked / Having been worked   6. reporting   7. illustrate
8. would have observed   9. depth   10. was regarded

II Reading Comprehension

1. business communication consultant   2. good business letters
3. impersonal, difficult or tedious   4. tired phrases   5. create an image

III Translation

Task 1

1. I'm green with envy when I go to Shanghai and see their pictures.
2. He is full of concern for the future.
3. Her competence is beyond doubt.
4. When he started criticizing my work, I really saw red.
5. Sunlight can promote growth.

Task 2

石油和天然气都用管道输送。这种管道从油田延伸至使用地点长达数百公里。如果你所在的城市使用天然气，那么当你扭开气炉时，你所用的管子，它的另一端可能在一千英里以外的地底下。

Key to supplementary exercises

Unit 11

I Vocabulary and Structures

1. taking   2. repaired   3. anxiety   4. work   5. likeliest   6. to finish
7. deadly   8. would never turn   9. Having ignored   10. pick up

II Reading Comprehension

1. pay the balance of $500   2. June 30   3. air freight   4. court proceedings
5. September 15

III Translation

Task 1

1. The boy managed to sort out those of the largest size.
2. I won't go swimming because I must look for my mother at the station.
3. The chairman couldn't get his son off the hook.
4. We were cut off in the middle of our telephone conversation.
5. The sun finally broke through the clouds.

Task 2

　　百事泰公司是全球最大的保健品生产和供应商之一。其业务遍及100多个国家和地区。郑州百事泰公司保健品有限公司是百事泰公司和郑州长征药厂新近联合成立的合资公司。

Unit 12

I Vocabulary and Structures

1. applying   2. stimulated   3. is used to   4. used to   5. criminal
6. Not having received   7. speaking   8. haven't   9. implication   10.agreeable

II Reading Comprehension

1. A   2. B   3. B   4. C   5. D

III Translation

1. It cleared up quickly after the rain.
2. For the whole afternoon my little brother hung on to me.
3. Regardless of the danger, he climbed the tower.
4. They were too young to be wised up to that kind of thing.
5. The teacher talked me into coming here.

Key to supplementary exercises

Revision 10-12

I Vocabulary and Structures

Section A

1. A   2. C   3. B   4. A   5. B

Section B

6. be informed require   7. intended   8. affects   9. will they look on   10. had been

II Reading Comprehension

Task 1   1. D   2. B   3. H   4. G   5. A   6. D   7. E

Task 2   8. 081-440-3174   9. 071-723-8818   10. 6315560

Task 3   11. Yes, they do.

          12. They have a two-day weekends.

          13. Yes, they do.

          14. Running, biking, playing volleyball and swimming are popular in summer.

          15. They work in their yards or in their houses.

III Translation

1. A   2. C

IV Writing

Weather in city:

It'll be cloudy today, and later turn to partly cloudy, with the north wind. The high will be eight degrees Celsius and the low four below zero. It is expected to be partly cloudy in the next two days. The winds will be calm with little change of the temperatures.